D0875323

CICS
A Programmer's Reference

CICS
A Programmer's Reference

Phyllis Donofrio

Intertext Publications
McGraw-Hill Book Company

New York St. Louis San Francisco Auckland Bogotá
Hamburg London Madrid Mexico Milan Montreal
New Delhi Panama Paris São Paolo
Singapore Sydney Tokyo Toronto

Intertext Publications/Multiscience Press, Inc.
One Lincoln Plaza
New York, NY 10023

McGraw-Hill Book Company
1221 Avenue of the Americas
New York, NY 10020

*This book is dedicated
to two very special friends,
Nils Ekberg and Barry Brooks
for without them,
none of this would have happened.*

Acknowledgments

The past several years have been truly memorable ones, especially in the professional contacts I have made. Those of us who dedicate most of our waking (and sometimes, it seems, sleeping) hours to support of this product know that the efforts are only made worthwhile through the friends and colleagues that we meet. These people have made this book possible though the support and confidence constantly provided.

Nils Ekberg (Metropolitan Insurance, Greenville SC) and Barry Brooks (Northeast Regional Data Center, Gainesville FL) have probably changed my life more than my own parents. They are the best friends anyone could ever have, and the most supportive people I have ever known. I may still not be fearless, but I'm much more confident than when I stood in front of 350 people at the that first memorable Share session.

The other people in the CICS project are all special, both customer and IBM reps. To name them all would take another book. This group is incredible, and produces the highest quality professional sessions I have ever been involved with. Any customer that has not been able to experience CICS sessions at Share is truly missing a special insight into the product. Thank you to everyone in the project for their support and assistance.

This past year has been memorable in the 'independence' that I have been able to realize. I recognize the education and unique experiences that my previous employer, Dun & Bradstreet Plan Services provided. I am still indebted to Al Stephan, who is probably the most unique Senior VP I will ever know. His installation continues to exist on the 'leading edge' of technology. The Database Administrator, Patty Pritchard, maintains one of the most challenging DB/2 environments in the industry. I am indebted to her for several of the figures and a great deal of the content in the DB/2 chapter.

I am deeply indebted to the Central Florida Regional Data Center and the University of South Florida Computing Center. They had confidence in the consultant, and gave me an opportunity. John Jackson will always be a special friend, and I appreciate the support of Ed Fischer, Director, and Barry Blonde, Manager of Technical Support. Of course, working with the systems staff was a special treat and I truly enjoyed the time spent with Lou, Dale, Debbie, Walter, George M., George D., Richard, Allen, Jim and Henry. The IBM SE at this account, Alan Stalvey, has been a friend for many years and I have always valued his committment to customers.

Most of the DL/I materials were compiled with the assistance of Jimmy Pittman, Director, and Jim Matthews, Technical Support, for the IMS/CICS at Deposit Guaranty National Bank in Jackson, Mississippi. These people are special friends and technical wizards with this database interface. Thanks for the time and energy required to produce the entire chapter.

Steve Ware is a CICS system programmer with Barry at NERDC. I owe him a great deal for his programming expertise and assistance with many portions of the book. He is truly talented, and I value his input and advice on any CICS support issue.

A special thanks to the entire IBM support structure. The folks at the Dallas System Center including Bob Yelavich, Bob Archambeault, Mary Ann Edwards, Phil Emerick and Bill Matthews have been a real inspiration. The CICS service group in Raleigh are dedicated and gifted. Jim Grauel will always be my hero, and his staff including Herb Williams have taught me so much.

The CICS development, test and change team staff in Hursley (including Eastleigh and Millbrook) have done an wonderful job with the product, especially Version 3. I treasure the friendships I have made, especially with Mike Jeffery, Andy Krasun and Tom Baldwin.

A special debt is due my special friend and series editor, Jay Ranade. His expertise in the publishing field has proven invaluable through both books. I owe a great deal of gratitude to all the people who have supported me though my publishing experiences. Alan Rose, Intertext Publications, has been so tolerant of my inexperience and his production talents have been appreciated during all phases of the book's assembly. I have also been fortunate to contribute regularly to one of the most popular technical journals in the world, the Enterprise System Journal. The publisher and Editor-in Chief, Bob Thomas, has been very supportive and has given me the opportunity to write articles that can be read by literally thousands of professionals. The research for those articles, and the feedback from readers have been incorporated into some of the chapters of this book.

In closing, I would like to extend a special thanks to a person who helped me though a very difficult time while this book was being developed. She taught me that all things are possible, and that while we can never avoid the constant struggles of daily life, we can learn to work through them . . . one day at a time. Thanks Mary Ann.

Contents

Preface

CICS continued to evolve through the 1980s and has now produced an entirely new product, with new code base and internals. CICS/MVS 2.1.1 will continue to be supported, but CICS/ESA 3.1.1 and CICS/ESA 3.2 will be the future of the product. Both system and application programmers will find enhanced function, but a new "look" to the CICS that has been supported for many years.

It has been said that of the Fortune 500 companies, 490 use CICS to process their business needs. Those that don't, use a specialized operating system for their unique industry, a control program that processes transactions similar to, but separate from CICS. Those 490 businesses depend upon the CICS product for their very existence, as was painfully evident a few years ago in the financial industry. The employees of these companies are constantly searching for additional assistance to support this enormous workload.

This book was created to fill a gap in documentation, a book on issues rather than technique. Many publications have been produced to explain skill and/or syntax of both COBOL and CICS programming. Once programmers were introduced to these skills, and the myriad of options available, they were expected to understand the "nuances" of the choices. Both the language (COBOL) and the product (CICS) are being enhanced, which means the options are not only increasing in numbers but complexity. This book does not address the multitude of options in syntax, but rather the ramifications of some of those choices. In other words, if the programmer chooses to use "X" option or parameter within a program . . . what are the implications of that choice.

Audience for the Book

This book can be used by both application and system programmers responsible for the development and support of CICS systems. Those administrators of databases (DBAs) may find relevant materials in the two chapters specifically dedicated to those topics, the CICS-DL/I and CICS-DB/2 interfaces. Both interfaces have experiences substantial changes in the past year, with the IMS/ESA Version 3 product, DBCTL and CICS/ESA Version 3. Although some material has been recently announced and shipped, many new issues, techniques and enhancements have been included in the chapters wherever possible.

The material in the book has been written for both the inexperienced and the veteran programmer. Some topics are "fundamental," and will assist even the unseasoned programmer, since they cover many basic issues of application development and CICS concepts and facilities. Other topics may present new materials to the accomplished technician, since I have attempted to include new facilities that have been recently announced or shipped. Hopefully, the materials will present new techniques or alternative methods to any reader.

Of course, in no way can these materials cover all issues, and all topics. Hopefully the numerous sections of each chapter will cover at least some of the items relevant to your responsibilities. I have compiled information from numerous sources, including many of my friends who are veterans of CICS programming. I am always receptive to additional material, and would accept input from anyone with further ideas. Send any comment or suggestions to me at: P.O. Box 1521, Lutz, FL. 33549.

Operating System Environment

This book has been written primarily for CICS/MVS 2.1.1 but includes a great deal of information from CICS/ESA Version 3. Many of the concepts are similar to situations that could be experienced in previous releases of CICS, or even CICS/VM and CICS/VSE. While CICS/ESA Version 3 contains enhancements to the programming interface, many of the internals from CICS/MVS 2.1.1 remain unchanged. Of course, Version 3 has removed all support for macro-level coding, and for that reason, no macro issues or examples were included. Some chapters contain information that would be relevant in the conversion from macro to commands.

Previous Knowledge of CICS

Although there are really no prerequisites, I have assumed that the reader understands the concepts of COBOL, especially CICS command level COBOL. Knowledge of, and the use of, the CICS APRM (Application Programmer's Reference Manual) is a must, since the basics of CICS programming are covered there. Knowledge of CICS concepts and facilities would certainly be helpful, but not necessary. Any knowledge of these concepts would enhance the reader's ability to absorb the issues within the book. Whenever possible, I cited specific manuals or other publications that could supplement the issue being discussed.

Benefits to the Programmer, and the Installation

I have found that few installations have formal procedures in place to guide or advise programmers in technique, and skill options. Some installations have subscribed to IBM (or other) vendor "question and answer" facilities to research specific problems. These facilities, however, are usually restricted to only the technical support staff, and not globally available to the typical application programmer. For that reason, this book has drawn some information from those sources to make them available to the programmers . . . who are the most affected by them. Use of this information may assist in the selection, and most productive use, of this research material, even for those installations who have not chosen to subscribe to the service.

Book Content

This book is compiled into four sections: CICS Application Programs, CICS Non-Database File Issues, CICS Database Issues, and CICS Program Services. Each section attempts to isolate specific corresponding issues into each chapter within the chapter. In some cases, the material may correspond in more than one chapter, since programming issues may transcend more than one heading. For that reason, material on a topic, such as COMMAREA may appear in more than one chapter since some issues deal with the program itself, and some may deal only with specific storage issues.

In the section on database issues, I have attempted to highlight some of the main issues that deal SPECIFICALLY with CICS. In no way are these chapters inclusive, or do they cover all database topics. The intent was to deal with the most current, and therefore the most relevant items that programmers may face when developing applications in these environments.

Summary

After reading all, or part of this book, I hope you will have discovered some new (and perhaps relevant) items that can be used to produce efficient CICS transactions. These materials are not necessarily novel, but in many cases, they have been previously undocumented or poorly documented. There are many misconceptions about CICS, and perhaps some of these have been made more clear.

CICS is the largest transaction processor in the mainframe world, and therefore the largest employer of application programmers. Perhaps some topics in this book will increase employability, but it is hoped that at least, it will increase the appreciation of CICS as a viable and resourceful product.

CICS Application Programs

Application Programming Issues

Many of the chapters in this book deal with specific topics that tend to group into clusters, but these topics warranted a separate chapter unto themselves. Other application issues are valid, yet are specific to the programming technique or process used by the programmer. This chapter will deal with many COBOL-related CICS concerns and attempt to answer many of the most common questions raised by programmers. While the topics are extensive, they are by no means totally inclusive. Every programmer faces unique problems, especially since he or she is presented with unique requests (some call them challenges and opportunities). This chapter will address some of the most common programming issues of CICS applications.

1.1 Pseudoconversational CICS Transactions

One of the primary differences between batch COBOL programs and CICS COBOL programs is the transaction-based environment of online programs. Batch programs (typically) read in large amounts of data (files), calculate or otherwise process the data, and then create new data and/or reports. CICS applications, however, must support a constant dialog with a terminal operator, and accommodate the steady stream of keyboard input to screen output common in these programs. This requires a new approach to application design: an interactive approach.

1.1.1 Interactive CICS Design

Any interactive application is designed to function via the typical inquiry/response strategy. The most common example would be:

Inquiry (keyboard) —> CICS —> Response (screen)

where the terminal operator enters an inquiry (an account number), the CICS application processes the request and returns the requested data to the operator's screen. What typically follows? The operator then contemplates the response and inputs a second request based on the results of the first. The outcome produces a continual repetition of the above scenario (inquiry/CICS/response) that must be accommodated by the design of the program.

This "interactive" requirement is normally accomplished by the "pseudo"-conversational technique used by most CICS programmers. The name implies that the terminal operator appears to be maintaining a constant conversation with the program (and CICS). In reality, however, the conversational procedure is simulated, or "pseudo." The technique, however, requires additional design considerations.

1.1.2 Saving Data Between Tasks

Why would CICS programs simulate this interactive environment instead of actually producing it? Consider the architecture of CICS itself and the fact that every piece of storage associated with the program must be maintained by CICS during execution. While the application is active in CICS, all program, data, and terminal storage must be physically sustained within the CICS system. If the interactive program is truly continual interactions of the

Inquiry (keyboard) —> CICS —> Response (screen)

routine, then each inquiry/response combination can be "encapsulated." In fact, each response component is probably followed by a (sometimes elongated) "think time" segment by the terminal operator. If the application is designed to be truly conversational, all task storage must be sustained by CICS during these think time segments. Most installations have found this to be extremely detrimental and resource consuming.

As an alternative, pseudoconversational applications use the response component as a logical ending point of the program. While a logical end, it is not the physical end of the application, since the next inquiry must continue the iterative process. To allow reinstatement of the program after logical end, the application must provide a vehicle for retaining a "restart" of the task. Reinstatement is necessary for two reasons:

1. All task storage is released by CICS at task termination. Task initiation must reference the previous execution.
2. The terminal operator is isolated from the simulated interaction and is not responsible for origination.

The normal vehicle for retaining data across multiple task executions is the CICS COMMAREA. While the application could also use temporary storage or the terminal control table user area (TCTUA), the COMMAREA is the most widely used technique.

With the CICS command:

```
EXEC CICS RETURN
    TRANSID(XXXX)
    COMMAREA(......)
    LENGTH(.....)
END-EXEC.
```

the application can end the current execution and RETURN to CICS. All task storage is freed, and CICS saves the information indicated by the COMMAREA in a reserved area. CICS then maintains this storage (above the 16-Mb line if CICS/MVS 2.1.1 or later) until that terminal initiates the next task.

What is stored in the COMMAREA? Whatever the application needs for successful reinstatement at next execution. Potential data stored might include:

- Status codes for execution or error conditions
- Control information for program logic
- Screen contents at last execution
- Partial contents of the data being processed

or any other fields significant to the environment at the time the task was terminated. The only limitations are the restrictions on the COMMAREA as imposed by CICS. (See the section of this chapter on DFHCOMMAREA.)

When the terminal operator initiates the next transaction (via any keyboard input), CICS returns control to the program as indicated by the TRANSID parameter of the RETURN. When the program regains control, the COMMAREA is automatically made available via the DFHCOMMAREA within the LINKAGE SECTION. This information is now available to the new task and can be processed as if the transaction had not terminated. The technique, however, released resources during the interval that could subsequently be utilized by other CICS tasks.

Most installations require pseudoconversational programming as standard procedure in any CICS design. While the technique is not mandated by CICS, it has become standard application design in most CICS systems.

1.2 Programming Restrictions

Most programmers are aware of the limitations of the COBOL language, some of which have been removed in VS COBOL II. Some individuals have "circumvented" the restrictions; some have ignored them, when possible. This section will not only identify most of the restrictions, but help explain why they exist.

1.2.1 Operating System Services

As documented in the Application Programming Reference Manual (APRM), OS/VS COBOL programs cannot (should not) use commands that require operating system services. These statements include:

ACCEPT	CURRENT-DATE	DATE	DAY
DISPLAY	EXHIBIT	INSPECT	STRING
UNSTRING	STOP RUN	TIME	

While these commands are documented with "cannot," most programmers are aware that they can, indeed, be coded and will not cause any abnormal termination of the program. In fact, they do not even cause warning messages during compilation of the program. Why should they be avoided?

Since CICS is a "subsystem," it attempts to encapsulate all processing within the CICS address space or multiple CICS systems. Programs issue CICS requests, and CICS becomes responsible for all management of storage, dispatch, I/O, etc. When a program issues a restricted COBOL statement, CICS management modules must relinquish control to MVS (the operating system) to satisfy the request. This can cause two very negative effects on the CICS region:

1. An SVC (supervisor call) must be made to MVS to execute the instruction.
2. A GETMAIN may be issued for OS storage to execute the instruction, which must be satisfied from OSCOR. This storage is never FREEMAINed by CICS, since COBOL expects the FREEMAIN to be issued at end-of-job (EOJ) and knows nothing about CICS task termination.

When an SVC is issued, the entire CICS address space may be placed into a WAIT state while the request is being processed. This can severely affect performance of the region.

Instructions such as STRING and UNSTRING require GETMAINs that allocate the required storage from OSCOR. Excessive use of these statements can exhaust the supply of OSCOR and cause an 80A abend of the entire CICS region.

1.2.2 Upper-/Lower-Case Translation

Many programs have been severely restricted by the inability to dynamically change the character translation within a program. While some applications wish to use lower-case characters within the text, not all require the support.

Prior to CICS/ESA Version 3, this translation was globally set in the definition of the terminal. The UCTRAN option could be set to YES or NO and would remain that value for every task executed on that device. Programmers, weary of this inflexible option, discovered the location of this setting within the internal CICS control block. Many installations currently have an ASSEMBLER routine that can be called by any program that, in effect, "flips" the setting of UCTRAN to lower case when necessary and then returns the field to its original value.

This is dangerous and unsupported, since every new version of CICS may change the location or value of this internal field. In addition, since many CICS terminals are now "auto-installed," the TCTTE is rebuilt every time the terminal logs off and back on. The content of the field cannot be guaranteed once changed.

UCTRAN by Transaction In the announcement of CICS/ESA 3.1, IBM finally provided a supported, flexible alternative. UCTRAN can now be defined at a transaction level, allowing applications that require the facility to utilize lower-case characters, while others need not. A new option to the online resource definition facility, CEDA can be used to

CEDA DEFINE PROFILE

with the UCTRAN for the profile of that transaction as either YES or NO. When the transaction is executed, therefore, the translation can be dynamically invoked for that task only.

Will this enhancement be provided in CICS/MVS 2.1.1? The announcement has not been made at the time of this writing. Only substantial persuasion from customers will encourage IBM to comply.

In addition to the programming restriction for UCTRAN, programmers need to realize that the lower-case TRMIDNT support has been removed when terminals are auto-installed or defined with RDO. In previous macro definitions, lower-case names could be used, since they were assembled and loaded into the module exactly as they were defined in the macro.

Since RDO-defined terminals are created with CEDA, the transaction only accepts A-Z, 0-9, $, @, and #. Any other characters will be rejected, and lower-case input will be "folded" into upper case.

Installations that use lower-case terminal names can continue to define these devices with macros but will eventually have to eliminate them. Any migration to CICS/ESA V3 will force the deletion, since terminal macros are no longer supported.

1.2.3 Enforcing Restrictions with COBOL II

As previously stated, there is currently no supported facility available to enforce the programming restrictions of OS/VS COBOL in CICS. Programmers must be aware of the impact of these statements and voluntarily avoid them.

In VS COBOL II, however, a facility has been provided to assist in enforcement. While some of the restricted instructions have been removed (see Chapter 2), some remain. A "reserved word table" has been provided in COBOL II, which can be defined by the installation. Any statements placed into this table can be flagged as either an error or a warning during the compile of the program. This mechanism, then, can be used to fail the compile of any programs that continue to use restricted COBOL statements.

1.3 Use of HANDLE

During execution, CICS transactions may be unable to perform the required process. In these cases, the CICS task is said to be in an "exception condition." This condition can be "handled" or not, depending on the logic built into the program. If an application program attempts to execute and an exception condition is detected, the program has three options available:

1. HANDLE CONDITION — take some predetermined action.
2. IGNORE or NOHANDLE CONDITION — take no action and return control to the next instruction following the failed command.
3. Terminate the task with the corresponding CICS ABEND code. This is the default and occurs when no HANDLE CONDITION has been provided.

Most installations choose to use either the first or second alternative, since task termination is not exactly a "clean" way to leave the transaction and the corresponding terminal operator.

There are more than 70 conditions that can occur in a CICS task, and new ones may be added in future releases of the product. The supported conditions are documented in the APRM in the section dealing with the EIB-EXEC Interface Block. This internal control block is always updated during an exception condition and contains the specific code corresponding to the condition.

Which technique should be used? The choice should be made based on the strengths and weaknesses of each method.

1.3.1 Detecting Exception Conditions

If the program chooses to take some action with the HANDLE mechanism, CICS performs the following steps:

1. The condition table is scanned to determine if an entry for this situation exists.
2. If no entry in the table is found, the task is either suspended or abended. The default is ABEND, but some CICS commands produce conditions for which the default is SUSPEND. The commands that default to SUSPEND are:

ALLOCATE	ENQ	GETMAIN
JOURNAL	READQ TD	WRITEQ TS

If the condition was not raised by one of those commands, and no entry in the table is found, the task terminates.

3. If an entry in the table is found, action is taken based on the HANDLE statement. If different actions are required for different conditions, multiple labels can be used in the command.

Most programmers use HANDLE for multiple executions of a single routine, a routine that can be used by conditions raised by many different commands. In fact, IBM recommends that HANDLE be used instead of IGNORE or NOHANDLE in those cases exactly. These "error routines" are provided within the program and are common to many conditions. Remember, a HANDLE CONDITION will remain active until an IGNORE is detected or until another HANDLE is specified for the same condition within the program.

Figure 1-1 contains a portion of a program that would check for the MAPFAIL condition and choose to HANDLE that situation. Note that with HANDLE, one specific condition can be tested, and a "generic" error routine can then be used to accommodate any other conditions that may be raised. In this example, a MAPFAIL error would branch to that specific routine, while any other error would branch to a general routine.

If, however, the program must detect conditions that are not raised often or are unique, HANDLE may not be appropriate. These situations may be more efficiently processed by testing RESP and RESP2.

Some installations believe that use of HANDLE is contrary to the concepts of structured programming. They may wish to preserve this logic in the mainline of the program and test response codes. Again, the decision needs to be made by the installation based on existing programming standards.

1.3.2 Alternatives to HANDLE

The programmer may wish to use an alternative technique, NOHANDLE or IGNORE. With NOHANDLE, CICS returns control to the next instruction in the program, therefore taking no action. This technique is more global then IGNORE, bypassing conditions for any command.

The RESP and RESP2 options can be used to detect the response of the command's execution. The RESP field contains the value of the condition that has been raised or can be used to test for a "normal" condition. The RESP2 field is used as a result of the INQUIRE

```
LINE       SOURCE LISTING

00317          05  BLLCELLS-BAR              PIC S9(08) COMP.
00318      EJECT
00319      PROCEDURE DIVISION.
00320      EJECT
00321      0000-PROGRAM-DCNESHUT.
00322  **      PERFORM SECURITY CHECK HERE...
00323  **      HANDLE SHUTDOWN TIME = '0000' TO NEVER SHUTDOWN.
00324  **      HANDLE SHUTDOWN IMMEDIATELY
00325
00326  *       SERVICE RELOAD BLLCELLS.
00327
00328          PERFORM 0100-INITIALIZATION THRU 0100-EXIT.
00329
00330          IF EIBTRNID = WS-CONS-TRANSID-1
00331  **         PROGRAM WAS STARTED VIA "TIME" AT CONSOLE
00332             ADD CODE TO VERIFY START AT CONSOLE
00333             PERFORM 0500-SHUTDOWN-TIME THRU 0500-EXIT
00334          ELSE
00335          IF EIBTRNID = WS-CONS-TRANSID-2
00336  **         PROGRAM WAS STARTED VIA "SHUT" AT CONSOLE
00337             ADD CODE TO VERIFY START AT CONSOLE
00338             PERFORM 0600-RECEIVE THRU 0600-EXIT
00339             PERFORM 0800-RECEIVE-CHECK THRU 0800-EXIT
00340          ELSE
00341          IF TERMINAL-INPUT AND EIBTRNID = WS-TRANSID
00342  *          PROGRAM WAS STARTED VIA A TERMINAL
00343             PERFORM 1000-PSEUDO-CHECK THRU 1000-EXIT
00344             PERFORM 2000-PSEUDO-RTN THRU 2000-EXIT
00345             PERFORM 9950-PSEUDO-RETURN THRU 9950-EXIT
00346          ELSE
00347          IF START-WITHOUT-DATA OR START-WITH-DATA
00348  *          PROGRAM WAS STARTED VIA INTERVAL CONTROL
00349             PERFORM 1110-SHUTDOWN THRU 1110-EXIT
00350          ELSE
00351  *          PROGRAM WAS STARTED VIA PLT
00352             PERFORM 1120-PLTI-RTN THRU 1120-EXIT.
00353
00354          PERFORM 9900-RETURN-TO-CICS THRU 9900-EXIT.
00355
00356      0000-DUMMY-EXIT.  EXIT.
00357      EJECT
00358      0100-INITIALIZATION.
00359
00360          EXEC CICS HANDLE CONDITION
00361              ERROR   (9700-GENERAL-ERROR-RTN)
00362              MAPFAIL (9750-MAPFAIL-ERROR-RTN)
00363          END-EXEC.
00364
00365          EXEC CICS ASSIGN APPLID(WS-APPLID)
00366              NETNAME(WS-NETNAME)
00367              STARTCODE(WS-START-CODE)
00368              USERID(WS-USERID)
00369              RESP(WS-RESP)
00370          END-EXEC.
00371
00372          EXEC CICS LINK PROGRAM(WS-JOBNAME-PGMID)
```

Figure 1-1   COBOL program using HANDLE Of MAPFAIL condition.

and SET commands. These commands are usually restricted, since they have the ability to change the value of CICS resources. The commands are not even documented in the APRM, since they are not considered common application functions.

While this technique is generally considered more efficient, there are some disadvantages. As previously stated, there are currently more than 70 conditions that can be raised, and each potential value may need to be accommodated differently. Future releases may introduce new conditions, which would have to be added to the program. This could be avoided with a preliminary test for DFHRESP(NORMAL). This "normal" test is not available with the normal HANDLE command, since it has no NORMAL condition that can be tested for in the options.

In addition, repetitious occurrences of response checking within the program could increase the size of the program and subsequent module size. This method is usually restricted to conditions that are only occasionally raised. Remember, also, that RESP checking implies the same environment as NOHANDLE. The program naturally falls into the next statement during execution of that portion of the logic.

Figure 1-2 shows a sample section of a program using RESP checking. Note that the first test is for DFHRESP(NORMAL), with all subsequent tests for specific conditions. One drawback of this procedure is the inability to test for a "generic" condition, as HANDLE can. All situations must be tested for. As previously stated, this can be repetitious and cause the module size to increase.

1.3.3 HANDLE ABEND

If the program did not wish to HANDLE the condition, and the task terminates abnormally, the HANDLE ABEND command can be used to direct control to an ABEND exit facility in CICS. The installation can then create an exit routine to gain control at the time of abnormal termination.

When the task abnormally terminates, CICS locates the active exit based on the "logical level" of the program. If the program has been LINKed to and does not contain an active exit, the ABEND passes control to the next higher level for existence of an ABEND exit. If both programs contain a HANDLE ABEND, the termination technique used in the abending program determines which, or both, exits are processed. Figure 1-3 shows the logic of the ABEND exit facility.

```
LINE        SOURCE LISTING

00933       5100-EXIT.   EXIT.
00934       EJECT
00935       6000-LINK-TO-WTO-SUBR.
00936
00937           EXEC CICS LINK PROGRAM(WS-WTO-PGMID)
00938                          COMMAREA(WS-WTO-COMMAREA)
00939                          LENGTH(WS-WTO-CALEN)
00940
00941           END-EXEC.
00942
00943       6000-EXIT.   EXIT.
00944       EJECT
00945       9000-HANDLE-RESP.
00946
00947           MOVE SPACES TO WS-MESSAGE-AREA.
00948
00949           IF WS-RESP = DFHRESP(NORMAL)
00950               GO TO 9000-EXIT
00951           ELSE
00952           IF WS-RESP = DFHRESP(ENDFILE)
00953               MOVE WS-ENDFILE-TEXT TO WS-MESSAGE-AREA
00954           ELSE
00955           IF WS-RESP = DFHRESP(DISABLED)
00956               MOVE WS-DISABLED-TEXT TO WS-MESSAGE-AREA
00957           ELSE
00958           IF WS-RESP = DFHRESP(DSIDERR)
00959               MOVE WS-DSIDERR-TEXT TO WS-MESSAGE-AREA
00960           ELSE
00961           IF WS-RESP = DFHRESP(DUPKEY)
00962               MOVE WS-DUPKEY-TEXT TO WS-MESSAGE-AREA
00963           ELSE
00964           IF WS-RESP = DFHRESP(ILLOGIC)
00965               MOVE WS-ILLOGIC-TEXT TO WS-MESSAGE-AREA
00966           ELSE
00967           IF WS-RESP = DFHRESP(INVREQ)
00968               MOVE WS-INVREQ-TEXT TO WS-MESSAGE-AREA
00969           ELSE
00970           IF WS-RESP = DFHRESP(IOERR)
00971               MOVE WS-IOERR-TEXT TO WS-MESSAGE-AREA
00972           ELSE
00973           IF WS-RESP = DFHRESP(LENGERR)
00974               MOVE WS-LENGERR-TEXT TO WS-MESSAGE-AREA
00975           ELSE
00976           IF WS-RESP = DFHRESP(NOTAUTH)
00977               MOVE WS-NOTAUTH-TEXT TO WS-MESSAGE-AREA
00978           ELSE
00979           IF WS-RESP = DFHRESP(NOTFND)
00980               MOVE WS-NOTFND-TEXT TO WS-MESSAGE-AREA
00981               MOVE JOBNAMEI TO NCC-JOBNAME
00982           ELSE
00983           IF WS-RESP = DFHRESP(NOTOPEN)
00984               MOVE WS-NOTOPEN-TEXT TO WS-MESSAGE-AREA
00985           ELSE
00986           IF WS-RESP = DFHRESP(SYSIDERR)
00987               MOVE WS-SYSIDERR-TEXT TO WS-MESSAGE-AREA
00988           ELSE
```

Figure 1-2   COBOL program using DFHRESP checking.

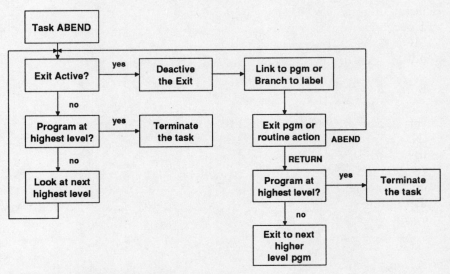

Figure 1-3 ABEND exit logic.

ABEND Exit Program Processing Within the exit program, logic may be necessary to accommodate dissimilar ABENDs from various programs. The ABEND code and TRANSID can be located via the EXEC CICS ASSIGN facility, but this will not produce the program name of the terminated task. The field is addressable to the exit program but must be located via CICS internal fields. While this is not recommended, the program name can be located in several places, one of which is the CICS control block TACB (Task ABEND Control Block). The TACB is created at abnormal task termination as an extension of the task's TCB (Task Control Block). As long as IBM documents these internals, it can be found as ABNDPRG field within the TACB.

CICS/ESA Version 3 continues to document this control block in the CICS Data Areas manual, so the location of the field can be discovered in that manual. Future versions of the product may not, and therefore may need to be located elsewhere.

HANDLE ABEND with CICS LINK vs. OS/VS COBOL CALL ABEND processing was changed recently and is now different if the program issues a CICS LINK or a COBOL CALL. The APRM has been updated to describe the change, and it explains the difference.

CICS LINKed-to programs have no active CONDITION or ABEND handling on entry. If an ABEND occurs during this time, CICS searches higher level programs and passes control to the first active exit program. If none can be found, the task terminates abnormally.

CICS CALLed programs have no active CONDITION or ABEND handling on entry. The called subprogram can issue

EXEC CICS POP HANDLE

to return the caller's conditions. The program must then "undo" this HANDLE with the corresponding PUSH HANDLE before returning control to the caller or an ABEND will result.

VS COBOL II does not support CICS HANDLE ABEND in a program using the CALL statement, and therefore suspends any HANDLE conditions. (See the VS COBOL II Programming Guide for more information.)

1.3.4 Miscellaneous Issues

Many more uses of HANDLE could be listed in this section but are too numerous to include. Two other items may be relevant to programmers, however. One deals with the conditions of the display device that has transmitted the request, the other with a relatively new condition for CICS-DB/2 tasks.

HANDLE AID The handling of AIDs (attention identifer) can be helpful within a program to create logic based on the terminal operator's input. Many programs check the value of data fields, thereby "editing" the data before processing. Some terminal functions can also be "edited," and the program can detect the existence (or not) of specific functions.

The available values for an AID are:

Constant	Description
DFHENTER	ENTER key
DFHCLEAR	CLEAR key
DFHPA1 - PA3	PA1, PA2, or PA3 key
DFHPF1 - PF24	24 PF keys
DFHOPID	OPERID or MSR
DFHMSRE	MSR extended
DFHTRIG	Trigger field
DFHPEN	Light pen

The HANDLE AID command can be used to branch to a specific location within the program if the AID is received from the device. These values apply only to the program in which it is specified and are active until task termination or another command is executed.

One common use of the AID value is to terminate the program and return control to CICS when the CLEAR key is used. Many other values can be used by the program, including specification of PF keys or the removal of function. Some installations choose to restrict the use of CLEAR and check for its value before returning control to the program.

While new technology provides enhanced function, some older devices (non-SNA) do not "reset" functions in all cases. One common use of the AID is to terminate the transaction with CLEAR and then reset the keyboard with FREEKB at the end of task.

HANDLE ROLLEDBACK   In recent releases of CICS, sync-point rollback can be utilized to return all resources to the starting point of the unit of work. If an explicit SYNCPOINT ROLLBACK is issued, the appropriate CICS management module notifies the task of the ROLLBACK.

The program can detect this condition with the

EXEC CICS HANDLE CONDITION ROLLEDBACK(label)

to accommodate this situation. The program can then take additional steps if necessary, aware that protected resources are being backed out. Of course, the program can choose to use the NOHANDLE option within the SYNCPOINT command.

1.4 XCTL, LINK, CALL

CICS program control directs the flow of operation within any application. The choice of technique, however, can affect both the efficiency and the performance of the task. The programmer has several choices to make and should base those choices on the results that are anticipated. Each technique possesses its own characteristics, advantages, and pitfalls to expect during execution. While some advice can be given, the programmer must choose the technique that most accurately reflects the most efficient execution environment.

1.4.1 Characteristics of the Program Control Commands

The most common program control commands are XCTL, LINK, and CALL. While most installations have used XCTL and LINK, there have been recent enhancements to the CALL facility that encourage increased consideration. This section will attempt to delineate the characteristics of each command, especially the unique attributes of each one.

1.4.1.1 XCTL   Control can be transferred from one CICS program to another with XCTL, allowing data to be passed to the target program via the COMMAREA option. Use of XCTL notifies CICS that no return to the originating program will be required. There are a few unique characteristics of XCTL which do not apply to the other control techniques.

1. The initiating program does not remain "associated" with the new program and therefore the CICS task. It can therefore be removed from CICS, and the associated storage freed. The initiating program is, in effect, terminated after the XCTL is issued.
2. XCTL produces a single "link level" of programs. When one program XCTLs to another, CICS establishes direct linkage with the target program. The previous program ceases to exist to CICS, and any residual data that is required must survive via the COMMAREA that is passed to the target program.
3. The target program, when complete, does not return control to the originating program. It returns control to CICS when complete. Since no return is allowed, the associated overhead with reinstatement to the original program by CICS is avoided. XCTL is therefore, by design, more efficient than LINK.

Figure 1-4 illustrates the logical flow of an XCTL from Program A to Program B. Note that once control is passed to Program B, no association exists to Program A, as if CICS initiated the task with Program B. Only a single logical level ever exists with XCTL.

1.4.1.2 LINK   When LINK is used, control is passed from one program to another, but additional processing is required since CICS must return control to the original program. Data can be passed to the LINKed-to program via the COMMAREA option. When the target program completes, control reverts to the instruction in the original program immediately following the LINK command.

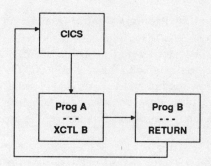

Figure 1-4 XCTL program flow.

The LINK command is very similar to the structured programming technique of PERFORM, where multiple logical levels of a program are established. In a PERFORM, however, the target routine is enclosed within the same program. LINK transfers control to an external program. Use of LINK also generates requests for storage, which contribute to the additional overhead associated with LINK.

Since the LINKed-to program is another (lower) logical level within the control hierarchy, it operates independently and does not "inherit" any conditions that were established by the originating program. Any HANDLE commands that were assigned in the first program are not transferred with the LINK and must be reestablished if necessary. Upon RETURN to the original program, however, the HANDLE commands that existed are restored.

Figure 1-5 illustrates the logical flow of a LINK from Program A to Program B. Note that once control is passed to Program B, the association remains to Program A and serves as the vehicle of return to Program B. Multiple logical levels can exist with LINK.

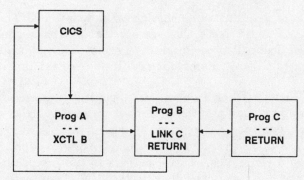

Figure 1-5 LINK program flow.

Figure 1-6 contains a sample portion of a program with LINK. Note that while the command must (should) have the program name, commarea, and length, these parameters can be "symbolics." The LINK command will then be executed with the current values as previously loaded by the program. One important factor to consider with LINK (as opposed to CALL) is that the LINKed-to program *must* be defined to CICS via RDO or PPT definition. In this example, the value of

WS-TIMEINT-PGMID

must exist as a defined program to the CICS region. The LINK process requires additional CICS module initialization for execution and, therefore, must be known to CICS as a program resource.

This requirement is immediately evident if investigating via a CICS trace of a LINK. Figure 1-7 contains a typical CICS trace of a program during the LINK process. Note that upon EIP LINK ENTRY (1), CICS instantly invokes PCP (Program Control Program) to perform a PPT LOCATE of the program. If the LINKed-to program cannot be found, the transaction will terminate with an APCP abend.

1.4.1.3 CALL The CALL command has been used very infrequently in CICS programming since it contains restrictions that have been both inconvenient and constraining. Full documentation on CALL restrictions can be found in the SC26-4045 VS COBOL II Application Programming Guide.

Within OS/VS COBOL, programs cannot CALL other programs that contain CICS commands. This restriction severely limits any programming potential and has caused most installations to use LINK when control needs to be transferred. As documented in the CICS APRM, the main program must be the only module containing the CICS interface stub. If the CALLed program contains commands, this cannot be possible.

Of course, an Assembler subprogram can be CALLed by a COBOL program (OS/VS COBOL or VS COBOL II) and can issue CICS commands. The Assembler program, however, is responsible for register preservation and restoration upon return to the CALLer.

IBM has subsequently enhanced support of COBOL, and in February 1989 announced added support for COBOL II that allows dynamic CALLs to subprograms that contain CICS commands. This new facility is further described in Chapter 2. The characteristics of

```
CICS/VS COMMAND LANGUAGE TRANSLATOR VERSION 1.7                    TIME 12.48 DATE 10 JULY 90   PAGE 17

LINE    SOURCE LISTING

00877           MOVE WS-JULDATE TO JULDATEO.
00878           MOVE WS-SYSDATE TO SYSDATEO.
00879           MOVE WS-SYSTIME TO SYSTIMEO.
00880           MOVE WS-NETNAME TO NETNAMEO.
00881           MOVE NCC-JOBNAME TO JOBNAMEO.
00882           MOVE NCC-APPLID TO APPLIDO.
00883           MOVE NCC-INITIAL-SHUTDOWN TO BEGSHUTO.
00884           MOVE NCC-CURRENT-SHUTDOWN TO CURSHUTO.
00885           MOVE NCC-SHUTDOWN-SET-BY TO SETBYO.
00886           MOVE NCC-SHUTDOWN-SET-DATE TO SETDATEO.
00887           MOVE NCC-SHUTDOWN-SET-TIME TO SETTIMEO.
00888           MOVE WS-MESSAGE-AREA TO MSGLINEO.
00889
00890       4000-EXIT.  EXIT.
00891       EJECT
00892       5000-CALC-INTERVAL-AND-START.
00893
00894           MOVE 'N' TO WS-ERROR-SW.
00895
00896           IF NCC-CURRENT-SHUTDOWN < '0000'  OR
00897                                    = '0000'  OR
00898                                    > '2359'
00899               MOVE 'Y' TO WS-ERROR-SW
00900               GO TO 5000-EXIT.
00901
00902           PERFORM 0200-ASKTIME THRU 0200-EXIT.
00903
00904           MOVE EIBTIME TO WDC-BEG-TIME.
00905           MOVE NCC-CURRENT-SHUTDOWN TO WDC-END-TIME.
00906           MULTIPLY WDC-END-TIME BY 100 GIVING WDC-END-TIME.
00907
00908           EXEC CICS LINK PROGRAM(WS-TIMEINT-PGMID)
00909                          COMMAREA(WS-DCNETINT-COMMAREA)
00910                          LENGTH(WS-TIMEINT-CALEN)
00911           END-EXEC.
00912
00913           EXEC CICS START TRANSID(WS-TRANSID)
00914                           INTERVAL(WDC-INTERVAL)
00915                           REQID(WS-REQID)
00916                           NOCHECK
00917           END-EXEC.
00918
00919           PERFORM 5100-SHUTDOWN-TIME-WTO THRU 5100-EXIT.
00920
00921       5000-EXIT.  EXIT.
00922
00923       5100-SHUTDOWN-TIME-WTO.
00924
00925           MOVE WS-JOBNAME            TO WWM-JOBNAME.
00926           MOVE WS-APPLID            TO WWM-APPLID.
00927           MOVE NCC-CURRENT-SHUTDOWN TO WS-STM-SHUT-TIME.
00928           MOVE WS-SYSTIME           TO WS-STM-CURR-TIME.
00929           MOVE WS-SHUTDOWN-TIME-MSG TO WWM-TEXT.
00930           MOVE WS-WTO-MSG           TO WS-WTO-COMMAREA.
00931
00932           PERFORM 6000-LINK-TO-WTO-SUBR THRU 6000-EXIT.
```

Figure 1-6   COBOL program using LINK.

CUSTOMER INFORMATION CONTROL SYSTEM - TRACE UTILITY PROGRAM   PAGE 3

TIME OF DAY	ID	REG 14	REQD	TASK	FIELD A	FIELD B	CHARS	RESOURCE	PROGRAM TRACE TYPE	INTERVAL
13:04:22.220608	F1	0048B8E38	4004	00315	001C2F30	010CA744	....		SCP FREEMAIN USER STORAGE	00.000000
13:04:22.220640	C9	504727B8	0004	00315	001C2F30	8C000038	....		SCP RELEASED USER STORAGE	00.000032
13:04:22.220672	E1	50396D42	00F4	00315	001C604C	00000208	....		EIP ASSIGN RESPONSE	00.000032
13:04:22.220672	E1	50396D9A	0004	00315	001C604C	00000E02	.---		EIP LINK ENTRY ①	00.000000
13:04:22.220704	F2	004DD12C	8204	00315	01000300	00000000	....	DCNE-JOBN	PCP PCP LOCATE	00.000032
13:04:22.220704	EA	404DF4E0	0003	00315	01000300	001C2214	...OD	DCNE-JOBN	TMP PPT LOCATE	00.000000
13:04:22.220736	EA	40476074	0005	00315	00000000	000ED6C4	..8..		TMP RETN NORMAL	00.000032
13:04:22.220768	F1	004B71C2	CC04	00315	000000F8	010CA744	..B..		SCP GETMAIN INITING	00.000032
13:04:22.220800	CB	5047277C	0004	00315	001C75E0	8C000108	....		SCP ACQUIRED USER STORAGE	00.000032
13:04:22.220800	F2	004B7530	8104	00315	01000300	00000000	....	DCNE-JOBN	PCP PPT LINK-CONDITIONAL	00.000000
13:04:22.220832	EA	404DF4E0	0003	00315	01000300	001C2214	...OD	DCNE-JOBN	TMP PPT LOCATE	00.000032
13:04:22.220832	EA	40476074	0005	00315	01000300	000ED6C4	...OD	DCNE-JOBN	TMP RETN NORMAL	00.000000
13:04:22.220864	F1	4040F078	8904	00315	001C0050	010CA744	..4..		SCP GETMAIN	00.000032
13:04:22.220896	C8	5047277C	0004	00315	001C2F30	891C0058	....		SCP ACQUIRED RSA STORAGE	00.000032
13:04:22.220928	F1	004B673E	CC04	00315	0000010A	010CA744	....		SCP GETMAIN INITING	00.000032
13:04:22.220960	C8	5047277C	0004	00315	001C75E0	8C000118	..0		SCP ACQUIRED USER STORAGE	00.000032
13:04:22.220960	E1	5039C0A8	0004	00315	001C7700	00000E08	....		EIP RETURN ENTRY	00.000000
13:04:22.220992	F1	004D59C	00F4	00315	001C76F0	010CA744	.0..		SCP FREEMAIN	00.000032
13:04:22.221024	C9	504727B8	0004	00315	001C76F0	8C000118	....		SCP RELEASED USER STORAGE	00.000032
13:04:22.221024	F2	004B7530	1004	00315	00000000	00000000	....	DCNE-JOBN	PCP RETURN	00.000000
13:04:22.221056	F1	604DF54A	4004	00315	001C2F30	010CA744	....		SCP FREEMAIN	00.000032
13:04:22.221088	C9	504727B8	0004	00315	001C75E0	891C0058	....		SCP RELEASED RSA STORAGE	00.000032
13:04:22.221088	F1	004B71C2	4004	00315	001C75E0	8C000108	....		SCP FREEMAIN	00.000000
13:04:22.221120	C9	504727B8	0004	00315	001C604C	00000000	.0..		SCP RELEASED USER STORAGE	00.000032
13:04:22.221152	E1	50396D9A	00F4	00315	001C604C	00000A02	....		EIP LINK RESPONSE	00.000032
13:04:22.221152	E1	50396E38	0004	00315	001C604C	00000A02	-...		EIP ASKTIME-ABSTIME ENTRY	00.000000
13:04:22.221184	E1	50396E38	00F4	00315	001C604C	00000A04	....		EIP ASKTIME-ABSTIME RESPONSE	00.000032
13:04:22.221216	E1	50396EFA	0004	00315	001C604C	00000A04	....		EIP FORMATTIME ENTRY	00.000032
13:04:22.221216	E1	50396EFA	00F4	00315	001C604C	00000A04	....		EIP FORMATTIME RESPONSE	00.000096
13:04:22.221312	E1	50398010	0004	00315	001C604C	0000060C	....		EIP STARTBR ENTRY	00.000000
13:04:22.221344	F5	00470CB0	F103	00315	00000400	00000000	....	NESH00	FCP CTYPE LOCATE	00.000032
13:04:22.221344	F1	4047BAB8	CC04	00315	001C75E0	010CA744	....		SCP GETMAIN INITING	00.000288
13:04:22.221632	C8	5047277C	0004	00315	001C75E0	8C000408	....		SCP ACQUIRED USER STORAGE	00.000064
13:04:22.221696	EA	4046804E	0003	00315	01000500	001C2214	....	NESH00	TMP FCT LOCATE	00.000000
13:04:22.221696	EA	40476074	0005	00315	01000500	000ED6C4	....		TMP RETN NORMAL	00.000032
13:04:22.221728	F5	40464E38	0045	00315	000000A4	04C4600	....		FCP RETN NORMAL	00.000032
13:04:22.221728	F1	004B71C2	CC04	00315	001C2F30	010CA744	....		SCP GETMAIN INITING	00.000000
13:04:22.221760	C8	5047277C	0004	00315	001C2F30	8C0000B8	....		SCP ACQUIRED USER STORAGE	00.000032
13:04:22.221792	F1	004B71C2	CC04	00315	001C79F0	010CA744	....		SCP GETMAIN INITING	00.000032
13:04:22.221792	C8	5047277C	0004	00315	001C79F0	8C000018	.0..		SCP ACQUIRED USER STORAGE	00.000000
13:04:22.221824	F5	5047277C	0004	00315	001C0104	010CA744	....	NESH00	FCP SETL	00.000032
13:04:22.221856	F1	50465B1A	8F04	00315	001C7A10	8F1C0118	....		SCP GETMAIN	00.000032
13:04:22.221888	C8	5047277C	0004	00315	88000000	001C7A90	....		SCP ACQUIRED FILE STORAGE	00.000000
13:04:22.221888	F0	50467830	0004	00315	01000000	010CA744	....		KCP WAIT+CANCADDR DCI=CICS	00.000128
13:04:22.222016	D0	504B4CE6	0504	00315	001C005B	010CA744	....		KCP DISPATCH	00.000192
13:04:22.222208	F1	50465CB4	8F04	00315	001C7B30	8F1C0068	....		SCP GETMAIN	00.000064
13:04:22.222304	C8	5047277C	0004	00315	88000000	44B50003	....		SCP ACQUIRED FILE STORAGE	00.000000
13:04:22.222304	F5	40464E38	0015	00315	000000A4	0000060C	....		FCP RETN NORMAL	00.000032
13:04:22.222336	E1	50398010	00F4	00315	001C604C	0000060C	....		EIP STARTBR RESPONSE	00.000032
13:04:22.222368	E1	50398150	0004	00315	001C604C	0000060E	.---		EIP READNEXT ENTRY	00.000032

Figure 1-7   CICS trace of COBOL LINK (CICS/MVS Version 2).

the facility, however, are relevant to the other program control commands.

CALL has many properties similar to LINK, since it passes control with expected return. CALLed programs, sometimes called subroutines, have advantages comparable to PERFORM, since they break a common task into a single, multi-executed module. This module can, therefore, be utilized by many main routines without redundant coding or debugging.

CALL has been used regularly by installations in the past, but only with Assembler routines. These routines, then, are link-edited into the main program and become separate CSECTs within the module.

Linkage in a CALLing Program   The COBOL program performing the CALL uses the following syntax:

    CALL literal-1
    or identifier-1

While most CICS COBOL programs use "literals" or program names in their calls, an identifier can be used. Use of CALL identifiers can significantly alter the way in which CICS deals with the program. This is most obvious when using DYNAMIC vs. STATIC CALLs and is discussed in the next section.

Use of CALL can be more efficient, since the subroutine becomes a part of the load module (a CSECT) and does not suffer the overhead of LINK. Figure 1-8 contains the linkage of a program containing a CALL. Note that the module DCNEAX00 has been created (1) but that it also contains a subroutine DFHDATE within the load module. When executed, CICS will load only DCNEAX00, and the subroutine will be CALLed when necessary.

The CALLed program, since not loaded by CICS, is actually "OS loaded," or loaded by the MVS program loader. When CALLed, CICS must use the MVS loader and store the program into OS storage, also known as OSCOR. For this reason, excessive use of CALL in CICS can fragment and overuse OSCOR resources. While the loaded subroutine may be reused once loaded, it is never deleted and remains resident in OSCOR. Unlike CICS program storage within the DSA, this storage is not compressed and reused. It remains "resident" for the life of the region.

The CALLed programs can be dynamically or statically included, specified by the option at link-edit time. The choice of static or dynamic link is both a performance and maintenance issue.

```
MVS/XA DFP VER 2 LINKAGE EDITOR      09:09:41  TUE  JUL 10, 1990
JOB DCNEAX00   STEP COBOL2   PROCEDURE LKED
INVOCATION PARAMETERS - LIST,MAP,LET,XREF
ACTUAL SIZE=(317440,86016)
OUTPUT DATA SET NER.S624.LINKLIB IS ON VOLUME SYS801
IEW0000   INCLUDE SYSLIB(DFHECI)


                        CROSS REFERENCE TABLE


CONTROL SECTION                 ENTRY
    NAME      ORIGIN  LENGTH        NAME      LOCATION      NAME      LOCATION      NAME      LOCATION      NAME      LOCATION
  DFHECI        00      48          DFHEI1        8        DLZEI01       8        DLZEI02       8        DLZEI03       8
                                    DLZEI04       8        DFHCBLI      26

  DCNEAX00      48     7CC
  DFHDATE *    818      F8          DFHDATEX    824

  IGZEBST *    910     1A8          IGZEBS2     A14


LOCATION  REFERS TO SYMBOL  IN CONTROL SECTION          LOCATION  REFERS TO SYMBOL  IN CONTROL SECTION
    B4         IGZEBST          IGZEBST                     DC         DFHEI1          DFHECI
    E0         DFHDATE          DFHDATE                     AA8        IGZETUN         SUNRESOLVED(W)
    AAC        IGZEOPT          SUNRESOLVED(W)
ENTRY ADDRESS    48


TOTAL LENGTH        AB8
*** DCNEAX00 REPLACED AND HAS AMODE 24
*** LOAD MODULE HAS RMODE 24
*** AUTHORIZATION CODE IS      0.

                                        50000000
```

Figure 1-8   COBOL program linkage control section.

STATIC vs. DYNAMIC CALL   Dynamic CALL is certainly the preference from a maintenance perspective, since any changes to the CALLed subroutine are automatically reflected at next execution. If the subroutine is changed frequently, the dynamic option may be necessary.

Static CALL is chosen more often, however, since the performance advantages are significant. If the CALLed subroutine is statically link-edited before execution, all linkage issues are resolved at the time the load module is created. The "clean" module is available to execute with the CALLed subroutine and performs much more efficiently than a dynamic CALL.

One important item to remember is the effect of compiler options on static and dynamic CALLs. Several references have been made to the NODYNAM compile option, the recommended choice. If, however, CALL identifier instructions are used, NODYNAM loses its effect, and all CALL identifier statements are dynamic. For this reason, installations should take note that the CALL technique can override compile time options and use CALL identifier with that knowledge.

The choice is always a trade-off. Static CALLs are always more efficient, but require additional link-editing of the main program every time the subroutine is modified.

1.4.2 Instruction Pathlength LINK vs. CALL

Since CALL is now available to programs written in VS COBOL II, many installations are now rethinking the programs containing LINK statements. As previously stated, LINK is not a trivial process for CICS and requires substantial overhead. Should programs be converted to CALL?

The decision is not simple. The syntax of the CALL is different from the LINK, since data is passed via variables in the CALL statement itself, not a COMMAREA. Performance is also an issue, especially if the CALL is dynamic rather than static.

The first dynamic CALL will certainly have similar properties to a LINK, since the routine will require locate and load. It will definitely have a longer pathlength than a static CALL.

The second and all subsequent dynamic CALLs of the same subprogram from the same main program will have a much shorter pathlength than a LINK. The benefit is provided by avoidance of redundant initialization of VS COBOL II within CICS.

When control is RETURNed to the CALLer, the CALLed subprogram remains in an initialized state. Any subsequent CALLs do not require reinitialization of the environment. This can substantially improve performance, but requires additional considerations with Working Storage data. Since Working Storage data begins as previously initialized, any INITIAL VALUE fields will not reflect any modifications and will begin with the values as reflected by the first CALL.

This can reduce the pathlength, since data need not be passed on each CALL. It also avoids the requirement for any COMMAREA to be passed, as is required for each EXEC CICS LINK.

1.4.3 CALL Effect on HANDLE

As documented in the CICS APRM, a CICS program that LINKs to another routine passes all conditions that are in effect. The LINKed-to program inherits any HANDLE conditions that were in effect. This does not occur with CALL. No condition handling is passed to the CALLed program and must be established upon entry.

Some programmers wish to transfer these conditions along with the CALL. This can be accomplished by "reverse" use of PUSH and POP. These commands are normally used to suspend condition processing during a LINK if the target program does not wish to inherit them. The command

EXEC CICS PUSH HANDLE

will suspend existing conditions at entry to LINK. The reverse, POP, will restore the original commands.

With CALL, these commands can be used in reverse to force condition handling to be inherited by the CALLed program. Upon entry to the CALLed subprogram, the command

EXEC CICS POP HANDLE

will reinstate any condition and abend handling state of the CALLer. At exit from the subprogram, a corresponding PUSH must be used to suspend the process before returning to the CALLer.

1.4.4 CALLed Programs that Manipulate Working Storage

In the CICS APRM, IBM reminds programmers that since CICS is a "multi-threading" environment, design should ensure that programs are "quasi-reentrant." This type of design requires that the programs be serially reusable between entry and exit. The CICS command level interface enforces this rule by providing a fresh copy of working storage at each invocation.

Use of CALL can complicate this process, especially if Assembler routines are CALLed that manipulate Working Storage. Remember, CICS can dispatch only a single task (except for subtasked processes such as VSAM and DB/2) at a given time from the active chain, but tasks can be interrupted during execution.

The CICS dispatcher gives control to a task, and that task will continue to execute until complete unless interrupted. What can interfere with execution? Control may be given up whenever CICS services are requested. These services are requested by practically any

EXEC CICS command

If control is relinquished, another task can execute until CICS is able to return to the interrupted task.

Assembler programs that modify Working Storage but do not contain any CICS commands will never be interrupted. They will retain control until the calling program RETURNs control or terminates the transaction.

1.5 DFHCOMMAREA

Use of the COMMAREA within programs is very routine, yet the techniques used for both storage and transfer of this data may impact both the CICS task and the system as a whole. Chapter 7 addresses some issues that deal specifically with the COMMAREA and its characteristics. This chapter will consider issues that relate specifically to the application program.

1.5.1 Program Allocation — Working Storage vs. Linkage Section

Programmers may pass data with COMMAREA in either XCTL or LINK conditions. This area may be defined in either Working Storage or in the Linkage Section of the program. The storage area designated in either technique must be addressable by the program at the time of XCTL or LINK.

In the CICS APRM, IBM states that the data should be specified in the Working Storage section of the originating program and in the

Linkage Section of the receiving program. This is a standard technique, but it is not necessary.

If the COMMAREA is defined in the Working Storage section, it then becomes a data area within the object module that is created and the subsequent load module. Potentially, a large COMMAREA defined within Working Storage could create an unnecessarily large load module. This could affect both the performance of the application, since the resources required to load the program would increase, and the performance of CICS as a system, since it would occupy more physical storage while executing.

If the programmer chooses to use the Linkage Section to define the COMMAREA, addressability is slightly more complicated. There is no way to guarantee that the label specified for the COMMAREA in the XCTL or LINK command is addressable at the time of execution. The status of the label is a function of the application logic and how the program is invoked.

COMMAREA in the Linkage Section When the program is translated, the CICS translator inserts an EIB as the first 01 level in the Linkage Section to ensure proper communication between CICS and the application program.

The second 01 level in the Linkage Section will be DFHCOMMAREA. If this section is used to define the COMMAREA, the programmer must use the first statement for a 01 named DFHCOMMAREA. If the programmer does not provide it, the CICS translator will create this 01 level regardless. Whether the program actually uses the COMMAREA created is irrelevant. The programmer then has the responsibility to ensure that the COMMAREA created is addressable.

If, therefore, the COMMAREA is defined in the Linkage Section, but no data is ever moved into the area, the EIB field indicating COMMAREA length (EIBCALEN) will be equal to zero. Any command specifying a COMMAREA will be invalid since the area is not addressable. This is especially common during the first pass through program initiation and transaction execution. If the transaction performs a

EXEC CICS RETURN
TRANSID(ABCD)
COMMAREA(label)
LENGTH(nnnn)
END-EXEC.

and the COMMAREA of the receiving program is defined in the Linkage Section of the program, it will not been initialized and will consequently contain an address of low values. Any subsequent use of this COMMAREA by the next pseudoconversational program will attempt to use an area addressed by low values, the contents of which are unpredictable (and usually undesirable). This can be verified by locating the address at task initiation. CICS stores the contents of DFHCOMMAREA into the TCTTE field TCTTEEIA (EXEC Interface Parm Address). If this field contains low values, the COMMAREA has not been properly initialized and the application will usually receive an INVREQ (invalid request) at initiation.

For this reason, many programmers continue to use the Working Storage section of the program for most COMMAREA definition.

In either technique, the program should always check the EIB field for length prior to command execution to ensure a valid content and establish addressability.

1.5.2 Size Calculation and Restrictions

The calculation and size restrictions of the COMMAREA must be considered by the programmer. Proper use of this critical data area creates optimum performance and reliability of the program.

Many times installations use a fixed size for most COMMAREAs, even though the applications may only use a portion of the area. There may be substantial savings realized by properly allocating the area for the amount of storage needed and no more.

During execution of the program, the COMMAREAs are stored in an area of CICS's DSA (Dynamic System Area) called "Shared Storage." This area is below the 16-Mb line, and therefore in contention by all other 24-bit programs. A recent announcement moved COMMAREAs "above the line," but only on the

EXEC CICS RETURN
 COMMAREA ....

implementation of data area. In all other uses of COMMAREA, the amount of storage requested must be loaded into the DSA, is not page "aligned," and can produce excessive fragmentation. CICS loads the data into the page size specified in the SIT (2K or 4K), wasting any unused space.

Installations can more efficiently use this space and avoid fragmentation by specifying the page size most suitable for their applications and defining COMMAREAs that utilize these pages most efficiently. Realize that CICS will require storage within these areas for control information (Storage Accounting Areas, etc.), which actually calculates to approximately 24 bytes.

4 Byte SAA
16 Bytes (Internal CICS Addresses)
4 Byte Length of Data Area

Using this calculation, COMMAREAs can be specified to utilize page sizes:

$(2K * n) - 24$ if page size = 2K

$(4K * n) - 24$ if page size = 4K

and allocate COMMAREAs that fit within the aligned blocks of storage within the CICS DSA. Of course, the amount of storage recovered would depend on the number of COMMAREAs at any given time and their size.

This storage can also be redistributed by using DFHTEMP main instead of COMMAREAs, since these data areas always reside above the 16-Mb line.

Size Restrictions and Limitations While most programmers are aware of the 32K size restriction of COMMAREA, this constraint can be further complicated if the installation is using ISC (Intersystem Communication). If two CICS systems are communicating, applications can transfer control across the link and therefore pass data.

Some customers have noticed that definition of these links with RDO (Resource Definition Online) restricts the maximum value of the field SENDSIZE for any SESSION definition to 30720. When transferring data between ISC sessions, the data must be contained within the RU (Request Unit) of the communications session. The architecture of transmission restricts the size of these RUs to 30720, and CICS cannot extend this restriction.

Installations that are passing COMMAREAs over an ISC link must be aware that 32K is not allowed, that the communication protocol further restricts this data size to 30720.

Further restrictions on size of COMMAREAs can be found in the CICS APRM (Application Programmer's Reference Manual). In the section "Passing Data to Other Programs," IBM states:

. . . the receiving data need not be of the same length as the original communication area; if access is required only to the first part of the data, the new data area can be shorter. It must not be longer than the length of the communication being passed, because the results in this situation are unpredictable.

Although unstated, the results are also usually undesirable. Many programmers have attempted this technique and achieved various results, including the total loss of COMMAREA and/or corruption of the data. The condition is caused by the actual machine instructions that are generated by the compiler for execution. If the MOVE instruction, such as

MOVE DFHCOMMAREA TO WS-COMMAREA ....

attempts to move an area that is greater than 256 bytes, a different instruction is generated than would be used to move an area that is 256 bytes or less.

The compiler generates an MVC (Move Character) instruction for any MOVE of COMMAREAs that are 256 bytes or less. The MVCL (Move Character Long) instruction is generated for the larger (> 257) request. This alternative instruction (MVCL) performs additional checking of send/receive size combinations. If any potential corruption of data can be detected (e.g., overlap), the transfer of data is terminated. In these cases, the programmer observes the apparent loss of data during the move. CICS does not detect the condition and returns no condition to the program.

For this reason, some programmers have successfully avoided the warning from the APRM when the receiving size is larger than the sending size, but less than 257 bytes. Be warned, however, that size variations in these passed data areas must conform to published support. For consistent results, use only techniques that are recommended by current documentation.

EXEC CICS RETURN TRANSID(xxxx) COMMAREA Enhancement   As previously stated, CICS/MVS 2.1.1 contains an enhancement that moves these COMMAREAs "above the line." Realize, however, the exact implementation of this new facility.

The COMMAREA is moved above the line between transactions and then passed to the next transaction (if it is AMODE(31)). Prior to this enhancement, the storage was acquired from the DSA and left there until requested by the next transaction.

Some programmers do not check to ensure that the COMMAREA length specified in the RETURN is indeed equal to the actual length of the data area. IBM recommends that programmers ALWAYS check the length of the area via the EIBCALEN field of the EIB and compare it to the size built in the program.

A new problem arises in CICS/MVS 2.1.1 when the values are not equal, especially when the data area being moved from DFHCOMMAREA is larger than the area in Working Storage. Prior to this implementation, the passed COMMAREA came from the DSA and, if not equal, at least contained valid data (from the DSA) that the program could accommodate, even if not used. When this storage is being returned from 31-bit areas of MVS storage, the resulting areas may be of unknown value and not even allocated or initialized. This MVS storage area cannot be assumed to contain data similar to DSA storage. Potential program checks and other unpredictable results can be expected. COMMAREAs should always be checked for proper and equal value when data is being transferred.

1.6 RES Compiler Option vs. CICS Residency

Programmers can make their programs resident in CICS for performance reasons. With this option, the program can be loaded a single time and remain for the life of the CICS region. In addition, installations can choose to establish residency for some COBOL management modules using the RES compiler option. The techniques used for these two approaches are very different.

1.6.1 Program Residency Specifications

Programs can be made resident within CICS via the RES=YES option in the program specification (PPT or RDO). If the program is defined as resident, it will be loaded into CICS at first reference and remain for the duration of the CICS address space. Of course, programs that are linked with AMODE(31) RMODE(ANY) will be loaded into extended storage (31-bit) rather than below the 16-Mb line and will not detract from the storage "below the line."

This can be a substantial performance advantage, depending on the operating environment. Programs loaded in extended storage will never be loaded again, even if unreferenced, yet the storage will not reduce CICS DSA storage. If the installation is experiencing a shortage of real memory and paging occurs, these resident programs may be paged-out. Paging, however, is much more efficient than program loading, since when the program is referenced, only the pages required for the request will be paged back in. If the installation possesses a CPU with expanded storage, paging will utilize this type of storage, making the paging process even more efficient.

While in the past many installations limited the residency of programs, since they would impact the available storage for CICS DSA, recent enhancements provide alternatives to make this facility more viable.

1.6.2 NEWCOPY Issues

One issue remains an obstacle to program residency. If the resident program is modified and relinked, it cannot be "refreshed" within CICS and retain residency. Programs that are "dynamic" and modified often are not good candidates for residency. When the command

CEMT SET PROG(xxxxxx) NEWCOPY

is used, the previously resident program is now nonresident for the remainder of the life of the CICS address space.

The reason for the removal of residency can be blamed on the CICS load logic. Resident programs are loaded during initialization into a "special" subpool in CICS, since they must be loaded and packed in the sequence of definition. This subpool is never compressed if storage becomes unavailable, as does the DSA during program compression, since the programs are defined resident and therefore never again loaded.

If CICS detects a request for NEWCOPY of the program, a modification has obviously been made. This could affect many characteristics of the module, especially the size, and it may then not refit into the previous slot. The NEWCOPY request must then move the program into the "normal" subpool within the DSA, which is continually scanned for program compression requirement. It cannot be reclassified as RESIDENT and is treated the same as all other CICS programs.

Use of CICS-resident programs is very installation-dependent, since it affects both performance of the application and the entire CICS system. While no recommendations can be globally made, any program that is used extensively, requires good performance, yet is seldom if ever "NEWCOPIED," may be a candidate for CICS residency.

1.6.3 RES Compiler Option

Installations may choose to incorporate some of the COBOL support modules within the CICS system or within the program modules for performance enhancements. COBOL library subroutines, required at execution time, can be made available to the CICS application via two techniques.

In the installation of either OS/VS COBOL or VS COBOL II, some product modules are eligible for LPA (Link Pack Area) and can be placed in this MVS "global" storage area if necessary. Any modules in LPA are addressable to any address space; therefore, they can be utilized by CICS directly from LPA storage.

Use of the NORES compiler option causes COBOL routines to be link-edited into the COBOL module. The use of RES in the COBOL compiler options causes the COBOL library subroutines to be loaded dynamically at run time. The combination of RES and NODYNAM with CALLed subroutines requires that the required library subroutines be permanently resident. If they are not, they will be loaded into the CICS address space during program execution. Storage fragmentation will result if a static CALL is made to a COBOL subroutine, since the library subroutines will never be deleted from OS storage.

On the other hand, overall DSA usage may be reduced with RES, since only one copy of the COBOL subroutine is necessary. With NORES, every COBOL program contains the subroutines linked into the program module, causing redundancy of code loaded into the CICS DSA at run time.

1.7 CICS/OS2 Issues

Many CICS systems people were amazed when CICS was announced to run on a personal computer, yet installations are using the new product for many innovative applications. While this platform may not be applicable to all installations, it provides facilities that are not, and may never be, available on the mainframe product. Programmers may wish to investigate this new offering for potential function in future development.

1.7.1 CICS/OS2 1.2 Characteristics

The most current release of the product is Version 1 Release 2. While previous releases provided many facilities including the CICS command level API for application development and VSAM file support, this release offers even more enhancements. Following are some of the features of CICS/OS2 that programmers may be interested in.

CICS API The command set for this product is much closer to CICS/MVS 2.1 than in the first release. The API now available to programmers includes most of the host commands, including:

- Extra-partition Temporary Data queues
- POST, WAIT, DELAY, FORMATTIME
- ENQUEUE, DEQUEUE, SUSPEND
- SIGNON and SIGNOFF
- SET and INQUIRE
- ISSUE PRINT, SEND TEXT

In addition, this product has something that the mainframe CICS does not: the capability for graphics or window development. CICS/OS2 applications can call Presentation Manager and Dialog Manager services from within the CICS transaction to exploit the full capabilities of OS/2EE. CICS applications are no longer restricted to the BMS services that confine mainframe transactions.

CICS/OS2 applications can utilize EDF (Execution Diagnostic Facility) for debugging or use the source level debug features of the COBOL compiler on the workstation.

One major enhancement in the new version is full bi-directional support of cooperative processing. In other words, CICS applications on the workstation or on the mainframe have full capabilities of Transaction Routing, Function Shipping, and Distributed Transaction Processing. Figure 1-9 demonstrates the full capabilities of communication between CICS/OS2 and the other CICS products. This true bi-directional capability provides the ability to place the CICS application at the optimum location. The addition of DPL — Distributed Program Link — provides even greater function within CICS to distribute processing requirements. This facility will be more fully described later in this chapter.

1.7.2 External Call Interface — Distributed Program Link

This facility should not be confused with the External Transaction Initiation facility. Both processes are fully documented in the CICS/OS2 System and Application Guide.

To: From:	CICS OS/2 OS/2 EE	CICS OS/2 DOS	CICS/ESA	CICS/MVS	CICS/OS/VS	CICS/DOS/VS	CICS/VM
CICS/OS2 OS/2 EE	LU6.2 DTP Dist. link Fn. ship Tx. route Net Bios Dist. link Fn. ship Tx. route	Not supported	LU6.2 DTP Dist. link Fn. ship Tx. route LU2 Fn. ship	LU6.2 DTP Dist. link Fn. ship Tx. route LU2 Fn. ship	LU6.2 DTP Fn. ship Tx. route LU2 Fn. ship	LU6.2 DTP Dist. link Fn. ship Tx. route LU2 Fn. ship	LU2 Fn. ship
CICS OS/2 DOS	Net Bios Fn. ship Tx. route	Not supported	LU2 Fn. ship	LU2 Fn. ship	LU2 Fn. ship	LU2 Fn. ship	Not supported
CICS/ESA	LU6.2 DTP Fn. ship Tx. route	Not supported					
CICS/MVS	LU6.2 DTP Fn. ship Tx. route	Not supported					
CICS/OS/VS	LU6.2 DTP	Not supported	Key to abbreviations:				
CICS/DOS/VS	LU6.2 DTP Fn. ship Tx. route	Not supported	Dist. link — Distributed CICS link DTP — Distributed transaction processing Fn. ship — Function shipping LAN — Local area network Tx. route — Transaction routing				
CICS/VM	Not supported	Not supported					

Figure 1-9 CICS/OS2 communication capabilities.

External Transaction Initialization gives the programmer the ability to invoke a specific CICS transaction or program from the Start Programs List. A program or transaction can be defined in the list and then invoked.

Rather than download data to the workstation, the application can be designed to execute required function within CICS/OS2 and then "link" to a program on the mainframe, returning to the workstation when complete. This facility is utilized by

EXEC CICS LINK PROGRAM(progext) COMMAREA(name)

where progext is a program defined to CICS/OS2 as a remote program in the host CICS. The program definition contains the SYSID of the host CICS system that will be the target of the program. The two CICS systems establish an LU6.2 connection for this communication, and the workstation transmits the request to the host.

Information is passed to the host via the COMMAREA for processing in the "linked to" program. When complete, the host program returns control to the workstation, again passing data back via the COMMAREA. This process can be very valuable to applications running on the workstation, since it avoids moving data to that location if not necessary. Many installations wish to distribute their processing, but not their data.

In addition, some data cannot be distributed to this environment. Both DL/I and DB/2 data cannot reside on the workstation, and therefore cannot be distributed. Applications in CICS/OS2, however, can use DPL to access these databases on the mainframe and process the results back on the workstation.

Many installations have attempted this process by "rolling their own" and writing APPC (Advanced Program-to-Program Communications) applications for workstation-to-host processing. This new facility provides SUPPORTED commands and a simple, straightforward technique for distribution of programs.

1.8 PL/I Programs

Some installations choose to code CICS applications in PL/I instead of COBOL. These programs have additional issues that need to be addressed.

1.8.1 CALL to COBOL II Restrictions

Restrictions exist for any applications that CALL subroutines of dissimilar languages within CICS. In the VS COBOL II Application Programming Guide, programmers are warned:

. . . No CALLs are allowed to or from PL/I programs . . .

The only supported technique to invoke programs with dissimilar languages is with LINK or XCTL commands, not with CALL. The restriction does not permit multi-language routines to be linked together for execution within CICS.

CICS performs the program loading and initialization process when the program is requested. This process occurs for the initial CSECT (code section) of the load module only, and therefore cannot reinitialize the environment for another language after execution has begun.

PL/I programs that wish to invoke VS COBOL II routines could, on the other hand, LINK to a VS COBOL II program that subsequently CALLed VS COBOL II subprograms.

1.8.2 Macro and Command Programs

PL/I programs can contain both macros and commands, although these programs will be unsupported in CICS/ESA 3.1 and must be converted to command-only.

Mixed-mode PL/I programs must follow a specific sequence of steps during the compile process:

- Execute the CICS macro-level preprocessor
- Execute the Assembler (F or H)
- Execute the CICS command-level translator
- Execute the PL/I compiler
- Execute the Linkage Editor

In this sequence, both the macros and the commands will be properly processed, translated, and compiled into an executable load module.

1.8.3 Version 2 Enhancements

PL/I Version 2 provides both processor and runtime performance improvements since it contains the ability to execute "preinitialized" programs. Unfortunately, these programs cannot be executed within CICS. Other enhancements are CICS-related, however.

Improvements in subscripting and allocation can be utilized by CICS programs including CMPAT=V2, which removes the previous restriction of halfword subscripts. While this provides the support for extremely large arrays, programmers should take care not to specify PL/I areas that would affect CICS performance.

An additional routine, IBMFXITA, can be used in CICS to exit routines to be invoked at both initialization and termination for control of execution options and error handling. Full documentation can be found in the PL/I V2 Installation and Customization Guide.

1.9 Miscellaneous Issues

Several items are popular issues, although they do not fit into any of the predefined section headings. Programmers should be aware of the following design considerations and potential hazards of the facilities.

1.9.1 Programmed Interface to Master Terminal Functions

Some installations have found the need to use some of the same functions as the master terminal transaction — CEMT. While programs cannot directly invoke the transaction, there is a "programmed interface" to the facility that can be used by any task for similar functions. Since this facility is very powerful, it is not documented by the APRM and is considered a "restricted" operation.

Use of the CEMT program DFHEMTA is documented in the CICS Customization Guide, but examples and addressing techniques are not provided. Many programmers have solved the problem themselves, but care must be taken to ensure that this facility is used properly and by personnel who are granted that authority.

SET/INQUIRE

These commands are also documented in the CICS Customization Guide and are considered "restricted" because of the power of their functions. The SET/INQUIRE commands are being enhanced, however, and may replace the programmed interface, since they have the capability to be secured.

In the CICS/ESA 3.1 Release Guide, GC33-0655, IBM announces the enhancements to these commands, with additional security for protection against unauthorized use.

The INQUIRE and SET commands will be restricted for:

PROGRAM	SYSTEM	TRANSACTION
TERMINAL	NETNAME	CONNECTION
TASK	FILE	DSNAME

to name just a few. In this way, extensive inquiry will be made available to programs, with the ability to change values with the corresponding SET. Not only are these facilities undocumented in the typical programming manual (APRM), the only information about them will be found in the new CICS/ESA System Programming Reference Manual.

1.9.2 Addressability to Internal Areas

Many programmers have complained that addressability to internal areas justifies the preservation of macros in their transactions. True, many techniques available to macro programs cannot be replicated in commands. The previously described enhancement in CICS/ESA 3.1 adds to command capability.

Other installations have resorted to user exits, most written in Assembler, to provide function that is unavailable by commands. These exits are also documented (some more completely than others) in the CICS/MVS Customization Guide.

Again, CICS/ESA 3.1 provides major enhancements in the customization interface and user exit facility. The enhancements in this version are substantial, and include:

- User exits that conform to MVS linkage conventions
- XPI (Exit Programming Interface) for CICS services
- New global user exits for the new domains
- New PLT initialization for prerecovery exit enabling

A table is provided in the CICS/ESA 3.1 Release Guide that identifies all the new CICS domains, the exit name, and all exit-specific parameters for addressing data within the domain. This will, no doubt, be more completely documented in other manuals of the product.

Installations must then prepare to migrate to these new exits and replace any routines currently in place that address internal CICS areas.

1.9.3 ASKTIME and FORMATTIME

As previously stated, CICS applications are restricted from issuing MVS commands or any COBOL statements that request operating system resources. Several of these restricted commands deal with time and date services such as:

CURRENT-DATE   DATE   DAY   TIME

Since these cannot (or should not) be used in CICS applications, programmers must utilize the supported commands ASKTIME and FORMATTIME for all "time-controlled" functions.

These commands are used to query the CICS-controlled clock and obtain the date and time for use within the transaction. Many CICS applications are driven by time-controlled events or at specific intervals. The clock within CICS provides the required data for interval or time functions.

At initiation, CICS updates the EIB with the current date and time. These values are not changed until the application issues

```
EXEC CICS ASKTIME
 END-EXEC.
```

to request that CICS update the EIBDATE and EIBTIME fields. Note that the subsequent option ABSTIME is not required for the update request.

CICS provides the current time in an "absolute" time format. Two fields, EIBDATE and EIBTIME, are updated for the requesting task to now contain up-to-date values. This absolute time is in milliseconds (since hour 0 of January 1) and fairly unusable until converted with

```
EXEC CICS FORMATTIME(timearea) ...
```

The options chosen in this second command allow the program total control over the format of the date and time. Some of the options allow characters for separation of the numbers and any sequence of month/day/year combination.

Use of these two commands prevents the need for requests to the operating system for either date or time and accomplishes the task in an efficient manner within CICS.

1.9.4 Compiler Options

COBOL programs must be compiled with proper options and cannot use some options available for batch COBOL programs. As with command restrictions, options cannot be used if they require the use of operating system services. CICS must be allowed to control the execution environment of all applications. The restrictions for both OS/VS COBOL programs and VS COBOL II programs are listed below.

OS/VS COBOL programs cannot use the compiler options:

COUNT	DYNAM	ENDJOB	FLOW
STATE	SYMDUMP	SYST	TEST

VS COBOL II programs cannot use the compiler options:

DBCS	DYNAM	GRAPHIC	NOLIB
NORENT	NORES	TRUNC	

1.10 CICS Data Tables

In CICS/MVS 2.1.1, IBM announced Data Tables, an enhancement to VSAM KSDS file processing. This facility could be a substantial benefit to CICS programmers, since it allows data to be "loaded" into the CICS address space for improved performance. When data is readily accessible to the program when requested, the task spends less time waiting for data and more time in productive processing.

The Data Tables feature is available as an additional license to CICS/MVS 2.1.1 and must be ordered separately. The feature is "bundled" into CICS/ESA Version 3 and is shipped with the base product.

1.10.1 Programming Considerations

Use of the Data Tables feature will require very few changes to the application. This facility allows the program to create, maintain, and access data stored within the tables. If the tables are maintained by CICS, existing applications can be run without any modifications. If the application wishes to control the table, additional considerations must be made.

In either case, the VSAM KSDS is defined to CICS as a data table with the new FCT (File Control Table) option

```
DFHFCT   TYPE=(CICSTABLE/USERTABLE)
```

and

```
SIZE=nnnn
```

The data is then accessible to the program via standard CICS commands, as supported by the API (Application Programming Interface). Each data table is identified with a VSAM KSDS, where the source data is stored before loading into virtual storage.

If the program uses data tables, it can choose between two types:

• CICS-maintained data tables
• User-maintained data tables

The difference between the two types relates to maintenance of the data and performance requirements.

1.10.1.1 CICS vs. User-Maintained Tables

CICS-Maintained Data Tables   These tables synchronize all modifications between the source data (VSAM KSDS) and the data table within CICS. Any change to one is automatically reflected in the other. Programs using CICS-maintained tables have the full command API support, including data integrity and recovery. Any request to the data table that cannot be satisfied (such as record not found) will be automatically routed to the source VSAM KSDS.

These attributes of CICS-maintained data tables allow existing applications to run intact, with no required modifications.

User-Maintained Data Tables   These tables are *not* synchronized with the source data and are, in fact, logically detached. The user program must reflect the change in the source data if required. The records in these tables, however, can be modified by the program as well as accessed.

Programs using these tables can use a subset of the command API and are restricted from some file control requests such as BROWSE. In addition, requests not satisfied by data in the table are not routed to the source data and return conditions such as NOTFND to the application.

While somewhat more restrictive, these tables provide optimum performance since *no* physical I/O is ever performed. All requests are satisfied from CICS virtual storage. This data, however, is not recoverable since modifications are not reflected in the source VSAM file.

1.10.1.2 Data Suitable for Tables

With integrity and recovery restrictions, not all types of data would be good candidates for these tables. Data that is accessed very frequently, yet seldom updated, would be able to take advantage of this facility. Many installations use storage areas, such as Main Temporary Storage, TCTUA, or CWA (common work area), to "load" data for CICS applications. Some have written their own interfaces to store data within CICS for all applications to reference.

Data Tables provide a supported, common facility for data that many applications will require. Some common uses include:

• Subset records or fields — selected records or fields can be copied from existing customer data into a table. Subsequent requests for this information can be directed to the data already stored within CICS without the overhead of full file or record processing.

- Demographic data — customer or product descriptive data can be stored when frequently requested. This information usually remains unchanged, yet is constantly required by CICS tasks.

One existing restriction of data tables is the single-system image that is created that prevents data sharing. Since the data is stored within the CICS address space, it is not available to other address spaces, either CICS systems or batch jobs. If another CICS region wishes to access the data, the VSAM KSDS source data is available but may not reflect any changes made to the table within the other CICS. The "second" CICS must load the data into its own table for either CICS-maintained or user-maintained access.

In addition, data integrity and recovery is not provided since user-maintained tables do not synchronize the data. Any failure of the address space will destroy the virtual contents of the data table.

Installations may find many good candidates for data tables, however, and be able to take advantage of the new facility.

1.10.2 Data Tables vs. LSR Buffers

Chapter 3 will deal extensively with CICS LSR (Local Shared Resources) programming issues. In that chapter, LSR is recommended for almost all CICS VSAM files, since the data loaded into LSR buffers is stored within available CICS virtual storage. How does that process compare with CICS data tables? Should VSAM files be moved from LSR buffers into tables?

Of course, the question can only be answered with extensive research. Not all data should be good candidates for tables, especially since LSR has been enhanced to provide very similar qualities. In both CICS/MVS Version 2 and CICS/ESA Version 3, LSR buffers can be defined to Hiperspaces (high-performance data spaces) and can then utilize expanded storage. If the customer's CPU contains adequate expanded storage, LSR buffers use this storage for improved performance.

Realize, however, that VSAM files defined to LSR pools are managed as buffers, which are actually pools of virtual storage based on the CI (control interval) size of the file. Only the active data within the file actually remain in the LSR buffers, so very large VSAM files are "cached" by the process. Active records remain in CICS LSR storage, and inactive records remain within the physical file on DASD. For this reason, very large VSAM files, or files with random access patterns within CICS, may not be good candidates for data tables.

Data that can be "subsetted" from the VSAM file and subsequently loaded within a table for frequent access performs better as a table than within LSR. This provides a more efficient use of storage within CICS if the access falls within the Data Tables feature restrictions. CICS-maintained tables perform optimally with full key nonupdated READ operations. Other requests, especially BROWSE operations, may not benefit at all.

In summary, the new Data Tables feature offers new alternatives to programmers and should be considered for future applications and existing programs.

2

VS COBOL II

VS COBOL II is the SAA (System Application Architecture) compliant language for most CICS applications. Of course, CICS can now support the C language, which is also SAA-compliant, but most installations will retain their commitment to COBOL. Since VS COBOL II is the generally accepted SAA language, it will therefore be required for any "portability" of applications across the SAA platforms. In other words, only VS COBOL II applications will have the ability to take source code from the MVS, OS/2, OS/400, and, now, VSE/ESA operating systems and recompile without changes for execution in the target system. This can provide substantial savings for installations in recoding efforts when the distribution of systems is required.

For these reasons and others, many installations are now actively migrating existing CICS applications to VS COBOL II. When a CICS application is converted from OS/VS COBOL to VS COBOL II, there are several items that must be changed in CICS to allow support of the new language. In addition, the application must contain changes that are necessary in the new language support. Following are highlights of the necessary CICS support required for COBOL II support and several items that apply specifically to programs that will be using the new facilities.

2.1 CICS Support of COBOL II

CICS applications can utilize COBOL II in any version of CICS, Version 1, 2, or 3. The changes are mainly in the new language modules that must be available to CICS and in the options that COBOL II now provides. One of the most significant advantages of using COBOL II is the virtual storage relief provided by the facility. This has always been a major factor in CICS, and installations are using many techniques to save storage or use it most efficiently. With COBOL II, program storage can be used in a 31-bit mode, relieving storage requirements "below the line."

In addition, the new "optimization" feature of VS COBOL II can substantially reduce the size of the resulting load module. Some installations have reported a decrease of 15–20% in the program size after converting to VS COBOL II. The combination of reduced program capacity and 31-bit exploitation provides substantial benefits in a CICS environment.

2.1.1 CICS Initialization Requirements

When an installation is beginning the conversion of any program, care must be taken to ensure that proper support is provided in the CICS regions that will be running the applications. Following is a list of items that must be changed or added into the CICS region or the program before the first execution can begin.

1. Do not use the ALOWCBL=NO option when installing the VS COBOL II product. The CICS translator generates a CBL statement, and this option will be incompatible with the CICS module produced.
2. Use the CICS translator option COBOL2 when preparing CICS programs. In addition, use the ANSI85 translator option if the program will implement the ANSI 85 standard.
3. Place VS COBOL II module IGZECIC into an MVS authorized library that will be available to the CICS region.
4. Place the additional VS COBOL II modules into an available DFHRPL library (more detail will be provided in the next section). Define these modules to CICS via RDO DEFINE PROGRAM commands. A list of programs is made available in the MVS library SYS1.SAMPLIB(IGZ9PPT).
5. Update the SIT with COBOL2=YES.
6. Use required VS COBOL II compiler options NODYNAM, RESIDENT, and RENT. This may be confusing, since programs with NODYNAM are allowed to have dynamic CALLs. This compiler option does not affect the support of dynamic CALL.

A complete explanation of installation issues can be found in the VS COBOL II Installation Guide and the VS COBOL II Migration Guide.

2.1.2 CCCA (CICS Command Level Conversion Aid)

A product has been made available to assist in the conversion of CICS programs to COBOL II. CCCA (product number 5785-ABJ) converts CICS (and non-CICS) programs from OS/VS COBOL to VS COBOL II. The primary facilities of CCCA enable one to:

- Convert most syntax differences between the two languages
- Eliminate conflict between variables and COBOL II reserved words
- Flag elements that cannot be directly converted
- Provide a statement-by-statement diagnostic listing including management reports
- Convert EXEC CICS commands into proper COBOL II format
- Remove/convert BLL (Base Locator for Linkage) references

Some installations may use this facility to reduce the conversion effort and time required. Locate the CCCA manuals for a full description of the product capabilities.

2.2 Program Calls with COBOL II in CICS

2.2.1 Dynamic Call Utilization

In an IBM announcement dated February 7, 1989, "CICS/MVS Version 2 Release 1 Enhancements . . . ," the following item can be found:

ENHANCED COBOL SUPPORT

VS COBOL II programs running under CICS can now use COBOL dynamic CALLs to invoke subprograms that contain requests for CICS services."

Of course, this enhancement will never be available in CICS/OS/VS 1.7. VS COBOL II programs will run in 1.7, but they cannot call programs that contain CICS commands.

With CICS/MVS 2.1.1, programs can dynamically call other VS COBOL II programs and have all the capabilities of a "main" VS COBOL II program. This facility provides execution of CICS commands within a dynamically CALLed VS COBOL II subprogram. Previous problems with the processing of normal and abnormal termination of these programs has been eliminated. The use of dynamic calls eliminates the need for CICS LINK and the corresponding COMMAREA. Data is passed instead via variables in the CALL statement itself.

The following chart summarizes the availability of CALLer and CALLed programs with VS COBOL II. The chart assumes CICS/MVS 2.1.1 environments or later.

CALLer Program	Type of CALL	CALLed Program
COBOL II	STATIC	COBOL II
COBOL II	DYNAMIC	COBOL II
COBOL II	STATIC	ASSEMBLER
COBOL II	DYNAMIC	ASSEMBLER

The "CALLed" program (if DYNAMIC) must be defined (via RDO) and available to CICS (in DFHRPL) as well as the main program. Previous supported CALLs did not require these definitions, but remember, previous CALLs were restricted to subroutines that did not contain CICS commands. These new CALLed routines may include CICS commands, and thus are not "OS loaded." CICS must locate the definitions for proper loading. If CICS is unable to locate the CALLed module in any DFHRPL library, the VS COBOL II message:

IGZ029I ...... ABCODE 1029

will result with a corresponding CICS transaction ABEND.

Application Changes When Using Dynamic Calls   Replacing existing LINKs in application programs with dynamic CALLs will require extensive changes to the source. In the calling program, the LINK and corresponding COMMAREA need to be replaced with the CALL pgm USING syntax with corresponding parameters to pass data. In the "called" program, changes need to be made to accept the new parameters rather than the previous COMMAREA. This would include changes to both the USING option and the LINKAGE section.

If the program is passing parameters and the CALLed program contains CICS commands (was translated with the CICS translator), the CALL statement must pass:

DFHEIBLK (CICS EXEC Interface Block) as the first parameter

DFHCOMMAREA as the second parameter

. . . followed by any other optional program parameters

Following is a sample of a VS COBOL II program that uses a DYNAMIC CALL to a VS COBOL II program translated by CICS.

```
....
Working-Storage Section.
    77  PROGA  PIC X(08) VALUE 'PROGA  '.
Procedure Division.
    CALL PROGA Using DFHEIBLK DFHCOMMAREA
            PARM1 PARM2.
....
End Program PROGB.
```

Be aware of performance changes that may occur in the CICS transaction. IBM has measured performance between LINK and the VS COBOL II static call and found that the static call performs better than the LINK. The dynamic call, however, may not perform as well as the static call and may produce additional overhead during execution time.

Complete coverage of LINK and CALL characteristics, with corresponding examples, can be found in Chapter 1.

2.2.2 CALLs to COBOL II from Assembler Programs

In the CICS Application Program Reference Manual (APRM), IBM documents that a CICS Assembler program cannot CALL a VS COBOL II program. The CALL was allowed in OS/VS COBOL but is not supported in VS COBOL II.

The problem is created by the manner in which VS COBOL II is initialized. CICS must recognize the COBOL II environment when the program is invoked and cannot do so if CALLed by an Assembler program. The APRM advises one to use EXEC CICS LINK from the Assembler program if transfer of control is necessary. The LINK allows CICS to recognize the COBOL II requirements.

2.3 CICS Issues with COBOL II

There are several issues that must be understood when converting OS/VS COBOL programs to VS COBOL II. Some are directly related to the fact that the program will be executing in a CICS environment rather than batch. This section will attempt to cover some of these concerns.

2.3.1 Working Storage Changes

Limitations on Size   Most programmers are aware of the 64K Working Storage size limitation for any OS/VS COBOL program. While there is no restriction listed for VS COBOL II, the technique that CICS uses to acquire the storage can transfer this limitation into COBOL II programs if not avoided.

The Working Storage for a COBOL II program is acquired via the

EXEC CICS GETMAIN FLENGTH(xxxxx)

CICS command. As documented in the APRM, the size of this GETMAIN request will be accommodated by the following table:

FLENGTH Vale	24-Bit	31-Bit
1–4095	BELOW	BELOW
4K–64K	BELOW	ABOVE
64K–1GB	N/A	ABOVE

Requests for storage acquired above the 16-Mb line may actually be loaded below the line if insufficient extended storage is available.

Note, however, that any requests from 24-bit programs for more than 64K are not allowed and will result in a length error.

If a VS COBOL II program is compiled with the DATA(24) option or link-edited with AMODE(24) RMODE(24) attributes, the CICS limitation (table above) applies and causes a COBOL II 1009 ABEND. The CICS GETMAIN cannot accommodate the request, even though it came from a COBOL II program.

To create a Working Storage size of greater than 64K, the COBOL II program must be compiled with the DATA(31) option and link-edited with AMODE(31) RMODE(ANY) attributes.

Working Storage Initialization   There are substantial differences in the manner by which VS COBOL II acquires and initializes Working

Storage. With OS/VS COBOL, CICS assumed the responsibility for allocating the storage and immediately initialized it to hex zeros.

In VS COBOL II, the runtime library routines pass the request to CICS to acquire the storage and do not initialize the contents. If the storage needs to be initialized, the runtime option WSCLEAR can be used to "clear" the area and force the hex zero values. While this option was not available in early releases of the product, it was made available in Release 2 and is documented in the SC26-4045 VS COBOL II Application Programming Guide.

The following items identify Working Storage considerations when using VS COBOL II programs that perform either LINK or CALLs.

CICS LINK   Working Storage is always initialized after the LINK to the new program, since control is being transferred to a new program or transaction.

VS COBOL II CALL   If the CALLed program uses the INITIAL option, Working Storage will be initialized at entry to the CALL.

If the CALLed program does not use INITIAL, Working Storage is initialized on the first CALL to the program and is in the "last used" state on any subsequent CALLs after the first.

Some programmers, in OS/VS COBOL, wrote routines to address fixed locations of Working Storage. For example, the first "77 Level" in the block of storage could always be located at the same offset in any program. Once found, the Assembler program could scan the rest of storage to locate compiler information such as TIME/DATE stamps or version levels.

Unfortunately, VS COBOL II was designed much differently. Working Storage does not even exist at the time the program is loaded into CICS, it is acquired (as previously explained) by CICS at the start of execution. Programs that expected fixed Working Storage contents will be affected by conversion to COBOL II and will probably not work at all.

Since Working Storage does not exist at program load, it also does not exist as part of the object module. The contents of this storage are defined by a "dictionary," from which Working Storage is built dynamically when the program is executed. The storage will be acquired above the line or below via the DATA compile option selection: DATA(31) above, DATA(24) below.

This feature, along with the OPTIMIZE option, tends to significantly affect the size and performance of VS COBOL II programs. As previously stated, COBOL II load modules are usually much smaller than previous OS/VS COBOL modules. Figure 2-1 contains a typical

OS/VS COBOL program. This particular example calls a date sub-routine and then compares that information to date/time received via the EXEC CICS ASKTIME facility. Figure 2-2 displays the subsequent linkage information, with a total length of this module as x"CD8" (1).

This program was recompiled with VS COBOL II, deleting the SERVICE RELOAD DFHEIBLK as required but with no other modifications. Figure 2-3 contains the resulting source, and, as shown, no changes were made. Figure 2-4 displays the linkage information from the new VS COBOL II output, with the new total length of x"AB8" (1). The decrease in size is significant and is representative of the savings that can be realized with VS COBOL II conversion.

2.3.2 OPTIMIZE Option

The OPTIMIZE option may be utilized in VS COBOL II during compile to enhance execution of the program. The VS COBOL II optimizer analyzes and eliminates unnecessary transfer of control within the program as well as instructions that are never executed. It may relocate PERFORM instructions to other locations in the program for improved performance.

CICS applications that are converted to VS COBOL II may experience some new messages and results when using the OPTIMIZE compiler option. This option is utilized to enhance performance of the program, but may actually change the way the program is executed.

When the VS COBOL II optimizer detects code that will never be executed, it actually deletes it from the resulting module and issues a warning message to the programmer. VS COBOL II can identify the value of data items tested in a condition and remove any subsequent instructions (ELSE . . .) if the value will never be reached. OS/VS COBOL does not have that capability.

Unfortunately, if a data item is modified via a CALL, but the data is not returned with the USING clause, VS COBOL II cannot recognize the modified value. The optimizer may remove code incorrectly due to the format of the CALL. Use the GC26-4047, VS COBOL II Language Reference Manual for more complete information on CALL syntax.

Of course, since performance and testing should be mutually exclusive, this option is not allowed with the TEST option. See Section 2.5 for use of the TEST option prior to use of OPTIMIZE.

7   DCNEAX00   8.45.17   JUL 10,1990

```
00164                    CALL 'DFHEI1'.
00165                    SERVICE RELOAD DFHEIBLK.
00166             0000-PROGRAM-DCNEAX00.
00167
00168                    PERFORM 0500-RECEIVE THRU 0500-EXIT.
00169
00170                    IF CALL-DFHDATE
00171                        PERFORM 0600-CALL-DFHDATE THRU 0600-EXIT
00172                    ELSE
00173                        PERFORM 0700-ASKTIME THRU 0700-EXIT.
00174
00175                    MOVE WS-SYSTIME TO WS-M-A-TIME.
00176                    MOVE WS-SYSDATE TO WS-M-A-DATE.
00177
00178                    PERFORM 9000-RETURN.
00179
00180               0500-RECEIVE.
00181
00182                    MOVE WS-RECEIVE-LENGTH TO WS-RECEIVED-LENGTH.
00183
00184             *EXEC CICS RECEIVE
00185             *          INTO(WS-RECEIVE-AREA)
00186             *          LENGTH(WS-RECEIVED-LENGTH)
00187             *          RESP(WS-RESP)
00188             *END-EXEC.
00189                    MOVE ' {              00100   ' TO DFHEIVO
00190                    CALL 'DFHEI1' USING DFHEIVO  WS-RECEIVE-AREA
00191                    WS-RECEIVED-LENGTH
00192                                      MOVE EIBRESP TO WS-RESP.
00193
00194
00195               0500-EXIT.  EXIT.
00196
00197               0600-CALL-DFHDATE.
00198
00199                    CALL 'DFHDATE' USING EIBDATE, WS-SYSDATE.
00200
00201               0600-EXIT.  EXIT.
00202
00203               0700-ASKTIME.
00204
00205             *EXEC CICS ASKTIME
00206             *          ABSTIME(WS-ABSTIME)
00207             *END-EXEC.
00208                    MOVE '¢              00116   ' TO DFHEIVO
00209                    CALL 'DFHEI1' USING DFHEIVO  WS-ABSTIME.
00210
00211
00212             *EXEC CICS FORMATTIME
00213             *          ABSTIME(WS-ABSTIME)
00214             *          MMDDYY(WS-SYSDATE)
00215             *          DATESEP('/')
00216             *          TIME(WS-SYSTIME)
00217             *          TIMESEP(':')
00218             *END-EXEC.
00219                    MOVE '¢ dc dc        00120   ' TO DFHEIVO
00220                    MOVE '/' TO DFHEIV9
00221                    MOVE ':' TO DFHC0011
00222                    CALL 'DFHEI1' USING DFHEIVO  WS-ABSTIME DFHDUMMY DFHDUMMY
00223                    DFHDUMMY DFHDUMMY WS-SYSDATE DFHDUMMY DFHDUMMY DFHEIV9
00224                    DFHDUMMY DFHDUMMY DFHDUMMY DFHDUMMY DFHDUMMY WS-SYSTIME
00225                    DFHC0011.
00226
00227               0700-EXIT.  EXIT.
00228
00229               9000-RETURN.
00230
00231             *EXEC CICS SEND
00232             *          FROM(WS-MESSAGE-AREA)
00233             *          LENGTH(WS-MESSAGE-LENGTH)
00234             *          ERASE
00235             *END-EXEC.
00236                    MOVE '        a      00132   ' TO DFHEIVO
00237                    CALL 'DFHEI1' USING DFHEIVO  DFHDUMMY DFHDUMMY
00238                    WS-MESSAGE-AREA WS-MESSAGE-LENGTH.
```

Figure 2-1 COBOL program with CALL.

```
MVS/XA DFP VER 2 LINKAGE EDITOR          08:45:27  TUE  JUL 10, 1990
JOB DCNEAX00    STEP LKED
INVOCATION PARAMETERS - LIST,MAP,LET,XREF
ACTUAL SIZE=(517440,92160)
OUTPUT  DATA SET CICS.TEST.DGLIB IS ON VOLUME SHPR00
IEW0000    INCLUDE SYSLIB(DFHECI)

                            CROSS REFERENCE TABLE

CONTROL SECTION                  ENTRY
  NAME    ORIGIN  LENGTH     NAME    LOCATION   NAME    LOCATION   NAME    LOCATION   NAME    LOCATION
 DFHECI     00      48      DFHEI1       8     DLZEIO1      8     DLZEIO2     8     DLZEIO3     8
                           DLZEIO4      8     DFHCBLI     26

 DCNEAX00   48     B96
 DFHDATE *  BE0     F8      DFHDATEX    BEC                                        50000000

 LOCATION REFERS TO SYMBOL    IN CONTROL SECTION     LOCATION REFERS TO SYMBOL    IN CONTROL SECTION
   658        DFHEI1              DFHECI                65C        DFHDATE             DFHDATE

 ENTRY ADDRESS    48

 TOTAL LENGTH     CD8
*** DCNEAX00 DID NOT PREVIOUSLY EXIST BUT WAS ADDED AND HAS AMODE 24
*** LOAD MODULE HAS RMODE 24
*** AUTHORIZATION CODE IS  0.
```

Figure 2-2   COBOL program linkage control section.

```
LineID PL SL                         DCNEAXOU  Date 07/10/90  Time 09:09:26   Page   8
----+-*A-1-B--+----2----+----3----+----4----+----5----+----6----+----7-|--+----8 Cross Reference
000162              0000-PROGRAM-DCNEAX00.
000163
000164                  PERFORM 0500-RECEIVE THRU 0500-EXIT.
000165
000166      1         IF CALL-DFHDATE
000167      1             PERFORM 0600-CALL-DFHDATE THRU 0600-EXIT
000168      1         ELSE PERFORM 0700-ASKTIME THRU 0700-EXIT.
000169
000170
000171                  MOVE WS-SYSTIME TO WS-M-A-TIME.
000172                  MOVE WS-SYSDATE TO WS-M-A-DATE.
000173
000174                  PERFORM 9000-RETURN.
000175
000176              0500-RECEIVE.
000177
000178                  MOVE WS-RECEIVE-LENGTH TO WS-RECEIVED-LENGTH.
000179
000180              *EXEC CICS RECEIVE
000181              **          INTO(WS-RECEIVE-AREA)
000182              **          LENGTH(WS-RECEIVED-LENGTH)
000183              **          RESP(WS-RESP)
000184              *END-EXEC.
000185                  MOVE  '¢             00100    ' TO DFHEIVO
000186                  CALL 'DFHEI1' USING DFHEIVO  WS-RECEIVE-AREA
000187                  WS-RECEIVED-LENGTH
000188                              MOVE EIBRESP TO WS-RESP.
000189
000190
000191              0500-EXIT.  EXIT.
000192
000193              0600-CALL-DFHDATE.
000194
000195                  CALL 'DFHDATE' USING EIBDATE, WS-SYSDATE.
000196
000197              0600-EXIT.  EXIT.
000198
000199              0700-ASKTIME.
000200
000201              *EXEC CICS ASKTIME
000202              **          ABSTIME(WS-ABSTIME)
000203              *END-EXEC.
000204                  MOVE  '¢             00116    ' TO DFHEIVO
000205                  CALL 'DFHEI1' USING DFHEIVO  WS-ABSTIME.
000206
000207
000208              *EXEC CICS FORMATTIME
000209              **          ABSTIME(WS-ABSTIME)
000210              **          MMDDYY(WS-SYSDATE)
000211              **          DATESEP('/')
000212              **          TIME(WS-SYSTIME)
000213              **          TIMESEP(':')
000214              *END-EXEC.
000215                  MOVE '¢ dc dc         00120    ' TO DFHEIVO
000216                  MOVE  '/' TO DFHC0010
000217                  MOVE  ':' TO DFHC0011
000218                  CALL 'DFHEI1' USING DFHEIVO  WS-SYSDATE DFHDUMMY DFHDUMMY
000219                  DFHDUMMY DFHDUMMY WS-SYSTIME DFHDUMMY DFHC0010
```

Figure 2-3   COBOL program source modified to OS/VS COBOL II.

```
MVS/XA DFP VER 2 LINKAGE EDITOR    09:09:41 TUE  JUL 10, 1990
JOB DCNEAX00    STEP COBOL2         PROCEDURE LKED
INVOCATION PARAMETERS - LIST,MAP,LET,XREF
ACTUAL SIZE=(317440,86016)
OUTPUT DATA SET NER.S624.LINKLIB IS ON VOLUME SYS801
IEW0000    INCLUDE SYSLIB(DFHECI)
```

CROSS REFERENCE TABLE

CONTROL SECTION

NAME	ORIGIN	LENGTH
DFHECI	00	48
DCNEAX00	48	7CC
DFHDATE *	818	F8
IGZEBST *	910	1A8

ENTRY

NAME	LOCATION	NAME	LOCATION	NAME	LOCATION	NAME	LOCATION
DFHEI1	8	DLZEI01	8	DLZEI02	8	DLZEI03	8
DLZEI04	8	DFHCBLI	26				
DFHDATEX	824						
IGZEBS2	A14						

```
                    50000000
```

LOCATION	REFERS TO SYMBOL	IN CONTROL SECTION	LOCATION	REFERS TO SYMBOL	IN CONTROL SECTION
B4	IGZEBST	IGZEBST	DC	DFHEI1	DFHECI
E0	DFHDATE	DFHDATE	AA8	IGZETUN	$UNRESOLVED(W)
AAC	IGZEOPT	$UNRESOLVED(W)			

```
ENTRY ADDRESS   48

TOTAL LENGTH    AB8
*** DCNEAX00 REPLACED AND HAS AMODE 24
*** LOAD MODULE HAS RMODE 24
*** AUTHORIZATION CODE IS    0.
```

Figure 2-4   COBOL II program linkage control section.

2.3.3 Data Items in Numeric Fields

Programs being converted to COBOL II must be aware of the restrictions (that are now much tighter) when moving data between fields. If two data items are defined as

```
01  NUM1    PIC X(7).
01  NUM2 REDEFINES NUM1 PIC S9(5)V99.
```

VS COBOL II will detect the sign on the second field, and restrict the type of data that can be moved to the field. Any attempt to

MOVE LOW-VALUES TO NUM2.

will cause an 0C7 ABEND (data exception). VS COBOL II rejects the MOVE statement since LOW-VALUES does not conform to the picture clause. A signed field causes COBOL II to internally convert the field to packed format prior to the MOVE, and LOW-VALUES does not qualify as that data type.

VS COBOL II is ensuring that the data item must conform to the PIC clause before the move or computation is made. Programmers may need to add additional statements to verify the content or type of the field prior to use.

2.3.4 STRING and UNSTRING

These two verbs, while allowed in OS/VS COBOL batch programs, are prohibited in CICS. The COBOL subroutine modules issued with these commands issue OS GETMAIN SVCs (supervisor calls), which are extremely detrimental to CICS and place heavy demands on CICS OSCOR requirements.

The following commands, which were previously not allowed, have had those restrictions lifted in VS COBOL II:

INSPECT   STRING
UNSTRING   USE FOR DEBUGGING

In VS COBOL II, the subroutine modules called with STRING and UNSTRING do not use OS services and are therefore allowed. The storage required is handled by the compiler rather than the operating system. Performance effects have been removed in CICS systems, any version.

2.3.5 BLL Cell Removal

Prior to VS COBOL II, any CICS application that utilized storage external to Working Storage was responsible for maintaining the areas and corresponding address for program storage requests. BLL cells (Base Locator for Linkage) were used to storage and manage these addresses by the application program.

In VS COBOL II, BLL cells must be removed since they will not be utilized to address any storage areas chained to the CICS control blocks. In addition, the corresponding SERVICE RELOAD statements should be removed since they will be treated as comments by the VS COBOL II compiler.

Application programs using the CALL interface to DL/I must also remove the BLL cell and corresponding statements that address the UIB (User Interface Block) and PCB (Program Communication Block). In VS COBOL II, the UIB can be directly addressed with

CALL 'CBLTDLI' USING PCB-FUNCTION,
      PCB-NAME,
      ADDRESS OF DLIUIB.

This process can be accomplished automatically by the CCCA product, described in Section 2.1. If the installation wishes to convert without the product offering, all BLL support must be removed manually. The process is documented in the VS COBOL II Migration Guide, G320-0562.

2.4 OS/VS COBOL and VS COBOL II in CICS

Applications written in both versions of COBOL can exist in the same CICS region. Certain restrictions apply, such as:

- OS/VS COBOL programs and VS COBOL II programs cannot be in the same run unit.
- CALL statements in VS COBOL II programs cannot be used to CALL any OS/VS COBOL program.
- CALL statements in OS/VS COBOL programs cannot be used to CALL any VS COBOL II program.

2.5 COBTEST Use in CICS

When CICS applications are written in COBOL II, they can be debugged with a new COBTEST facility. This aid to problem determination can be invoked from within CICS, similar to the CEDF (execution diagnostic facility) transaction. The program must have been previously compiled with the FDUMP or TEST option. The TEST compiler option will be invoked during execution and will direct all output requested (with COBTEST commands) to CICS temporary storage when the transaction completes normally. The FDUMP option will direct a VS COBOL II dump to CICS temporary storage if the transaction completes abnormally.

When the transaction is complete, or when an ABEND is detected, COBTEST generates output which is directed to a temporary storage queue. The queue name is always CEBRtttt, where tttt = the terminal identifier used in the interactive test. If the program completed normally, and the TEST compiler option was specified, a summary of the program is produced in the queue containing some trace and program analysis.

If the program terminated abnormally, and FDUMP was requested, a small formatted dump will be produced in the queue. Included in this dump will be:

Completion Code
PSW (Program Status Word) Contents
Program and GP (General Purpose) Registers
Time/Date Stamp from Compile Time
Working Storage and Linkage Section Pointers

Programmers should be aware of the resource consumption of this facility and use it in CICS with care. Not only can these two compiler options consume additional virtual storage, they can exhaust temporary storage resources. The records written to temporary storage are *not* deleted after creation. It is the programmer's responsibility to delete these records. If not deleted, they can cause shortages of temporary storage, with corresponding performance degradation or system failure.

In addition, the FDUMP option does not support the previous OS/VS COBOL SYMDMP (symbolic dump). This compiler option must be removed, as well as STATE and FLOW, since the debugging tool produces similar data as a replacement.

COBTEST with CICS LINK   If the program being tested uses CICS LINK statements instead of COBOL CALLs, only one of the programs can be compiled with TEST. If both programs use TEST, the debugger may produce unpredictable results when control is returned to the invoking program. It makes no difference which of the two is compiled with TEST, but both cannot be.

Complete documentation on this facility can be found in the SC26-4049, VS COBOL II Application Programming: Debugging.

2.6 VS COBOL II for CICS/VSE Version 2.1

In the IBM announcements dated September 5, 1990, a new product emerged for the users of VSE operating systems. Not only did IBM announce new hardware and a new VSE/ESA operating system, but a new version of CICS appeared: CICS/VSE Version 2.1. This new version of CICS will be available only in VSE/ESA, therefore only on the new ESA-compatible machines. The new CICS/VSE, however, has the full support of VS COBOL II Version 1 Release 3.2.

With CICS/VSE 2.1 and the new VS COBOL II, applications can be developed that meet the intermediate level of the ANSI 1985 COBOL standard, and some features of the high level. These applications can then be ported for execution in the other operating systems and therefore CICS.

This new COBOL II release provides several tools for the conversion/migration from DOS/VS COBOL to VS COBOL II:

- MIGR — A migration flagging tool on DOS/VS COBOL to identify source statements that will require modification.
- CCCA — The Command Level Conversion Aid to convert source statements to VS COBOL II syntax and format.
- COBOL/SF — The Structuring Facility to transform old DOS/VS COBOL statements into structured VS COBOL II.

In the CICS/VSE 2.1 announcement, IBM also included a "Statement of Direction" to allow this product extended storage exploitation. Future releases will, therefore, utilize the extended capabilities of VS COBOL II to execute in 31-bit mode, even in VSE/ESA. These announcements, with existing support, continue to justify the customer's investment in VS COBOL II conversions.

CICS Nondatabase File Issues

3

VSAM File Processing

Many CICS problems are a direct result of incorrect or invalid utilization of VSAM files. Since VSAM is the most widely used non-database access method in CICS, a thorough understanding of these types of files can produce efficient and stable applications. The following sections deal with the most common problems and issues of VSAM file processing.

3.1 VSAM File Issues

While many VSAM issues deal with specific facilities, such as LSR and OSCOR, others are global to the access method. This section will address those global items that many programmers face when utilizing VSAM resources.

3.1.1 CI and CA Splits

A CI or CA split occurs when an update request requires more space than can be provided by that particular CI or CA. VSAM attempts to add or update a record, finds insufficient space to fit the data, and therefore "splits" the CI or CA. The original CI or CA is broken into equal quantities of records, and approximately half of the records are moved into a new CI or CA. The original CI or CA now contains adequate freespace to add new records, and the new CI or CA is also only half full. Of course, the new CI or CA is allocated in a new location on the storage device. The data, therefore, is no longer contiguous on the media, and requests for records on the new CI or CA will require additional effort on the part of the DASD to locate. In addition, large numbers of I/Os take place during the split and impact performance of the data request. For this reason, CI and CA splits are usually monitored, and VSAM files are "reorganized" on a regular basis to remove splits and ensure adequate performance.

Effect in CICS Previous releases of CICS had a significantly negative impact on CICS. Changes have been made in CICS to file control to reverse this process. LSR file requests are now issued synchronously, and an exit is used during the physical I/O of the split. Other CICS work can then continue during the split of an LSR file. NSR (non-shared resources) files continue to be processed in the original manner and will cause CICS work to wait during a split.

Since the CICS CSD (CICS System Definition) and the RSD (Resource Definition) files are "normal" VSAM files, they are also subject to CI and CA splits.

Both files should be monitored and managed as normal VSAM files and reorganized on a regular basis. In fact, these files can significantly impact performance of the CEDx transactions and even CICS start-up and shut-down. A CICS COLD start rebuilds the RSD with the contents of the CSD and can therefore take significantly longer if either or both of the files contain large numbers of CI or CA splits.

CI or CA Splits and Use of LSR When a CA split occurs, the newly created CA is formatted BEFORE any data is loaded into it. In an NSR file, the formatting is performed one track at a time. If the file has been placed into an LSR pool, the formatting is performed one CI at a time. For this reason, files that must endure excessive CA splits may not be good candidates for LSR. Of course, action could also be taken to avoid CA splits and leave the file in LSR.

In summary, CI and CA splits always impact CICS performance and should be monitored on a regular basis. Use techniques to avoid CI and CA splits, or reorganize VSAM files on a regular basis to remove them.

3.1.2 FCT Specifications

The File Control Table has been replaced in CICS/ESA with online resource definition capability (RDO); therefore, FCT specifications apply only to CICS/MVS Version 2. The file definitions in RDO, however, contain similar parameters for specification of file characteristics. The FCT must contain entries for files that will be accessed by any program or transaction and describe to CICS how that access can or cannot take place. While the file entry (DD name) must exist to CICS at initialization time, characteristics of files can be modified "on the fly" via CICS-supplied transactions.

A FCT entry can be specified LSRPOOL=n, where n = 1 – 8. Since CICS now had the capability of eight LSR pools, each file entry contained the ability to select a specific pool. The default is 1; therefore, if no LSRPOOL parameter is coded into the FCT for the file, it will be an LSR file and use pool 1. If the file is not a good candidate for LSR, or the programmer wishes to explicitly remove it from LSR processing, the FCT for the file must be coded with LSRPOOL=NONE. The file will then be classified as NSR-type.

FCT Entries for VSAM Clusters with Alternate Indexes (AIXs) Since an AIX is basically a KSDS (key sequenced dataset), the FCT entry contains the same requirements as a KSDS. Calculate the AIX strings and (if not placed into LSR) data and index buffers accordingly. Remember, however, that the number of strings for the base cluster must equal the total for its own requirements PLUS the strings required for the AIXs.

CICS provides the facility by default for data integrity of AIXs.

In addition, it allows access to the same dataset with multiple FCT entries. The programmer could use DSNSHR to use one FCT entry for the file for update and another for read only.

Multiple FCT Entries for the Same File If multiple FCT entries contain the same VSAM cluster, CICS will build only a single VSAM control block structure for the file. The CICS implementation of file control provides dataset integrity even if multiple applications attempt to update the same file via different FCT definitions.

SHRCNTL Macro This entry is significant in that it tells CICS which and how many buffers to allocate for each LSR pool. Since CICS can support eight LSR pools, there can be eight entries to specify different numbers for each size buffer in the different pools. In this way, an installation can tailor the resources for each LSR pool (and the storage allocated) and "tune" LSR. The SHRCNTL macro can also be coded to default, with RSCLMT. If only RSCLMT is coded with a percentage (it defaults to 50%), CICS calculates allocation amounts for BUFFERS and STRNO based on the files contained within the FCT. This may not be an optimum value (defaults seldom are), but releases the installation from the calculation requirements. IBM recommends that explicit SHRCNTL definitions be coded for each LSR pool.

SHRCNTL Macro with RSCLMT Defaults Some installations have very dynamic FCTs with files being added and removed frequently. In other cases, installations may have multiple "administrators" of the FCT for test CICS systems and even require that application programmers manage the FCT for the test system themselves. In this case, many programmers may be adding files and reassembling the table, without the knowledge or desire to update the SHRCNTL macro with the required buffersize for the new files. Allowing CICS to calculate the required buffers from defined files ensures that at least the minimum buffers are built to support the requirements within the FCT. Remember, if the SHRCNTL macro is explicitly coded with buffersizes and counts, any requests for additional buffersizes within that LSR pool after initialization will fail. In other words, if an FCT entry contains LSRPOOL=n and the CI size of that file is not explicitly coded in the BUFFERS= parameter of the SHRCNTL macro relating to that pool, CICS will not build a buffer set for that CI size. If the CI is larger than any buffers created for that pool, CICS cannot open the file. The file would have to be re-created with a CI size accommodated by the already-built buffer pool or removed from LSR.

This is one of the few cases that has prompted some installations to use a nonexplicitly coded SHRCNTL macro and merely allocate a percentage with RSCLMT.

Figure 3-1 contains a sample FCT with three LSR pools, each with a different percentage allocation to be used in the calculation. The first pool will use 30%, the second 40%, and the last 40%. As shown, each pool must be built individually and can be "tuned" for various files within the pools.

File Resource Definitions in RDO While previous versions used the table macro, CICS/ESA Version 3 allows these definitions to be created and managed dynamically. The CEDA transaction, as with other definitions, allows the file to be DEFINEd into a group, and then INSTALLed within the running CICS system. In addition to the specifications that were available with the FCT macro, new options can be used such as:

Opentime   (Firstref/Startup)
DATATABLE Parameters
AUTO JOURNALLING   including recovery parameters
DATABUFFERS   (1–32767)
INDEXBUFFERS   (1–32767)

```
******
* CICS FCT SHRCTL MACRO WITH WITHOUT EXPLICIT LSR POOLS       23120000
*           CALCULATE WITH 30 % ALLOCATION                    23140000
******                                                        23151000
                                                              23152000
       DFHFCT TYPE=SHRCTL,LSRPOOL=1,                         *23160000
              RSCLMT=30,                                      23180000
              KEYLEN=40,                                     *23190000
       DFHFCT TYPE=SHRCTL,LSRPOOL=2,                         *23201000
              RSCLMT=40,                                      23202000
              KEYLEN=50,                                     *23204000
       DFHFCT TYPE=SHRCTL,LSRPOOL=3,                         *23206000
              RSCLMT=40,                                      23208100
              KEYLEN=20,                                      23210000
                                                              23220000
       DFHFCT TYPE=FINAL                                      23230000
       END
       .
*
```

Figure 3-1   Sample FCT with three LSR pools.

The ability to isolate index from data buffers has never been available in previous versions. As further explained in Section 3.2.1 of this chapter, buffer utilization can be substantially affected by these sizes. CICS/ESA Version 3 provides customers with the ability to buffer the index and data components of VSAM files independently via the new dynamic definitions.

In addition, LSRPOOLs can be defined via the RDO facility, and managed dynamically. The pools can be DEFINEd, each with individual buffer sizes for optimum performance. A typical LSRPOOL in CICS/ESA Version 3 definition may look like:

```
Lsrpool                 LSRPOOL1
Lsrpoolid:              1   (1–8)
Maxkeylength:               (0–255)
SHarelimit:                 (1–100)
STrings:                    (1–255)
DATA BUFFERS
DATA512:                    (3–32767)
DATA1K:                     (3–32767)
. . .
INDEX BUFFERS
INDEX512:                   (3–32767)
INDEX1K                     (3–32767)
```

Both data and index buffers can be specified to a maximum of 32K size if required by the application. In addition, LSRPOOL definitions can contain HIPERSPACE DATA and INDEX buffers which have a maximum size of 16MB. These definitions can substantially impact the performance on CICS applications, especially those with high VSAM I/O rates. This enhancement exists only in CICS/ESA and will not be available in previous versions.

As with FCT table definitions, the SHRLIMIT value can be used to allocate a percentage of the maximum amount of resources in the pool. Unlike previous versions, however, these pools and the file definitions are dynamic. If inadequate buffersizes exist in the pool, the definition can be changed, or the file can be moved to another pool with an adequate buffer size. This new facility provides a great deal of new function and flexibility.

3.1.3 VSAM Options

The VSAM options used during the IDCAMS DEFINE can impact both performance and recovery capability of CICS files. The previous section identified FCT definitions, such as LSR pools, that are affected by the CI size specified for the file. Many other parameters can affect CICS processing of the file, especially SHAREOPTIONS.

SHAREOPTION 4 This option specifies that the records must be read directly from the storage media (DASD) for each request, ignoring any index records that may be in virtual storage buffers and therefore available for "look-aside" processing. Some installations use this SHAREOPTION to attempt to write integrity for files shared across multiple CICS regions or systems. Since VSAM files can really NEVER be completely guaranteed for integrity when shared by multiple address spaces for update, this may create a false sense of security. SHAREOPTION 4 also significantly increases I/O activity against the file and will always negatively impact any CICS file.

SHAREOPTIONS(4,4) will not allow a CI/CA split to occur and returns a NOSPACE condition to the application if any CI or CA requires split processing, even if other portions of the file contain free space. The options can be changed (via IDCAMS ALTER) to 2,3 to allow records to be added.

UPGRADEable AIXs If the VSAM AIX is defined with UPGRADE, the user is requesting that the AIX be updated to reflect any and all changes in the VSAM base cluster. This will, of course, cause additional I/Os, since any CICS application that adds or updates the base cluster will trigger the request to VSAM to reflect these changes in the AIX. If the base cluster has multiple upgradable AIXs, VSAM will "synchonize" all AIXs automatically with any updates. Applications that require optimum performance may not wish to incur the overhead of this process. The alternative would be to specify the AIX NOUPGRADE and rebuild the AIX on whatever schedule is required for accuracy of the contents.

Figure 3-2 contains a catalog listing (via LISTCAT) of a typical alternate index. Note that the MVS catalog is aware of the AIX status of the file and the corresponding cluster and path associations. The file contains the attribute UPGRADE and will therefore be kept in synchonization with the base if at all possible.

```
IDCAMS  SYSTEM SERVICES                                                 TIME: 14:03:13        06/22/90        PAGE    2

   INDEX ------ USFV.SA.AMF003.BROWSE.AIX1.INDEX
   IN-CAT --- CATALOG.USF
   HISTORY
     DATASET-OWNER-----(NULL)        CREATION------------1990.172
     RELEASE------------2            EXPIRATION----------0000.000
     PROTECTION-PSWD----(NULL)       RACF----------------(NO)
   ASSOCIATIONS
     AIX----USFV.SA.AMF003.BROWSE.AIX1
   ATTRIBUTES
     KEYLEN------------4             AVGLRECL-----------0             BUFSPACE-----------0             CISIZE-----------4096
     RKP---------------5             MAXLRECL-----------4089          EXCPEXIT--------(NULL)           CI/CA------------10
     SHROPTNS(2,3)  RECOVERY         UNIQUE      NOERASE             NOWRITECHK   IMBED               NOREPLICAT   UNORDERED
     NOREUSE
   STATISTICS
     REC-TOTAL---------34            SPLITS-CI----------0             EXCPS------------227             INDEX:
     REC-DELETED-------0             SPLITS-CA----------0             EXTENTS-----------3             LEVELS-----------2
     REC-INSERTED------0             FREESPACE-%CI------0             SYSTEM-TIMESTAMP:               ENTRIES/SECT----11
     REC-UPDATED-------0             FREESPACE-%CA------0                  X'A249C205C5619B02'        SEQ-SET-RBA----40960
     REC-RETRIEVED-----0             FREESPC-BYTES----36864                                          HI-LEVEL-RBA-----0
   ALLOCATION
     SPACE-TYPE--------TRACK         HI-ALLOC-RBA----176128
     SPACE-PRI---------1             HI-USED-RBA-----176128
     SPACE-SEC---------1
   VOLUME
     VOLSER-----------USERAC         PHYREC-SIZE-------4096           HI-ALLOC-RBA----40960           EXTENT-NUMBER----1
     DEVTYPE---------X'3010200E'     PHYRECS/TRK-------10             HI-USED-RBA-----4096            EXTENT-TYPE-----X'00'
     VOLFLAG----------PRIME          TRACKS/CA---------1
     EXTENTS:
     LOW-CCHH-------X'01DD0000'      LOW-RBA-----------0              TRACKS------------1
     HIGH-CCHH------X'01DD0000'      HIGH-RBA--------40959
   VOLUME
     VOLSER-----------USERAC         PHYREC-SIZE-------4096           HI-ALLOC-RBA----176128          EXTENT-NUMBER----2
     DEVTYPE---------X'3010200E'     PHYRECS/TRK-------10             HI-USED-RBA-----176128          EXTENT-TYPE-----X'C0'
     VOLFLAG----------PRIME          TRACKS/CA---------15
     EXTENTS:
     LOW-CCHH-------X'01BF0000'      LOW-RBA---------40960            TRACKS-----------450
     HIGH-CCHH------X'01DC000E'      HIGH-RBA-------163839
     LOW-CCHH-------X'01E00000'      LOW-RBA--------163840            TRACKS-----------45
     HIGH-CCHH------X'01E0000E'      HIGH-RBA-------176127

   PATH ------- USFV.SA.AMF003.BROWSE.PATH
   IN-CAT --- CATALOG.USF
   HISTORY
     DATASET-OWNER-----(NULL)        CREATION------------1990.173
     RELEASE------------2            EXPIRATION----------0000.000
     PROTECTION-PSWD----(NULL)       RACF----------------(NO)
   ASSOCIATIONS
     AIX-----USFV.SA.AMF003.BROWSE.AIX1
     DATA----USFV.SA.AMF003.BROWSE.AIX1.DATA
     INDEX---USFV.SA.AMF003.BROWSE.AIX1.INDEX
     DATA----USFV.SA.AMF003.BROWSE.DATA

IDCAMS  SYSTEM SERVICES                                                 TIME: 14:03:13        06/22/90        PAGE    3

   INDEX---USFV.SA.AMF003.BROWSE.INDEX
   ATTRIBUTES
   UPDATE
```

Figure 3-2   LISTCAT catalog listing of VSAM AIX.

3.1.4 VSAM vs. Database (DL/I or DB/2)

Many installations struggle with the choice of retaining native VSAM files in their applications or moving toward a database design. While this may be both a technical and political decision within the installation, several questions need to be asked before "scrapping" a great deal of investment in existing code and converting to any new access method.

The most important differences deal with the facilities available to preserve data integrity and the ability to share data across concurrently executing address spaces or MVS systems. IMS/DB and DB/2 contain a logging facility for online and batch updates, with utility facilities to provide both forward recovery and backout. While VSAM updates within CICS can be logged for forward recovery and backout, VSAM provides no support for logging batch updates to the file.

Can VSAM files be shared by both CICS and batch jobs? Yes, using SHAREOPTIONS(2,3) the file can be opened for update by CICS and then accessed for read-only by any batch job. This will ensure that only one address space updates the file at any given time. Batch jobs that attempt to open that file for update (once CICS has opened the file for update) will fail with VSAM return codes, indicating that the file is unavailable for that type of access.

The CEMT facility (master terminal operator) can be used to SET the file in CICS to read only, no update, add, or delete. A batch job could then be run that updates the file, since update authority has been released by CICS. Recovery of the file, however, is impacted since the forward recovery facility in CICS will be unaware of all updates made "outside" of CICS. A full backup prior to the batch update could reduce the exposure. In summary, VSAM files are simply not designed to be updated via multiple sources with full integrity. If that requirement is necessary, then the data will need to be placed within a database manager.

3.1.5 Alternate Indexes (AIX)

VSAM AIXs are very useful for access into VSAM files via alternate keys. While the primary key provides the main access into the file, alternate indexes assist programs to locate specific records within the file via other fields. AIX processing improves the performance of many CICS applications but requires additional concerns, some of which have already been discussed in previous sections of this chapter.

AIX Definition An alternate index is DEFINEd as a normal VSAM cluster, with the AIX operand. A second command, BLDINDEX, is necessary, which uses the base cluster as input, the AIX (previously defined) as output. This would correspond to the REPRO function used to load a normal KSDS. See the Access Method Services Reference Manual corresponding to your specific level of DFP (Data Facility Product) for exact syntax of the command.

Use of the UPGRADE option during the DEFINE AIX is necessary to reflect changed data in the AIX when the base cluster is modified. The previous catalog report identified the attribute required for upgrade functions. Performance impact of this option is discussed in Section 3.1.3.

AIXs in LSR (Local Shared Resources) Beginning in CICS/VS 1.7, full support of AIXs (even upgradable) is provided in any LSR buffer pool. Since multiple AIXs can use additional virtual storage, use of LSR will minimize the storage used and improve performance.

After the AIX is built, the DEFINE PATH command must be used to build a path entry. In the command, PATHENTRY refers to the AIX previously defined. When the path is opened to process data records, both the AIX and the base cluster are opened. The name used in the DEFINE PATH command is then used in the CICS FCT (file control table), NOT the AIX name. CICS then uses the path to process data via the AIX.

The AIX, however, can still become "out of synch" with the base cluster, even if UPGRADE has been specified.

An MVS cancel of CICS or an MVS system failure followed by a CICS emergency restart can produce an inconsistency between the AIX and the VSAM base cluster. This remains a problem in both CICS/VS 1.7 and CICS/MVS 2.1, and IBM's advice is to use BLDINDEX after such a failure to rebuild AIXs or to use forward recovery.

CICS can now accommodate (and open) an empty VSAM base cluster, yet it still cannot accommodate an empty AIX.

Both the AIX and the PATH must be created, and the AIX must be loaded with BLDINDEX prior to the CICS OPEN, or CICS will fail the open request with DFH0964I with VSAM return codes 0008,00A0. If the installation intends to consistently require CICS to open an empty base cluster, an alternate index cannot be used.

3.2 LSR (Local Shared Resources) and NSR (Nonshared Resources)

One of the most controversial, and often misunderstood, facilities in CICS is LSR. This facility can provide substantial performance benefits for VSAM files, yet can also produce some of the most confusing CICS errors and problems. This section will deal with many LSR issues and attempt to solve the many mysteries of LSR.

3.2.1 Virtual Storage Utilization

While many customers avoid LSR because of storage shortages, many use LSR to reduce storage shortages. Does LSR use more storage than NSR, and how can the storage utilization be minimized? Storage will ALWAYS be a concern in CICS, so management of storage used by LSR facilities will always be an issue.

If files were migrated from NSR to LSR, CICS will realize VSCR (Virtual Storage Constraint Relief) — the amount would be dependent upon several factors.

Storage savings would be realized in several categories, including OSCOR, CSA, and SQA.

OSCOR: NSR files require 5 – 8K per file
             LSR files require 2 – 3K per file
CSA: NSR files require 1200 – 1500 bytes per file
             LSR files require NO CSA except 112 bytes if
             SHAREOPTIONS are 3 or 4.
SQA: NSR files require 240 bytes per VSAM string
             LSR files NO SQA, since strings are in the LSR pool

In addition, each NSR KSDS requires one more data buffer than strings (specified) to accommodate CI or CA splits. LSR does not require this additional data buffer and saves the virtual storage of this buffer for each file.

Since use of LSR reduces CSA and SQA storage requirements, the installation may realize additional virtual storage available for CICS (private area).

LSR Effect upon DSA Even though VSAM (with LSR) allocates the buffers above the 16-Mb line, storage is required below the line for control blocks. The amount of storage and the number of control blocks remaining below the line decrease with higher releases of

DFP. The most recent releases of DFP (such as 2.3 or 3.1) move more control blocks above the line, and therefore provide the most virtual storage relief. If an installation used an older release of DFP and defined the maximum LSR buffer pools (8) with multiple sub-pools for different size buffers, the size of the DSA would reflect the control blocks that were built to accommodate the request.

DL/I Effect upon LSR Storage DL/I indeed uses CICS LSR pools. The DL/I pool (0) is built during DL/I initialization and will extend the LSR pool by the definition in the DFSVSAMP specification. It does not, however, utilize any OSCOR. In most cases, CICS VSAM files and DL/I databases will reside in different LSR pools. Incorrect specification in the SHRCNTL macro can, however, create conflict. If, for example, the SHRCNTL macro only contained definitions for 2K and 4K buffers, the DFSVSAMP specification provided for 2K, 4K, and 8K buffers, CICS VSAM files could conflict with DL/I databases in the 8K pool. Normally, the VSAM file would fail to open since no buffers were large enough. The DFSVSAMP definition would have created the available pool and placed the DL/I databases in conflict within the 8K pool. If native VSAM files use this 8K pool, they will be in contention with the DL/I data stored in the same pool. Proper review of the SHRCNTL macro should be performed on a regular basis for tuning.

LSR Buffers on Page Boundaries In the CICS Resource Definition Macro manual (DFHFCT TYPE=SHRCTL), IBM states "VSAM allocates buffers for each particular size on a 4K byte (page) boundary." If the installation, therefore, specifies a count of buffers that results in less than 4K bytes (or a multiple) for the pool, virtual storage will be wasted. For each buffer size, calculate a number of buffers such that the total allocation reaches the 4K boundary, since it will be allocated by VSAM regardless.

LSR CPU Utilization vs. NSR Although LSR increases throughput by eliminating physical I/Os, using large LSR pools has been known to increase CPU time due to the searching required to detect whether the CI is already in storage. DFP 2.3 has provided a new buffer hashing algorithm to reduce CPU requirements for large buffer pools. Installations that are constrained in CPU utilization should utilize DFP 2.3 to decrease CPU requirements of LSR.

3.2.1.1 Buffer Pool Utilization Starting in DFP 2.3, separate LSR buffer pools can be utilized for VSAM indexes and data, thereby isolating the index from the data and avoiding performance conflicts. Does CICS support separate LSR pools for the data and index component?

No, all buffers for the VSAM file will go into that pool, both index and data with CICS/Version 2. Not until V3 can customers isolate these buffers. CICS/MVS 2.1 does not have the ability to explicitly separate the data from the index buffers. The installation can, however, define the VSAM cluster with a different CISIZE for the data and index component. If the cluster was defined with a 2K CISIZE for the index and a 4K CISIZE for the data component, VSAM would manage the components into separate subpools within the same LSR pool. This could improve performance somewhat.

Rules of Thumb for Multiple LSR Pools There are no definite rules, but a few hints can be followed:

- Heavily browsed datasets should be placed in their own pool
- High-performance datasets with the same CISIZE should be in separate pools to keep from invalidating each other's buffers
- Isolate the index from the data buffers with different CISIZEs (or with CICS/ESA)

CICS LSR Pools and DFHSM If the SHRCNTL macro has been coded to use RSLMCNT (nonexplicit) for pool construction, it utilizes the catalog to build pools based on CISIZEs of all files. When DFHSM migrates a dataset, either to Level 1 or 2, it modifies the catalog to reflect the fact that the data no longer reside on "active" DASD. In addition, the catalog no longer contains information of CISIZE for the migrated file. CICS cannot, then, anticipate the size of the pool required and may not create a pool to accommodate this file. The OPEN, when requested by the application, will fail. The only alternative would be to remove this file from LSR or explicity code the SHRCNTL macro with the buffer size required to accommodate that file.

NSR FCT Specifications In all versions of CICS, the default definition for an FCT entry implies LSRPOOL=1 and will be used if no other LSR pool is requested. Explicit avoidance of LSR requires LSRPOOL=NONE to be specified in the FCT for the file.

"Total Number of Requests Waited for Buffer": This statistic for VSAM files in LSR indicated that one of the following conditions has occurred:

- No buffers are available to satisfy the request
- The CI (control interval) is locked by VSAM

The first condition is caused by a lack of buffers and can be easily avoided by increasing the number of buffers in the pool used by that file. The second condition is caused when VSAM locks a CI from an exclusive control request. When a CI is locked and the buffer containing the CI is in LSR, any read request for a record in the locked CI will produce a wait condition, reported in these statistics. More information on this deadlock condition can be found in Section 3.2.4.

3.2.3 SHRCNTL Calculation

Since IBM recommends that SHRCNTL be explicitly defined, rather than defaulted, the proper counts and sizes can be calculated with existing information from CICS.

The CICS shutdown statistics are an excellent source of the actual file requests and LSR hit ratios. The statistics show both by LSR pool and by file which files are receiving benefit from LSR and which are incurring physical I/O. Review these statistics on a regular basis and continue to modify the SHRCNTL macro to add or delete buffers from LSR pools.

3.2.4 Deadlock Issues with LSR

Many deadlock or file enqueue problems are discussed in Section 3.3; however, some of those issues are directly related to LSR processing. Programmers should be aware of techniques that must be used if files are placed into Local Shared Resources.

Programming Issues Relating to LSR Files   Programmers must realize that they are unable to use read for update inside a browse sequence. In other words, if a browse is initiated, it must be completed with an "End Browse" before the "Read for Update" is requested. Failure to end the browse can result in a deadlock. In fact, Browse, Massinsert, and Read for Update will all hold the CI for an extended period of time and potentially produce a deadlock condition.

How can programmers classify potential candidates for LSR and those that would not be good candidates since they could produce deadlock conditions during execution?

It is first important to understand the conditions that result in the deadlock. Lockouts occur when some CI is held for exclusive ownership for an extended period of time, and another request is issued for exclusive control of that same CI. A single task can even create a lock within itself if it requires multiple exclusive control of the same CI.

Requests that require exclusive control are Update, Add, and Delete. If the file has *only* these attributes (i.e., no Browse), it can still be a good candidate for LSR. If, however, an application issues requests exclusive control (Read for Update, Massinsert, Write, or Delete) and the resource is also required for shared ownership (Browse and Read), potential deadlocks can occur if the file is in LSR.

See Section 3.3.4 for a complete scenario of potential deadlock situations within an application and how to avoid it.

3.2.5 NSR vs. LSR

Many issues concerning NSR vs. LSR have already been raised. In conclusion of the discussion of LSR, a few questions remain to be answered.

Although IBM seems to recommend in almost all cases that files be placed in LSR, there are some instances where NSR is preferable.

There are very few situations that warrant removing a file from LSR. The primary purpose of using LSR is to reduce virtual and real storage utilization by sharing resources (buffers). As mentioned in the previous section, some files have attributes that produce deadlock situations and may need to be removed from LSR. If a file is browsed heavily, NSR may be preferable since read ahead is not performed by LSR. If the browse requests consistently remain in the same CI, however, LSR can provide high "lookaside" ratios and improve performance.

Installations should review the file statistics of their CICS systems on a regular basis and evaluate whether LSR is providing the service as described.

3.3 Deadlocks, Enqueues, and Wait Issues

Some of the most confusing problems that programmers face when using VSAM resources occur when the application is affected by record enqueues or deadlocks. This section will deal with these issues, the conditions that cause them, and the most common solutions to the problems.

3.3.1 Conditions Creating a "Deadly Embrace"

What conditions cause the potential for a "deadly embrace" in a CICS VSAM environment?

Consider the following: A VSAM CI contains multiple records including record #A and #B

- Transaction #1 accesses (for update) record #A
- Transaction #2 accesses (for update) record #A
- Transaction #1 accesses (for update) record #B

A potential "deadly embrace" will occur within Transaction #1 if it attempts to access record #B without having rewritten record #A. CICS prevents this from occurring for command level applications by prohibiting more than a single outstanding update to any single CI. In addition, Transaction #2 will wait until the REWRITE operation has been performed by Transaction #1.

There is only one way to terminate two transactions once they become locked in this "deadly embrace." If the transactions are held by some CICS resource enqueues on the record ID (key) while performing an Update, the DTIMOUT parameter in the PCT or Transaction RDO definition would ABEND one or the other if they are deadlocked for more than the time period specified. When CICS detects a deadlock for any of the following:

- SOS (short on storage)
- Temporary storage
- Enqueue
- Remote System Link Request

it places the task on the SUSPEND chain and invokes the DTIMOUT facility for the transaction. After the specified time is exceeded, CICS terminates the suspended task with an AKCS abend.

If, however, the deadlock was caused by VSAM's exclusive control of the CI during update, the tasks would be on the active chain waiting (via the RPL) for the I/O to complete or the CICS event to occur (via the FCT exclusive control wait byte). These transactions are not affected by the DTIMOUT parameter since they are not suspended and would have to be removed via the CEMT PURGE function. An enhancement has been made to FCP (File Control Program) recently to change the way exclusive control conflicts are managed. See Section 3.3.4 for a complete explanation of the enhancement.

3.3.2 Deadlocks across Multiple CICS Regions

There are some specific "deadlock" detection techniques in a multi-CICS environment, such as with ISC.

If Transaction #1 runs on CICS1, Transaction #2 runs on CICS2. Transaction #1 needs to update data on CICS2; however, Transaction #2 is holding the resource for update. Meanwhile, Transaction #2 needs to update data on CICS1 that Transaction #1 is holding.

The ISC (or more specifically LU6.2 architecture) does not directly address this problem. The installation must invoke the RTIMEOUT function to cause the deadlock to be broken after the specified time value has been exceeded.

3.3.3 Deadlocks with Databases (IMS or DB/2)

Many database manager issues will be discussed in a subsequent chapter; however, specific questions can arise dealing directly with deadlock or wait conditions. This section will attempt to cover many of these problems.

There is a recommended way to code the RCT (in DB/2 — CICS environment) option to protect against deadlocks and the backout of all updates as a result of a deadlock in a CICS application.

The ROLBI and ROLBE parameters in the RCT affect deadlock rollbacks. In the event of a deadlock, the transaction that DB/2 chooses as the victim must either commit or rollback updates done since the last commit point. With ROLBE = YES, the application program has no choice and the rollback is done. With ROLBE = NO, the application can decide whether to rollback or commit. Regardless, the program MUST check the SQL return code for a -911 or a -913 and take appropriate action.

If the SQL return code is -913 and ROLBE = NO was specified, the program could choose to commit or rollback and could decide to either terminate or retry the updates.

If a CICS transaction accesses both DB/2 and IMS/DB data, the IRLM (lock manager) is responsible for detecting and resolving a deadlock when one transaction has a lock on a DB/2 resource and is waiting for a lock on an IMS resource, while a second transaction has a lock on that IMS resource and is waiting for a lock on the DB/2 resource.

Deadlocks are detected by the IRLM (for both DB/2 and IMS) via the IRLMWAIT parameter specification of the DSNTIPI install panel. This can be modified later by reassembling the DSNZPARM macro and changing the value of IRLMWT. While the default is 60 seconds, the range can be from 1 to 3600 seconds.

There is no correlation between the DB/2 ownership of locks and the IMS ownerships of locks. The inability to continue will appear as a timeout, whether from DB/2 or from IMS.

In addition to the deadlock detection time value in the IRLM, CICS has the TIMEOUT parameter to detect inactivity at a terminal. This could be used to force a CICS and/or a VTAM session termination and logoff.

3.3.4 VSAM Exclusive Control Wait

While some deadlocks can be detected and purged with "timeout" values, VSAM exclusive control waits are not affected since they stay on the active chain for the duration. Is there any way to break this wait and purge one of the tasks?

When VSAM receives a request for a CI under exclusive control, this request is queued (deferred) if it is the first one in conflict. If this is a subsequent (second, third, etc.) request, it will receive an ILLOGIC error indicating the exclusive conflict, and the application can choose to "handle" the request.

The queued request scenario is explained completely below and will be managed differently if the installation has not installed the enhancement to file control. It is therefore possible to purge the task creating the conflict, the first task that is holding the CI and causing the exclusive control deadlock.

While two CICS "enqueues" for the same resource from the same task do *not* create a problem, two VSAM exclusive requests for the same CI from the same task *is* a problem. If the program holds a record for update in a CI while attempting to ADD, DELETE, or even BROWSE another record in that same CI, an exclusive control wait can occur within a single CICS program.

VSAM Exclusive Control Conflict Enhancement   VSAM Deadlocks caused by exclusive control conflicts are pervasive and extremely disruptive in many CICS systems. Installations have been struggling for years to avoid (if possible) or at least diagnose and correct tasks that cause or become victims of VSAM deadlocks. Database managers (such as IMS or DB/2) contain deadlock detection mechanisms to "break" the impasse between two requests. CICS has never contained any logic to detect and correct a similar situation with VSAM deadlocks.

VSAM Deadlock Logic What causes a VSAM deadlock (sometimes known as a "deadly embrace")? Consider the following scenario:

Task 1 — Issues a BROWSE to an AIX (alternate index) which is defined to LSR (Local Shared Resources). The BROWSE request creates a shared "enqueue" on the CI (control interval).

Task 2 — Issues a WRITE to the base cluster (also in LSR) of this AIX. Since the AIX was defined UPGRADEable, the request generates the subsequent WRITE to the AIX. This UPDATE request requires exclusive use of the AIX CI, which is already held (SHARE) by Task 1.

Task 1 will then attempt to gain shared control over the base CI to locate data on behalf of the BROWSE through the AIX. Task 2 already holds exclusive control over the base CI via the WRITE request. The result is a deadlock with Task 1 having control of the resource that Task 2 is attempting to UPDATE, and Task 2 having control of the resource that Task 1 is attempting to BROWSE via the AIX.

In the past, FCP (File Control Program) detected the inability to accommodate the requests, but issued a WAIT and left the task on the ACTIVE chain. The result: both tasks remained ACTIVE, with a WAIT reason (TCATCDC TCA field dispatch indicator) of X"43" — wait for I/O. If this became a problem (and it usually did) for the installation, a dump was usually taken, and the control blocks could be investigated to determine which tasks were causing the deadlock. Usually one task could be found that was holding the exclusive control over the resource and the appropriate program(s) analyzed for improper logic.

A single CICS application can deadlock itself if a BROWSE request is issued, followed by an UPDATE request within the same CI. The programmer may not be aware of the physical location of the data and that it may exist within the same portion of the VSAM file.

This problem could not only be caused by program logic, but by poorly defined or heavily inserted VSAM files. A CA (control area) split in a VSAM file causes an exclusive control enqueue on all CIs in the CA during the split. Any CICS request during the split will return an exclusive control conflict to the task.

New Logic for Deadlocks IBM has recently changed the logic in FCP and completely transformed the way CICS handles deadlocks. In recent maintenance to CICS, FCP is "amended" to detect the conflict and place the task on the SUSPEND chain rather than the ACTIVE chain. In addition, these tasks on the SUSPEND chain will contain a new SUSPEND code of X"1F" (TCATCDC content) to indicate the exclusive control conflict.

Installations with CICS/MVS Version 2 can install this enhancement with APAR PL52316, available at CICS maintenance level 9003. As promised, IBM is no longer enhancing CICS/OS/VS 1.7, and the APAR is not available in that version.

One justification for the change is that if the task is suspended, it is eligible to be "timed out" via the DTIMEOUT option. In a transaction definition (PCT or RDO), an installation can use DTIMEOUT with a specific time limit. Any task on the SUSPEND chain will be terminated after this time limit if a deadlock is detected.

New AKCW ABEND Code   While all previous tasks that were terminated via the DTIMEOUT value received an ABEND code of AKCS (deadlock timeout), any that are now terminated due to the ECC (exclusive control conflict) will receive an AKCW ABEND. This new ABEND will differentiate ECC terminations from other deadlocks such as temporary storage or remote system links.

To produce the ABEND, the installation must use the DTIMEOUT parameter for the transaction. The syntax of the option is

DTIMEOUT={NO/numeric value}

The default value, if uncoded, NO, will not terminate the task and will leave it suspended. To terminate any suspended task with a TCATCDC value of X"1F," a DTIMEOUT value MUST be coded for the associated transaction ID.

The numeric value in the option is the length of time as

MMSS = minutes/seconds

with 70 minutes 00 seconds as the largest possible interval. If DTIMEOUT is coded, the task will be terminated with an AKCW ABEND if suspended for longer than the interval.

Most installations have not coded and therefore not used this option for most transactions. This new "enhancement" in FCP may cause many installations to rethink their decision and use the ECC logic to break deadlocks. In a test CICS system, this option could be used with new applications to diagnose potential flaws in update logic.

VSWA Enhancements   The VSWA (VSAM Work Area) is a block of storage built for the task when FCP receives a request for VSAM data. The storage can be found in the "chain" of all storage areas for the task and is identified by the X"8F" type in the first byte. The VSWA is always analyzed when diagnosing VSAM problems or deadlocks, since it contains the RPL (Request Parameter List) and subsequent request conditions. The VSWA now includes additional information when FCP has detected an ECC.

While the VSWAEMA (Error Message Area Address) always existed, it now will be updated with the relevant information from the ECC. The address pointed to by VSWAEMA will be a message area with:

"RPLADDR" + 4 bytes of the RPL this request is waiting for

"TASKNUM" + 3 bytes of the associated task number

"TRANSID" + 4 bytes of the associated trans id

"FCTNAME" + 8 bytes of the associated filename

Of course, if the task number and trans id in these fields are the same as the suspended task, then the application contains an error in logic, since the task has deadlocked itself. If, however, the information points to another task, then an ECC across two tasks has occurred, and the scenario may be unavoidable. At least this new information in the VSWA will decrease the diagnosis time and assist in the identification of problem transactions and files.

Figure 3-3 contains a portion of a transaction dump with the storage chains for the task. Note that the VSWA for the task (storage type 8F) begins at X"00020430" (1). At offset +50 is the address X"000205C8" (2). This address points to the VSWAEMA (Error Message Area). This block of storage can be found at the top of the report, beginning at address X"000205C0" (3). It is then obvious to locate the remaining vital items of this conflict via the following "map" of the new VSWAEMA contents. The preceding map (above) contains the offsets within the error message area, and the specific contents from the example. As shown, the task currently on the SUSPEND chain is waiting on Task #33, which currently has file FILEA exclusively enqueued via transaction CECI. This scenario was, of course, manually created, but is very representative of typical exclusive control conflicts within a CICS application.

```
CICS 2.1 TEST                                                                                   42  15:55:33 07/12/90
     0000  42000068 00000000 00020010 001A038A  0001EF48 00020424 00000000 000AE918  *..............................Z.*
     0020  0001EF48 0001ED78 0001E8D4 0002041E  00000000 001F3FE0 0019FDE8 00199E54  *..........M.............Y.....*
     0040  0001E2C0 0001E190 001F6600 FE01E5E8  F000D2C3 001F0AA8 00000000 00000000  *..S..........VYO.KC...........*
     0060  00000000 00000000                                                         *........                       *

    TASK STORAGE 000205C0 (3)

     0000  8C000088 00020550 D9D7D3C1 C4C4D940  7A400000 0001D678 40404040 40404040  *........RPLADDR  ....O.        *
     0020  40404040 40404040 E3C1E2D2 D5E4D440  7A400003 3C404040 40404040 40404040  *        TASKNUM  ...            *
     0040  40404040 40404040 E3D9C1D5 E2C9C440  7A40C3C5 C3C94040 40404040 40404040  *        TRANSID  . CECI         *
     0060  40404040 40404040 C6C3E3D5 C1D4C540  7A40C6C9 D3C5C140 40400000 00000000  *        FCTNAME  . FILEA  ......*
     0080  00000000 00000000 8C000088 00020550                                       *................                *

    TASK STORAGE 00020550

     0000  8F020068 00020430 C0000000 00000000  00000000 00000000 00000000 00000000  *................................*
     0020  00000000 00000000 00000000 00000000  00000000 00000000 00000000 00000000  *................................*
     0040  00000000 00000000 00000000 00000000  00000000 00000000 00000000 00000000  *................................*
     0060  00000000 00000000 8F020068 00020430                                       *................                *

    TASK STORAGE 00020430

     0000  8F010118 10020410 0000004C 0281E3C4  40000000 1C080014 00000000 00000000  *..............TD................*
     0020  00199ED4 00000000 00020560 00020418  40860000 00000000 00000050 00000050  *...M............................*
     0040  00000000 00000000 00000000 00000080  000205C8 90199E54 00000000 0001D670  *...................H..........O.*
     0060  00000000 00000000 0001D670 00000000  00000001 00000000 00040000 00000000  *..............O.................*
     0080  00000000 00000000 00000000 00000000  00000000 00000000 00000000 00000000  *................................*
     00A0  00000000 4019E722 00000000 00000004  00020438 00020374 5019E506 00000000  *.......X.................V......*
     00C0  00199ED4 00020010 0019C598 0019D598  00199E54 00020550 00020430 0001E190  *...M......E...N.................*
     00E0  00000000 0001E190 001F6600 00000000  00000000 00000000 00000000 00000000  *................................*
     0100  00000000 00000000 00000000 00000000  00000000 00000000 8F010118 10020410  *................................*

    TASK STORAGE 00020410

     0000  8C000018 0001EF40 F0F0F0F1 F0F0F0F0  F0F1F0F0 00000000 8C000018 0001EF40  *........000100000100...........*

    TASK STORAGE 0001EF40

     0000  8C000088 00020000 C6C9D3C5 C1404040  00000000 08199E54 00020418 00060006  *........FILEA   ................*
     0020  8001EB09 07801850 00000000 00000000  00000000 00000000 00000000 00000000  *................................*
     0040  00000000 00000000 00000000 00000000  00000000 00000000 00000000 00000000  *................................*
     0060  00000000 00000000 00000000 00000000  00000000 00000000 00000000 00000000  *................................*
     0080  00000000 00000000 00000000 00000000  00000000 00000000 00000000 00000000  *................................*
     00A0  00000000 00000000 FF000000 00000000  00000000 00000000 8C000088 00020000  *................................*

    TASK STORAGE 00020000

     0000  8C000408 0001EE70 FE01E570 05180588  480003D0 0001E580 00000000 00000000  *...........V.......
     0020  00000000 00000000 00000000 00000000  00000000 00000000 00000000 00000000  *...................
     0040  00000000 00000000 00000000 00000000  00000000 00000000 00000000 FD0203E0  *...................
     0060  F500C6C3 0019A588 01000000 00000000  801BA1BA 00000000 00000000 00000000  *5.FC...............
     0080  801BA28C 00000000 00000000 00000000  801BA33A 001BC814 02814684 00020158  *...................
     00A0  00000000 00000000 00000000 00000000  00000000 00000000 00000000 00000000  *...................
     00C0  00000000 00000000 00000000 00000000  00000000 00000000 00000000 9019A828  *...................
     00E0  8019A82C 8019A840 9019A850 8019C2D8  A019A878 9019C06C 00000000 00000000  *..............BQ..
     0100  00000000 00000000 00000000 9019A864  9019A898 00000000 00000000 00000000  *...................
     0120  00000000 00000000 801B8326 00000000  00000000 001BC814 02814684 00020158  *...................
     0140  00000000 00000000 00000000 00000000  00169E70 A019C542 801988DE 0001E5E8  *...................
```

Figure 3-3 CICS transaction dump.

```
CICS 2.1 TEST                                                                                42  15:55:33 07/12/90
0000    42000068  00000000  00020010  001A038A    001EF48  00020424  00000000  000AE918  ...........Z...
0020    0001EF48  0001ED7B  0001EB04  00020041F   0001EB04  0001F3FE0 0019FDEB  0019E654  .........M....V...
0040    00000000  00000000  00000000  00000000    00000000  00000000  00000000  00000000  ................
0060    00000000  00000000  8F020068  00020430

TASK STORAGE 00020430
0000    BF01011B  10020410  0000004C  02B1E3C4    40000000  1C080014  00000000  00000000  ...........TD
0020    00199ED4  00000000  00020560  00020418    40B60000  00000050  00010670  ...........H...
0040    00000000  00000000  00010670  00000000    00205CB  90199E54  00040000  00000000  ...........O...
0060    00000000  00000000  00000000  00000000    00000001  00000000  00000000  00000000  ...........V...
0080    00000000  4019E722  00000000  00000004    00020438  00020374  5019E506  00010E190  .....X.........
00A0    00199ED4  00020010  0019C598  00190598    00199E54  00020550  00020430  00001E190  .....M....E...N...
00C0    00000000  0001E190  001F6600  00000000    00000000  00000000  00000000  00000000  ................
0100    00000000  00000000  00000000  00000000    00000000  00000000  8F010118  10020410

TASK STORAGE 00020410
0000    BC000018  0001EF40  F0F0F0F1  F0F0F0F0    F0F1F0F0  00000000  BC000018  0001E140  ...0001000000100...

TASK STORAGE 0001EF40
0000    BC000088  00020000  C6C9D3C5  C14D4D40    00000000  0819E654  00020418  00000016  .....FILEA
0020    8001EB09  078D1B50  00000000  00000000    00000000  00000000  00000000  00000000  ................
0040    00000000  00100000  00000000  00000000    00000000  00000000  00000000  00000003  ................
0060    00000000  00000000  00000000  00000000    00000000  00000000  00000000  00000000  ................
0080    00000000  FF000000  00000000  00000000    00000000  00000000  BC000088  00020000  ................
00A0    00000000  00000000  00000000

TASK STORAGE 00020000
0000    BC000408  0001EE70  FE01E570  051B05B8    4B0003D0  0001E580  00000000  00000000  ...........V.....
0020    000000Q00 00000000  00000000  00000000    00000000  00000000  00000000  FD0203E0  ................
0040    00000000  00000000  01000000  00000000    8018A1BA  00000000  00000000  00020015B ...........FC
0060    F500C6C3  0019A5B8  00000000  00000000    8018A33A  0018C814  02814684  00020015B .....BQ.......
0080    8018A28C  00000000  00000000  00000000    8018C814  02814684  00000000  9019AB28  .........M.....
00A0    00000000  00000000  00000000  00000000    A019AB78  9019C06C  00000000  9019AB28  ................
00C0    00000000  00000000  00000000  00000000    9019A898  9019C20B  00000000  00000000  ................
00E0    8019A82C  B019AB40  00000000  00000000    9019A898  9019A864  00000000  028140B4  ...........H...
0100    00000000  00000000  00000000  00000000    0019E70  028140B4  80191518  00191518  ...........E....V
0120    00000000  00000000  80188326  00000000    A019E70  A019512   B019HH0E  00191518
0140    00000000  00000000  00000000  00000000
```

Figure 3-4   CICS transaction dump with message area.

3.3.5 VSAM String Waits

VSAM strings can improve or degrade performance, depending on specifications that the installation uses. The utilization of VSAM strings can and should be monitored to ensure optimum performance. Several issues dealing with VSAM strings and string waits will be discussed to attempt to resolve and possibly avoid potential problems.

Tasks Holding VSAM Strings   In the CICS Problem Determination Guide, IBM has provided a section entitled "Debugging VSAM File Control Waits." In this section, IBM suggests that each VSWA (VSAM System Work Area) control block represents one string. Actually, however, not all VSWAs represent a held string. VSWAs are acquired before strings are assigned.

If the programmer is "chasing" control blocks, the VSWA for any file points to a PLH (place holder). The PLH points back to the RPL (request parameter list) contained within the VSWA for that file. Since there is a PLH for each real VSAM string, the ones that are active should point back to the owning RPL contained in the VSWA. The VSWA has a pointer back to the owning TCA, and the programmer could then find the task that "owns" that string.

This method requires analysis of a CICS dump to identify these control blocks and owners. The simplest technique would be to use the SDUMP facility of CICS to produce a SYS1.DUMPx and then format the dump with DFHPDX (CICS formatted dump facility for SDUMPS).

CICS shutdown statistics can show string waits while the maximum concurrent active strings are less than the total.

If a VSAM file uses LSR, any STRNO parameter specified in the FCT is used solely by CICS to limit the number of I/O requests for records within that specific file.

If, for example, the installation specified STRNO=4 in the FCT, CICS will never issue more than four concurrent VSAM I/O requests for records within that file. If the LSR pool had 10 strings, at least 6 of the strings in the pool will be used to satisfy requests for other files in the same pool.

While file statistics are maintained by CICS, LSR pool statistics are maintained by VSAM and requested by CICS when necessary. Often CICS considers strings in use while VSAM records less than the same number of concurrent requests. The CICS strings are acquired prior to issuing the request to VSAM and are not released until the requesting task is redispatched following completion of the VSAM I/O operation.

Calculating VSAM Strings   There exists a calculation to determine VSAM strings to avoid or to reduce string waits.

The number of strings is normally dependent on several factors. One factor would be the I/O activity of the VSAM file. Another could be the performance requirements or even virtual storage available, if that resource happens to be in short supply. Of course, in the calculation of VSAM strings, more is always better if performance is an issue. A very active file will need more strings to maintain fast access time.

Probably the best technique would be to do a "best guess" calculation and then closely monitor the CICS shutdown statistics. If no string waits ever occur, the allocation was probably too high, and resources are being wasted. If a high number of string waits occur regularly, the calculation was probably low and should be increased. Again, monitor the results until the string wait value remains relatively low on a consistent basis.

Specific techniques can be used by an application to reduce or avoid string waits.

VSAM holds the string from the time that a file request is issued until the request is implicitly ended. In the case of a Browse, the VSAM string is held for the entire length of the Browse, until the ENDBR is issued (or until the task ends). The program could reduce string waits by shortening the length of the Browse, or ensuring that the ENDBR is issued rather than leaving the release to task termination.

In the case of a Read or Update, strings are held until the data CI is rewritten after update. If index set records are retained within buffers (such as LSR), string retention can be reduced.

Again, careful monitoring of the shutdown statistics and review of applications that appear to cause excessive string waits can relieve most VSAM string waits.

3.3.6 Sharing CICS Files with Batch Jobs

CICS and VSAM work together to attempt to avoid deadlocks and enqueues when resources are accessed from multiple applications within CICS. Additional issues arise when address spaces other than CICS wish to share VSAM resources (files) and avoid enqueue conflicts.

Customers cannot use VSAM Shareoption 4, perform Enqueue/Dequeue processing within the program, and provide integrity of shared datasets between CICS and batch jobs.

IBM does not recommend, and CICS does not support, the sharing of VSAM files with batch jobs in update mode. Database managers such as DB/2 and IMS/DB are available to provide this requirement.

In fact, both ENQ and DEQ are MVS calls which violate the CICS defined application interface standards of not issuing MVS calls. Installations that utilize these techniques place themselves at risk and can violate the integrity of the data being processed.

If a batch job requires access to a CICS VSAM file, Shareoption 2 should be used and the CICS CEMT command should be used to either close the file entirely to CICS, or change the access options to read-only.

3.4 VSAM Subtasking

In a CICS environment, the installation can decide to "turn on" and utilize the VSAM subtasking facility. Many people are unaware of this facility or are unsure if it would be beneficial to their specific environment. This section will deal with the impact of VSAM subtasking and whether it could provide performance advantages in different environments.

Activating VSAM Subtasking The VSP= parameter in the SIT specifies whether or not to activate subtasking: a value of YES indicates the customer wants to utilize the facility.

3.4.1 Utilization Decisions

In almost every case, if CICS is running on a uniprocessor, i.e., a single-CPU environment, VSAM subtasking should not be used, since there is only a single CP (central processor) that can be used to dispatch all work. An example of a uniprocessor would be an IBM/3083 or IBM/3090 model smaller than a 200-class machine.

The CICS VSAM subtasking facility should also be considered for any CICS system utilizing more than 80% of the processing capacity of a multi-processor. IBM usually recommends that if the processor is running at less then 80%, subtasking may not be necessary and may, in fact, degrade performance.

In most installations, CICS environments with high VSAM file activity running on a diadic (2-CPU) or higher can benefit from subtasking.

In a recent announcement concerning CICS, VSAM subtasking was enhanced to reduce processor overhead. The change attempts to improve performance of the facility.

IBM discovered that in some BROWSE operations, the record requested was already in a VSAM buffer, and the CPU cycles consumed by the VSAM subtask was a significant amount of the total path length. This produced a situation where the cost of subtasking actually reduced or eliminated any benefit to the customer. The change to subtasking is an attempt to limit the use to instances when VSAM I/O would actually be required to satisfy the request for the record. If the record was expected to be found in a VSAM buffer, subtasking would be avoided.

3.4.2 Measuring Effectiveness

If a customer was utilizing VSAM subtasking, it is possible to calculate the amount of processing done by the VSAM subtask.

Utilizing the IBM facility CICSPARS (performance analysis product), locate the "CICS Total" report. The "Total Subtask Time" plus the "Total SRB Time" could be the combined amount of processing eligible to execute on any secondary processor (diadic or above) concurrent with primary processor (maintask).

If the customer was utilizing other vendor performance packages, the same fields should be reported. Locate these two fields in the particular reports provided.

3.4.3 LSR and CA Split Issues

VSAM subtasking can have an effect on files placed in LSR.

The problem arises when the LSR pool is efficiently utilized and therefore has a high "look-aside" ratio, since most of the requests will be satisfied in the buffer. In these cases, dispatching a secondary task to perform (or in this case, *not* perform) I/O is unnecessary.

Installations that are utilizing LSR may wish to use VSAM subtasking with caution and review the costs. As stated above, IBM is attempting to enhance subtasking to accommodate this problem. Since it is clear that CICS wishes to continue to exploit N-way architecture and provide even more subtasking facilities in CICS, future enhancements are inevitable.

VSAM subtasking can also affect the performance of CA splits in CICS.

When a CA split occurs, the entire CICS address space will wait while the CA split is being processed. If VSAM subtasking is used, the I/O subtask TCB is placed into the wait, not the CICS task. This is true only for NSR files.

Using LSR, neither the VSAM subtask nor the CICS task is placed into the wait. VSAM has been enhanced to invoke an exit while waiting for the I/O, and CICS processing will continue for other requests.

In summary, subtasking has potential benefits during a CA split only in the case of NSR files.

3.5 ESDS (Entry Sequence) and RRDS (Relative Record) Datasets

Although many CICS VSAM files are KSDS (key sequence) type, there are situations that may arise that either do not require a file to contain a key or require the data to be stored in a different format. ESDS and RRDS files can be used in CICS for many different reasons, some of which are discussed in this section.

3.5.1 Characteristics

There are some primary differences between ESDS and RRDS type datasets, and the typical KSDS dataset.

To begin with, ESDS and RRDS files have no index component; they consist of only a data component. For this reason, VSAM does not utilize an index level to search for the record, and any index-related specification (such as BUFNI) has no meaning.

In addition, ESDS and RRDS files do not split, either CA or CI, and therefore must be allocated accordingly. An ESDS can contain an AIX (alternate index), but RRDS datasets cannot have AIXs.

Records are loaded similarly in both ESDS and RRDS type datasets.

Records are loaded sequentially into an ESDS, as they are entered. New records are added to the end of the ESDS. When VSAM adds a record, it returns the RBA (relative byte address) of the record to the application program. A CICS application could, therefore, access the record directly via an index based on the RBA returned.

If an ESDS is accessed sequentially, records are retrieved in the order in which they were stored. For this reason, ESDS files are often used for a journal or log.

In an RRDS, records are added by the relative record number and occupy a "fixed-length" slot. This number can be assigned by the application program or, if not, will be assigned by VSAM. If the program allows VSAM to assign the number, new records are added to the end of the RRDS. If the application assigns the relative record number, the record is added according to the number assigned and can therefore be placed anywhere within the RRDS.

Since records are stored and retrieved within the slot (previously allocated), the slot can contain actual data or be empty. Records can be inserted, moved, or deleted without affecting the location or any other records within the RRDS. Records can be accessed sequentially or directly via the relative record number. An RRDS could, therefore, be accessed as much as a KSDS (key sequenced) but without the overhead of the index search to locate any specific record.

3.5.2 Performance

ESDS files in CICS are not buffered for output as are KSDS files.

The CICS WRITE of an ESDS results in the entire CI being written to DASD. A serial write into an ESDS, therefore, can produce excessive I/Os since each write will rewrite the entire CI, not just the single record.

Input buffering offers the same performance advantages of KSDS files, and ESDS files (especially when initially loaded) are excellent candidates for LSR processing.

There are some performance issues relating to recoverable ESDS files.

The characteristics of recovery with mass insert produces one VSAM write per CICS write. CICS will serialize writes to an ESDS by "locking" the base cluster. If a Write with mass insert discovers that another task owns the buffer, an ENQREQ produces a one-two-one match of VSAM writes to CICS writes for the multiple requests. The ENQREQ is required to prevent a deadlock between the cluster lock and the CI lock between two transactions.

This situation is driven by the mass insert request, not necessarily the recovery option. Other VSAM files using mass insert (such as KSDS) would perform similarly.

3.6 OSCOR Issues

The use of CICS storage, particularly OSCOR, is both confusing and frustrating to many CICS support personnel. A great deal of time can be spent tuning OSCOR requirements, and different versions of

CICS utilize OSCOR very differently. Overspecified values for OSCOR can produce wasted resources; underspecified values can produce system failures. This section will attempt to unravel the mysteries of OSCOR and provide insight into the facility.

3.6.1 What Goes into OSCOR?

The CICS SIT (system initialization table) contains the value for CICS to use for OSCOR=nnn, where nnn equals the amount of bytes to allocate. The default value is 8196 bytes, which is approximately enough to suport 4 VSAM files with CI sizes of 1K. Obviously this is inadequate and should be calculated by the installation for optimum value.

The CICS Performance Guide contains a section covering OSCOR and gives some recommendations regarding calculations.

In earlier CICS versions, all files (whenever opened) acquire storage from OSCOR for buffers and control blocks. The amount of OSCOR required for each file depends on the level of CICS and the level of DFP that the installation is using. More current releases of CICS combined with more current releases of DFP move buffers and control blocks into extended storage and decrease the OSCOR requirements. In addition, NSR files use more OSCOR than LSR files and must be accommodated in the calculation.

3.6.2 OSCOR Fragmentation

OSCOR can become "fragmented," and little can be done to reclaim storage. OSCOR cannot be "compressed" the way the CICS reuses DSA storage after program compression. The only way to reclaim fragmented OSCOR would be to shut down and restart CICS. Many installations start CICS as a started task to ensure that the storage is allocated "cleanly" at each startup. If CICS is run as a job (started via a JES initiator), the installation should make sure that the initiator (and subsequent address space) is intact every time by draining and restarting the initiator before each CICS startup.

3.6.3 Dynamic Open/Close

The dynamic Open/Close facility for files could affect utilization of OSCOR.

As previously stated, in some CICS versions most files, whether OPEN=INITIAL, OPEN=DEFERRED, or opened and closed during CICS execution, use OSCOR for control blocks. The amount varies depending on LSR/NSR utilization and levels of both CICS and DFP. If insufficient OSCOR is available during dynamic OPEN of a file, a CICS system failure occurs and is explained in Section 3.6.4. If sufficient OSCOR is available, but inadequate storage is available in other categories, other problems could result.

One example would be the inability of VSAM to acquire storage for catalog or VVDS (VSAM volume dataset) processing. A message such as:

IEC161I 037(050,016,IGG0CLE4)...

would indicate the VVDS management could not obtain adequate storage during the open process.

A facility to monitor OSCOR utilization after successive VSAM file open/close requests is available from IBM.

An IBM facility called VSMR (Virtual Storage Monitor Resource) can be used to monitor used and free OSCOR. If this monitor is utilized before and after each open/close, values can be calculated to observe the effect.

Also, an IBM publication, "Virtual Storage Tuning Cookbook," discusses OSCOR and can be used to monitor utilization. Of course, there are additional products available from other vendors to provide similar results.

3.6.4 80A Abends

CICS will abend with an 80A if inadequate OSCOR is available, which MVS defines as a GETMAIN failure. Since to use OSCOR is basically an MVS GETMAIN of storage, if the CICS address space is unable to accommodate the request, MVS treats it as a failure of storage acquisition and produces the 80A.

3.7 VSAM in an AS/400 and PS/2 Environment

As installations decide to distribute both processing and data, the issues of moving and accessing the data in the remote locations will raise additional problems for the application. The AS/400 and the PS/2 are two of the most widely used and accepted processors in a nonmainframe distributed environment.

3.7.1 DDM from the AS/400

If an AS/400 uses a DDM (Distributed Data Manager) request to communicate with multiple CICS systems via ISC, can data be function shipped from a second CICS to the first and then returned to the AS/400?

No, the AS/400 must establish sessions individually with each CICS region and request data directly from each CICS system separately.

The limitations are produced from the most restrictive system, in other words, although VSAM in MVS supports variable length records, the AS/400 does not. For that reason, variable length records are not supported in an AS/400-to-CICS DDM environment. If either system does not support a feature, DDM sessions cannot use the feature. Other limitations would be the lack of update capability via the AIX (alternate index), the ability to process ESDS only sequentially.

DDM can be used to transfer an AS/400 file to a CICS system executing on an MVS host.

The CPYF command (on the AS/400) has the ability to copy a file either from the AS/400 to CICS or from CICS back to the AS/400. The file (if transmitting from the AS/400) must already be created (allocated) on the host CICS system before the copy begins. For complete syntax and description, see the AS/400 publications covering CPYF.

3.7.2 OS/2 VSAM Support

The CICS/OS2 announcement contained a statement that its VSAM was "compatible" with the host. This raises many questions, some of which will be covered in this section.

CICS/OS2 does not contain VSAM utilities (such as IDCAMS) to process the VSAM data under OS/2.

There are no VSAM utilities since all VSAM support is provided by CICS/OS2 and not specifically by the operating system (OS/2). To create VSAM files, the programmer must use CICS facilities: create an FCT entry, open the file (as with CEMT), load the data via program writes, and then close the file.

CICS/OS2 cannot utilize catalogs for VSAM access as in MVS since OS/2 does not utilize catalogs.

Variable length records are supported for both KSDS and ESDS files. The maximum LRECL for KSDS and ESDS files is 9999; for RRDS the largest record is 4092. Other than maximum LRECL, the size of the VSAM file is only limited by the amount of DASD space available on the PS/2.

If there are no utilities to support VSAM files, how would files be "ported" from one environment to the other (MVS to OS/2 and back)?

The files are not directly transferrable, but can be downloaded from host to workstation via function shipping requests. In other words, an application can be initiated on CICS/OS2, request the data from the host, and function ship the records down to the CICS/OS2 system. The application would then create the OS/2 file by normal write instructions (and could even extract only a portion of the records). Perhaps future releases of the product will produce an easier way to download files.

3.8 Function Shipping and ISC with VSAM Files

Since many installations share data across multiple CICS systems, host computers, and distributed systems, the issues dealing with file sharing are even more complicated. Previous sections in this chapter dealt with file integrity across multiple CICS applications in the same CICS region. The issues covered in this section will be related to multi-CICS environments.

There are substantial differences between sharing VSAM files across multiple CICS regions as opposed to function shipping to a single FOR (file owning region).

Function shipping is the only technique recommended for sharing a single VSAM file with integrity. Any other method will violate VSAM integrity and produce (in IBM's words) unpredictable and undesirable results.

Even if all but one of the CICS regions were read only (one could update), read integrity could not be guaranteed. Of course, if all the CICS regions were read only (*no* update), then sharing is definitely possible, but integrity is not an issue since the file will never be updated.

If data needs to be shared among multiple CICS systems, a database manager (such as DB/2 or DL/1) should be used.

There are some integrity exposures if a database manager (such as DB/2) is used with CICS/MRO (multi-region option).

If MRO detects an in-doubt situation, the architecture of LU6.2 utilizes "syncpoint" processing. During MRO processing of the syncpoint, DB/2 will produce a request to continue or ABORT. If the DB/2 response is ABORT, then CICS will drive the MRO session with a backout request. If the response from DB/2 is continue, CICS will produce a commit. If the MRO session fails prior to the commit, CICS will ABEND the task, which will cause DB/2 to backout the updates.

The only exposure exists if the FOR ABENDS before the (phase 2) syncpoint is completed. CICS emergency restart will decide whether to backout or commit the resources, but a discrepancy will exist. CICS messages noting the problem will be produced when the session is reestablished.

3.8.2 FCT (File Control Table) Requirements

A file is defined differently in the FCT to establish the remote access requirement.

VSAM files that physically exist in another CICS region and are accessed via MRO contain only a few additional items. The TYPE=REMOTE entry in the FCT identifies to CICS that the file will not be found in the base system, SYSID= defines the remote CICS system that would contain the resource, and RMTNAME= can be used to specify the name by which the file is known to the system in which it resides. This last item is optional and allows the same file to be referenced in multiple systems, using a different name in each system.

The KENLEN and LRECL items in the FCT must be accurate for each file defined as TYPE=REMOTE, since a value cannot be coded that would accommodate the maximum value to be found.

"Generic" values should not be used for key lengths. CICS copies the amount of data specified by KEYLEN into the TIOA. If the area is larger than the actual key, a program check could occur. Of course, there are also performance issues involved when excessive amounts of data are stored or transferred unnecessarily.

3.8.3 CICS Transactions and VSAM Requests

In the CICS Performance Guide, Intercommunications Section, IBM states that dataset (VSAM) requests are recorded under the CSMI transaction while DL/I requests would be logged by CSM5. Would the installation assume, then, that all VSAM requests handled by intercommunications facilities thereby show up as CSMI I/O?

The mirror transaction (CSMI or CSM5) is created by the first function ship request. All subsequent calls to that region from the transaction that created the mirror transaction will use that mirror regardless of the function.

If, therefore, a request for VSAM data caused the mirror to be created, the CSMI transaction would be created. If, however, the request was for DL/1 resources (such as a PCB CALL), then CSM5 would be the transaction.

CICS also introduced a "reusable" mirror concept to improve performance. Mirror transactions are suspended when completed and can be resumed on behalf of a new request rather than creating a new transaction. For this reason, DL/1 requests and VSAM requests may be recorded under either transaction.

4

CICS Temporary Storage and Transient Data

Use of temporary storage within CICS is both straightforward and (if used properly) efficient. Temporary storage gives the application program a vehicle to perform I/O and share that data across applications without distinctly defining any files. This data can be much more dynamic, therefore, since the creation and deletion is handled by the application. There are limitations, however, and recovery issues that should be understood. This chapter will attempt to deal with many issues of temporary storage utilization.

4.1 Temporary Storage Utilization

The use of temporary storage can pose many decisions to the application programmer. In addition to read/write architecture, programmers need to be aware of proper and improper uses. In order to make the right decision, understanding the characteristics of temporary storage is necessary.

4.1.1 Characteristics

Temporary storage records are written/read from queues that can either reside in CICS main storage or on auxiliary storage (DASD). In the case of TS (temporary storage) AUX (auxiliary), the data is stored in a preallocated VSAM dataset defined to CICS via the DFHTEMP DD in the startup JCL. Since this file is both known and managed by CICS, the application program does not need to perform any file definition or open/close processing.

Temporary storage records (Main or AUX) are logically grouped into "queues" much the same way that partitioned datasets (PDSs) are grouped into members. The queue name is a unique identifier created dynamically when the queue is generated. The queue name must be unique whether it is built in MAIN or AUX.

Most installations develop a naming convention for queue names that becomes standard for all applications. Since the TS queue can be (and usually is) read by any transaction within the CICS region, a uniform queue name would be useful. Normally, the queue name contains some combination of the terminal ID, application code, and sequence number but cannot be larger than 8 characters.

The most widely accepted use of temporary storage is to save data between pseudoconversational tasks. Since this (pseudoconversational) technique is advised in most CICS installations (to conserve resources and improve performance), tasks return control to CICS, and all storage relating to the task is deleted by CICS. Temporary storage records can serve as a "save area," by using the transaction identifier (4 characters) and the terminal ID (4 characters) as the queue name to return control when the operator (or terminal) requests dispatch.

Other typical uses of TS are to communicate between CICS applications or as a "scratch pad" within a single application to reduce the storage required by the task. This technique can be used as an alternative to COMMAREAs passed in a LINK or CALL statement. The storage area is then not part of the program, such as Working Storage, and can decrease the size of the load module. The decision to use TS instead of COMMAREA must be made based on storage size, type, and life span.

Limits to the Number of Records or Size of a TS Queue   Any single TS queue cannot contain more than 32767 records. While the TS VSAM dataset for TS AUX queues can be any amount of cylinders, it is predefined and allocated. As with any VSAM dataset, it can become full and return an "out of space" condition to the application. The installation would then need to delete any unnecessary queues (perhaps not cleaned up or deleted by the application) to make space available. The VSAM dataset could be made larger, but only after CICS has come down, since DFHTEMP cannot be deleted during CICS execution.

Some installations limit the use of temporary storage by applications or force them to use either TS MAIN or AUX.

If the SIT is coded with TS=(,0), no TS AUX will be allowed by CICS. Any request will automatically be changed by CICS to MAIN.

Use of TS MAIN can normally not be restricted, except for internal installation standards. This resource needs to be monitored closely to detect excessive utilization.

Guidelines are available to use when creating the TS AUX VSAM dataset for performance or DASD utilization. The CICS Operations Guide (CICS/MVS 2.1 or CICS/ESA 3.1) contain information relating to definition of the TS VSAM dataset. In the CICS/MVS 2.1 Performance Guide, IBM states that CI (control interval) size can impact transfer efficiency, and that a smaller CI size is desirable if access to TS is random, while a larger CI size would be preferable for sequential usage. Also, this publication recommends the use of secondary extents for efficient DASD utilization. The primary allocation will be used under normal situations, and the secondary allocation can be available during "peak" requests. Read this material more completely if TS AUX or MAIN performance is an issue.

There are, however, some limitations or hazards to consider when reading records from a TS queue. Most programmers avoid using the NEXT option with the READQ command. Realize that multiple tasks can read from the same queue. The NEXT option returns the next record (to the current record) read by ANY CICS application. If a program executes a READQ, continues processing, and then requests a READQ NEXT, there is no guarantee which record will be returned, and it could potentially (and no doubt probably) *not* be the next sequential record from the first one read. It is, in fact, impossible to predict which record will be returned with this technique.

TS Queue Deletion   Individual records can be "logically" deleted from the queue but are, in fact, not physically deleted until the entire queue is deleted. The application must create a "delete flag" and interrogate this flag to determine any logically deleted records. The DELETEQ command deletes the entire queue, regardless of the number of records left in the queue. This command is therefore recommended when an application is prepared to terminate and would be used to "clean up" resources before returning control to CICS.

Installations must develop standards to enforce deletion of queues after the queues are no longer needed. Use of temporary storage without cleanup can waste resources. Even when using TS MAIN, the resources consumed by CICS can become excessive if records are created and never deleted, especially if CICS is left up (not recycled) for long periods of time. With many installations implementing continuous operations, CICS may keep executing for many days. Resources not deleted could impact both performance and availability.

COBOL II Use of TS   Applications that use COBOL II may find TS MAIN records with DATAIDs of CEBRxxxx, where xxxx = the terminal id. These entries are created when a COBOL II program ABENDS within CICS and are intended to be used during debugging. They contain compile information and other data normally found in a transaction dump. More information pertaining to this facility can be found in Chapter 2.

Using CEBR (the browse transaction), programmers can view these records to determine the problem and what caused it. Programmers need to realize, however, that although CICS writes these TS MAIN records "above the line," it does not take responsibility to delete them. They remain until TS MAIN is recreated during CICS startup (since it is nonrecoverable). Installations can review the shutdown statistics for TS MAIN usage. While excessive COBOL II TS MAIN utilization can increase the extended private area (and therefore the working set size), this should only be a problem in test CICS regions which would incur large numbers of COBOL II ABENDS.

Because excessive COBOL II ABENDs produce excessive use of TS MAIN, the installation may wish to prevent these records from being written. There are no parameters or options currently available to turn this facility off. CICS has a program error program, DFHPEP, however, which the installation could use to purge these queues with a "user-written" program when a program ABEND has occurred.

CICS utilizes TS MAIN or TS AUX when routing CICS messages via CMSG.

If an application routes messages to CICS users via the BMS ROUTE command, the CICS transaction CSMG is invoked. The messages are stored in TS AUX (unless specifically not requested in the SIT) as logical messages, with one created for each terminal type, not for each terminal. These logical messages remain until delivered to all eligible terminals.

Terminals that are eligible for autoinstall but not yet logged on may be eligible for the message, but since the terminal control blocks have not been built, they will not be considered eligible to receive the message.

4.1.2 TS MAIN vs. AUX

Many decisions regarding TS queues deal with the selection of MAIN or AUX. Both types of temporary storage have strengths and weaknesses and need to be analyzed when making this decision. Auxiliary temporary storage is recorded on the DFHTEMP VSAM dataset; records written to TS MAIN are written within the CICS system itself.

When CICS receives a request (WRITEQ) to TS MAIN, it writes the record to "main" storage, or storage within CICS's address space. If the installation is running MVS/XA and the comparable CICS/VS or CICS/MVS that contains "XA-support," the records are written "above the line" or above 16 Mb. When CICS writes these records above the 16-Mb line, it must execute an MVS GETMAIN for each record. This can produce excessive overhead, especially for large numbers of small records. For this reason, any record less than 1024 bytes is written within the CICS DSA (dynamic storage area). Applications are unaware of this automatic facility within CICS and cannot override the direction of the record.

In either case, TS MAIN is much more efficient than AUX, since all I/Os remain within CICS and do not require physical I/O to DASD. This increased access speed can enhance performance for most CICS transactions.

Although TS MAIN is so much faster with less overhead, there are disadvantages to using it. One substantial limitation of TS MAIN is the lack of recoverability. TS MAIN records can never be recoverable and exist only while that CICS region remains operational. If the region should fail, the contents of TS MAIN are lost, since the address space no longer exists.

Another point to remember about TS MAIN is that since all records are written to CICS storage, the memory requirements of CICS increase as TS MAIN utilization increases. Installations that are restricted or close to the limits of their CPU may see additional problems from excessive TS MAIN utilization. TS MAIN should be limited to nonrecoverable data with low volume and a short life span. And, of course, these queues should be managed by the application and deleted as soon as possible.

If the installation chooses to specify TS AUX as the default (by indicating strings and buffers in the TS parameter of the SIT), TS MAIN may be used (and override the AUX request) in some situations.

CICS/MVS 2.1 (since it is an XA-only version) writes DTB (dynamic transaction backout) buffers and overflow buffers to TS MAIN "above the line." The previous release (1.7) allowed the installation to specify a SIT parameter with DTB=(MAIN/AUX), but the current release ignores the option and always writes to MAIN. If necessary, an installation can calculate the effect of converting TS AUX utilization to TS MAIN and the subsequent storage requirement.

CICS provides TS statistics at shutdown. One entry identifies "Peak Storage Used for TS MAIN"; another is "Peak Number of CIs in Use" (TS AUX). If all TS AUX is converted to TS MAIN, CICS would replace the CIs used from DFHTEMP to TS MAIN records. The installation could multiply the peak CIs in use by the CI size of the DFHTEMP dataset to get a ballpark figure of the amount of storage required to replace the TS AUX writes. Figure 4-1 contains a sample CICS shutdown report containing TS statistics. Note the values in both "Peak Storage Used for TS MAIN" (1) and "Peak Number of CIs in Use" (2). In this example, very little storage would be required to convert these TS AUX requests to MAIN.

Of course, converting TS AUX to TS MAIN would remove all recoverability potential for the data. Most installations retain some use of TS AUX for queues that require recovery. If the installation wishes to retain some utilization of TS AUX for recovery, these queues must be specified to recover data in case of CICS failure.

TS AUX queues can be made recoverable via the TST (Temporary Storage Table). The parameter DFHTST TYPE=RECOVERY identifies the characters of the DATAIDs to be protected in case of transaction or system failure. Refer to CICS/MVS Resource Definition Macro for the full syntax of this table.

While all TS AUX is recovered during a WARM start of CICS, only those queues specified in the TST are recovered during an EMERGENCY restart. If CICS is started as COLD, recovery for any queues, even if specified in the TST, is ignored and all temporary storage is lost.

4.1.3 Storage Issues

Applications using TS MAIN or AUX may wish to utilize techniques that take advantage of both performance and storage consumption. This section will address several issues dealing with efficient utilization of temporary storage.

An application has very little control of TS AUX for efficient utilization of storage within DFHTEMP. Space required (or used) by the DFHTEMP VSAM dataset is usually not affected by the CI size specified, since CICS attempts to optimize the space. TS MAIN records

```
INTRAPARTITION DATASET STATISTICS
CONTROL INTERVAL SIZE                          1,536
NO. OF CONTROL INTERVALS                         460
PEAK NO. OF CIS IN USE                              1
NO. OF TIMES NOSPACE OCCURRED                      0

NO. OF WRITES TO DATASET                           0
NO. OF READS FROM DATASET                          0
NO. OF FORMATTING WRITES                           0
NO. OF I/O ERRORS                                  0

NO. OF STRINGS                                     3
NO. OF TIMES STRINGS ACCESSED                      0
PEAK NO. CONCURRENTLY ACCESSED                     0
NO. OF TIMES STRING WAIT OCCURRED                  0
PEAK NO. OF STRING WAITS                           0

************* TEMPORARY STORAGE STATISTICS *************
NUMBER OF PUT/PUTQ REQUESTS (MAIN)               201
NUMBER OF GET/GETQ REQUESTS (MAIN)               199

①  PEAK STORAGE USED FOR TS MAIN                 1,976

NUMBER OF PUT/PUTQ REQUESTS (AUX)                  0
NUMBER OF GET/GETQ REQUESTS (AUX)                  0

PEAK NUMBER OF TS NAMES IN USE                     1
NUMBER OF ENTRIES IN LONGEST QUEUE                1

QUEUE EXTENSION THRESHOLD (TSMGSET)                4
NUMBER OF TIMES QUEUE CREATED                    12
NUMBER OF QUEUE EXTENSIONS CREATED                 0

CONTROL INTERVAL SIZE                          4,096
NO. OF WRITES GREATER THAN CISIZE                 0

②  NUMBER OF CIS IN TS DATASET                   300
PEAK NUMBER OF CIS IN USE                          1
NO. OF TIMES AUX STORAGE EXHAUSTED                 0

NUMBER OF TS BUFFERS                               3
NO. OF TIMES BUFFER WAIT OCCURRED                 0
PEAK USERS WAITING ON BUFFER                       0
NUMBER OF BUFFER WRITES                            0
(NUMBER FORCED BY RECOVERY RQMTS)                0
NUMBER OF BUFFER READS                             0
NUMBER OF FORMATTING WRITES                        0

NUMBER OF TS STRINGS                               3
PEAK NUMBER OF STRINGS IN USE                      0
NO. OF TIMES STRING WAIT OCCURRED                 0
PEAK USERS WAITING ON STRING                       0

NUMBER OF I/O ERRORS ON TS DATASET                0
```

************* JOURNAL CONTROL STATISTICS *************

JOURNAL ID	NO. OF RECORDS WRITTEN	NO. OF BLOCKS WRITTEN	BUFFER FULL	NO. OF TIMES... SHIFTED-UP	AVE. O/P BLK SIZE	LAST BLOCK WRITTEN	VOLSER	NO. OF TAPES OPENED	SCRATCH TAPES LEFT
SYSTEM-LOG	394	111	0	0	1,515				
2	273	120	8	8					
17	5	5	0	0	248				
19		0	0	0					
18		0	0	0					

Figure 4-1   CICS shutdown statistics for temporary storage.

are written to a CI containing sufficient space in one of the TS buffers. If insufficient space exists in any of the buffers occupied by a TS CI, a CI with sufficient space will be located via a scan of the byte map.

When the application writes a TS AUX record larger than the DFHTEMP LRECL, the record spans two (or more) CIs to accomodate the request. In other words, CICS manages the TS AUX records within the dataset, and the application has little control over the use of storage within DFHTEMP.

TS Compression   If a write to TS AUX is performed, CICS calculates the number of nonempty CIs in temporary storage. If more than 75% of the CIs are not empty (full or partial), CI compression is performed to reclaim space.

These compressions are reported in the shutdown statistics and should be monitored, since excessive compressions can impact performance. A high number of compressions would indicate that more than 75% of the DFHTEMP VSAM dataset allocation was constantly being utilized. Increasing the size (allocation) of the dataset can reduce those compressions.

The CI size of DFHTEMP can have an impact on storage utilization or performance. The CICS/MVS Performance Guide states that buffer waits can occur if the required control interval is unavailable (in a locked buffer) even if other buffers are available. If the CI size of DFHTEMP is too large, there would be a greater possibility of this happening.

The installation should monitor the TS AUX shutdown statistics for buffer waits. These waits can be caused by insufficient buffers or by the CI size specified at DFHTEMP creation. In addition, the statistic for "No. of writes greater than CI size" would indicate that the CI size was decreased too much and needs to be larger.

If the number of buffers is increased to improve performance or decrease the buffer waits, it can impact the virtual storage that CICS uses "below the line."

Although most VSAM buffers are "above the line," TS AUX buffers are not. Installing a new version of DFP will have no impact on this problem, since the CICS temporary storage program manages the buffers, not DFP.

Use of Temporary Storage in CICS is very common, for it serves as an important location for an application to temporarily record small portions of data. For this reason, TS should be managed efficiently for optimum performance.

4.2 CICS Transient Data

Many programmers use transient data in CICS when sequential processing is required. These sequential files can be used for either input or output, serve as a way to process data by CICS, and also make the data available to other systems. Use of transient data (TD) facilities can provide enhanced function and serve as a "bridge" to outside resources.

Several issues will be covered in this section dealing with TD "destinations" or queues and when they can be most functional for an application.

4.2.1 Use of Transient Data (TD)

Transient data is used by an application when sequential data needs to be created, read, or "passed" to another destination. For this reason, TD "files" are sometimes called "queues," as they are handled much like sequential TS (temporary storage) queues. In addition, since the data is frequently passed to another location (printer, transaction, tape, etc.), the term "destination" is sometimes used to identify TS. Whether the term used is TS queue or TS destination is strictly semantics, and they mean basically the same thing.

On the other hand, there are two distinctly different types of TD queues: intrapartitioned TD, and extrapartitioned TD. Each has its purpose and function; however, there are similarities in each.

4.2.2 Characteristics

Some characteristics are the same for both types of transient data, such as location in the CICS DCT and command syntax. All TD queues must exist in the DCT (Destination Control Table), which must have been assembled prior to the initialization for the TD queue to be available. The queue names must be defined in this table and cannot be larger than 4 bytes (characters). In addition, the CICS commands to utilize either type of TD are the same, whether creating, writing, or reading the queue.

Although a physical dataset exists, as DFHTEMP exists, TD queues are not processed as TS queues, and no changes to existing records in the queues are allowed. Also, each extrapartitioned TD queue is defined in the DCT (TS queues are dynamically defined) and a different physical dataset can exist to match these DCT entries. In TS AUX, all queues share the same dataset DFHTEMP.

TD Queues Uses   Many applications use TD destinations to pass data to another CICS application via intrapartition TD or to make data available to another application, such as a batch program, via extrapartition TD.

In recent releases of CICS, however, other facilities have been made available to perform many of these functions. A VSAM ESDS (entry sequenced data set) is now a fully supported file structure for CICS and can be used to process sequential files. VSAM also provides better recoverability and has a full-function access method for processing outside of CICS.

If an application program needs to pass data to another application, TS MAIN is now much more efficient and does not take virtual storage from the CICS storage area "below the line." Intrapartitioned TD could be replaced by TS MAIN for improved performance.

Many programs still use TDQs, however, for routing messages, collection of data for processing at a later time, reporting of statistics, etc. The ability to set "trigger levels" gives TDQs an advantage over other facilities since data can be "batched up" and controlled to process "asynchronously" the transaction writing to the queue.

Trigger Levels in Transient Data   When the DCT definition is created, it can contain an entry such as

```
DCT TYPE=INTRA,
   DESTID=MESS,
   TRANSID=MESG,
   TRIGLEV=25
```

In this example, an intrapartitioned TD queue has been defined and will contain records written to it by any transaction. When the number of records in the MESS queue reaches 25, the transaction MESG will be automatically started by CICS.

This process is called ATI (Automatic Task Initiation) and is similar to the EXEC CICS START command. The transaction MESG will be initiated and will probably be written to process the records in the TDQ. More on trigger levels will be covered in the following section.

4.2.3 Intrapartitioned Transient Data

In order to fully understand the differences between these two types of TD, it must be understood that they are truly designed for separate functions. Much as their titles, intra- and extra- as the first component, they process and make data available either within or outside of CICS.

Intrapartitioned TDQ An application would use intra-TDQs as a "repository" for many applications to write data into, and then be processed later by a different transaction. This is a very frequently used method of intra-TDQ.

It allows the installation to collect data during the execution of CICS and then asynchronously (and automatically) process the data without operator intervention. This automated facility is fully controlled by the application and can even route the processing of this data outside of CICS in batch mode. This can remove unnecessary processing requirements from CICS and reduce both storage and CPU consumption.

Although intra-TDQ output can be processed "outside" of CICS, only CICS transactions can participate in intra-TDQs. The file is a single (predefined) dataset, DFHINTRA, and is processed only via CICS commands within the transactions.

Reuse Although the previous example defined an intra-TDQ, one parameter was omitted. REUSE can be coded YES or NO for these queues and identifies to CICS how space will be managed. When a record is read by a transaction, it is logically but not physically deleted. If REUSE=YES is indicated, the space for the logically deleted record can be used by another transaction. If REUSE=NO is selected, the intrapartition CI (control interval) space is not reclaimed until a transient data purge request is issued. Of course, all selections have a price to pay. Reuse of the space provides better space management, but loss of recoverability. Only REUSE=NO records are recoverable, but, of course, hold the intrapartion CI for much longer before releasing.

Reuse with DESTFAC The CIs are not reused any differently if the destination is a terminal or a file. If the DCT contains DESTFAC=TERMINAL or DESTFAC=FILE, the control intervals will be made available. Since CICS implements the process somewhat differently, however, the customer may see the TERMINAL CIs set to zero and reused immediately. The FILE CI is flagged for reuse, but will be utilized only when the next request is received.

Recoverability   Intra-TDQs can be made recoverable at three levels: logical, physical, or no recovery. This is specified within the DCT entry via the DESTRCV parameter. As the default is NO, the customer must specify the type of recovery required.

Physical recovery is the least significant recovery and is similar to no recovery. In physical recovery, however, any data remaining in the intra-TDQ is retained and available after a CICS system failure.

Logical recovery compares more closely to normal CICS recovery and allows recovery and backout during task or system failure. This process requires exclusive control over the queue until the transaction or unit of work has completed and may produce performance problems. In any recovery issue, performance must be compared to the need of data integrity.

NOSUSPEND   When an application issues a READQ TD for an intra-TDQ, use of NOSUSPEND will allow the application to only retry the request or wait for some period of time and retry. If, instead, the NOSUSPEND option is used, CICS will take control and resume the task as soon as possible when the resource is available. This should be more efficient, since CICS handles "dispatchability" much better than the application and can more efficiently manage the contention within the intra-TDQ.

4.2.4 Extrapartitioned Transient Data

Extra-TDQ data is processed in the other direction from intra-TDQ data. Records can be created by programs outside of CICS (batch jobs, etcs.) to be used by CICS transactions as input. Each extra-TDQ is a separate physical file, defined in the DCT and identified within the CICS JCL as a DD (data definition) statement. For example, if the DCT statement was coded:

```
DCT TYPE=EXTRA,
    DESTID=OUT1,
    DSCNAME=DESTOUT,
    OPEN=INITIAL
DCT TYPE=SDSCI,
    DSCNAME=DESTOUT,
    TYPEFILE=OUTPUT
```

This would define an extra-TDQ with the (destination) name OUT1. It would also, however, require a physical file to be created and a JCL statement to appear in the CICS startup, such as

//DESTOUT DD DSN=CICS.EXTRA.DESTOUT,DISP=SHR

EXEC CICS INQUIRE and SET with Extra-TDQ   Although transient data files are defined to CICS via DD statements and within the DCT, use of EXEC CICS INQUIRE and SET is not supported for these files. INQUIRE and SET is restricted to datasets defined in the FCT (File Control Table).

These extra-TDQs are, however, accessible via CEMT SET OPEN/CLOSE and may be manually opened and closed by the CEMT command or via the programmed interface to CEMT.

OSCOR Requirement for Extra-TD   CICS/MVS 2.1 opens extra-TD in DFHTDRP, during CICS initialization and after OSCOR is created. The result is that storage for OPEN=INITIAL extrapartitioned files is taken from OSCOR and must be considered in the calculation, or an ABEND S878 can result.

To calculate the OSCOR requirement (and addition), multiply the BLKSIZE of the file by the BUFNO (from the SDSCI of the DCT entry) and use this number of bytes as a conservative estimate. If inadequate OSCOR is available, reduce the BUFNO.

4.2.5 Trigger Levels

This facility is available with intra-TD and can be advantageous in many numbers of cases. Customers have used this facility in many ingenious ways and continue to produce ATI (automatic transaction initiation) tasks for CICS processing.

4.2.6 Terminal vs. File Related

When a trigger level is reached, a task is initiated to process the records. If the destination facility (DESTFAC) is a terminal, the task cannot start until the terminal is available. Once available, CICS assumes that separate tasks will process these records. Tasks are initiated by CICS until the queue is empty (QZERO). Terminal-related tasks normally issue a single READQ TD request, process the data, and return to CICS, where another task is started until the queue is empty.

In contrast, DESTFAC=FILE tasks must read all records from the queue and process before issuing a RETURN to CICS. For this reason, CICS initiates these tasks every time it detects the trigger level has been exceeded. If multiple transactions are writing into the intra-TDQ, CICS will dispatch another task every time the level has been exceeded. If another record is written before the queue has been deleted, i.e., the trigger level has been exceeded by two, there would be two concurrently executing tasks.

To serialize the process or ensure that only a single task is running at any time, the TERMINAL facility must be used. Of course, CMXT could also be used to restrict the transaction to a single execution.

Trigger Levels vs. START   Application programs can cause ATI processing with the EXEC CICS START command instead of intra-TD. Several factors should be considered before choosing between the two.

START has more options and can initiate work not based on trigger levels, but upon a specific time or interval. If time is the more important factor, START is more flexible. If the activity is volume-related or related to X number of records being written, intra-TD is the better way.

Intra-TD requires extensive DCT entries, which may require maintenance in more than one CICS region. In addition, tables that must be assembled do not produce available resources until the region is recycled. IBM may change this in future releases of CICS, since tables are being replaced by RDO (Resource Definition Online). For the present, however, START is easier to set up and make available to the application.

Intra-TDQs are recoverable (if defined as such) and can provide integrity for records that may be difficult to recreate. START facilities are primarily designed for tasks that are single requests and easily recreated.

CICS Database Issues

CICS DL/I Databases

In the early releases of CICS, access methods were elementary and contained no "database" components. Data could not be structured, and elements could have no relationships to each other. Even now, the only "native" access method to CICS is VSAM, and not only are relationships unavailable, but integrity of the data is very difficult to maintain. DB/2 or DL/I must be used from CICS to provide any database manager functions to an application.

Before DB/2 became available, DL/I was the only IBM facility that CICS applications could utilize for database functions. This language is a component of IMS/VS, another IBM transaction processor. IMS/VS contains two elements: the database system (DB) and the data communications feature (DC). This structure allows customers to utilize only the elements of IMS/VS necessary to specific applications.

The database system IMS/VS DB can use DL/I to create and access IMS databases. The DL/I language allows application programs to reference the data, while IMS manages the integrity and recoverability of the data. This becomes critical to the CICS program and the levels of recovery required.

The data communication feature IMS/VS DC extends the function of DL/I to the online, real-time processing environment. This feature allows communication between IMS databases and other connected devices, such as online terminals. As an alternative, many installations choose CICS to communicate with external DL/I databases and return results to the transaction for additional processing. This mechanism can be invoked via a "call" to DL/I or via a command-level interface. These two techniques will be discussed in a later section of this chapter.

Using CICS, DL/I databases can be accessed in the online environment and processed interactively rather than in batch. Since networks have become extensive and information needs to be available to installations in the most timely manner, real-time access to the data is mandatory. This chapter will deal with the IMS/VS features as implemented within CICS and many issues that must be addressed when a CICS application processes DL/I databases, whether local or remote (as in IMS/ESA Version 3 with DBCTL).

5.1 Virtual Storage Issues

Many installations are struggling with virtual storage limitations in their CICS systems, and without CICS/ESA, most of the CICS processing is still within the 16-Mb virtual storage area. Some installations are even resorting to MRO (Multi-Region Option) to "break" CICS systems into multiple regions that can support the level of transaction volume required. Since CICS is a multi-user single address space, all resources (data, programs, control structures) to support the applications must reside within the CICS address space while processed by the application.

This problem can be compounded by external database managers, since additional resources must be defined to CICS to support the enhanced function. In addition to the CICS code and the native VSAM resources, installations using DL/I must include all necessary support for the database interface. The amount of virtual storage needed has decreased recently, or at least been moved "above the line," and finally out of CICS entirely with DBCTL but installations need to be aware of these allocation issues and ensure that storage is used efficiently.

5.1.1 Version/Release Changes

In the IMS/VS Version 2.2 Installation Notebook, IBM attempts to notify customers of potential impact during migration to this release. One entry notes an increase in CSA utilization to support enhanced VTAM terminal functions and corresponding PSB (program specification block) pool size. Customers must realize, however, that IMS/VS is a very sophisticated subsystem, and not all facilities of IMS are utilized by CICS. In fact, this PSB pool increase only affects the IMS DC environment, not the CICS local DL/I environment.

IMS/VS 2.2 does, however, contain modifications that affect virtual storage utilization in CICS. Some control blocks increased in size, but some (namely DBRC) decreased. Of course, since some installations use DL/I without DBRC (Data Base Recovery Control), the impact on virtual storage utilization will vary based upon functions utilized. See the Installation Notebook for details that relate to specific customer configurations.

One constant complaint from customers, both CICS and DL/I, is the need for data buffers to enhance performance, yet decrease the amount of virtual storage consumed by these buffers. In recent releases of CICS, most VSAM buffers for "native" VSAM file processing have been moved "above the line," freeing a great deal of virtual storage for other purposes. Unfortunately, IMS/VS 2.2 has not provided the same relief.

In IMS/VS 2.2, the database buffers remain below the 16-Mb line. All virtual storage to support both DMB and PSB pools must be allocated in this storage area, regardless of the version of CICS utilized. The only version of IMS that truly provides virtual storage constraint relief is IMS/ESA 3.1.

In addition to buffers, CICS must provide virtual storage for the "threads" or connections to the DL/I resources. This thread storage can be significant if many concurrent threads are used and not released. The following table shows the IMS/VS releases and the amount of virtual storage required for DL/I threads.

IMS/VS Release	Virtual Storage Per Thread
Prior to 1.3	3K
IMS/VS 1.3	9K
IMS/VS Version 2	9K
IMS/ESA 3.1	12K

5.1.2 IMS/ESA 3.1

CICS customers may choose to install IMS/ESA 3.1, thus moving a great deal of virtual storage utilization within CICS above the 16-Mb line. IBM publishes data concerning the savings, noting 2–3K bytes per database. Of course, the most substantial savings will be in the use of IMS/ESA 3.1 with CICS/ESA 3.1. A new address space, DBCTL, will be available, moving all local DL/I resources out of CICS entirely and defined as remote DL/I (similar to the technique used by DB/2). This DBCTL address space will now contain the DL/I pools and buffers, allowing CICS access (although remotely). Customers with MVS/ESA operating systems can expect these new versions of the subsystems to extensively exploit extended storage (31-bit mode). The new technique will extend the path length, however, of the application since the request must be processed "externally."

Additional enhancements are being made to virtual storage utilization in both LSR (Local Shared Resource) pools and Hiperspace (High-Performance Data Spaces). These advantages are being made available as an SPE (Small Programming Enhancement) which is installed via the service process. Installations with IMS/ESA can order APARS PL58292 and PL58295 for the support.

The SPE adds the following features to IMS/ESA 3.1:

- Multiple LSR Pool Support
- Hiperspace Buffering Support

plus a facility to separate data and index buffers within shared pools.

5.1.2.1 Multiple LSR Pool Support   This new feature allows the definition of multiple VSAM subpools of the same size within the same LSR pool. Specific DL/I databases can then be dedicated to a subpool for performance improvements. The previous rule for CICS VSAM pools remains; that is, pools 1 through 8 are still reserved for native VSAM files. The new DBRC feature will further reserve pool 15 for CICS local DL/I support. The maximum LSR pools/poolids allowed is 16, however, which substantially improves availability for subpool definition.

5.1.2.2 Hiperspace Support   MVS/ESA 3.1 provided enhancements to virtual storage utilization beyond 31-bit addressing. Installations with this version of the operating system and expanded storage on their mainframes can extend usage of main storage to "high-performance" spaces, or "Hiperspaces." Use of Hiperspaces allows movement of data from expanded storage to real storage without any physical I/O requirements to DASD (disk).

The Hiperspace facility with the new multiple VSAM LSR pools will allow "preferred" DL/I databases to be defined to a specific LSR subpool, backed by Hiperspace support.

Of course, the ideal situation would be a CPU with adequate real storage to support large buffers without paging, but this may not be possible. Expanded storage is much less expensive than real storage and can, therefore, be used to support large buffer pools. Installations will probably choose to combine real with expanded storage for optimum performance. Any performance advantages of buffering depends upon the access techniques of the data. If the data cannot be found in the buffer, whether in virtual storage buffers or Hiperspace, physical I/O will result. Only frequently used data remain in buffers. Any random reads of data by the program, even databases, may result in performance problems. Proper design of the program and access techniques will always affect performance.

5.1.2.3 New Pool Definition Statements The enhancements to DL/I resources in CICS are made available via the previously identified service (SPE) and then utilized via new definitions for the features. Following are the additional statements or new options to existing statements for LSR pool and Hiperspace support.

POOLID for Subpool Definition Multiple pools must be defined via the POOLID statement for each shared resource pool. This statement is then followed by the VSRBF to define the subpools within that pool. The syntax of the POOLID statement is:

POOLID=id,FIXDATA=YES/NO,FIXINDEX=YES/NO,
FIXBLOCK=YES/NO,STRINGNM=n   .

The first POOLID statement will define the default shared resource pool (Shared Pool 0), and subsequent statements will define pools 9–14. Each statement defines one shared resource pool. The ID of the POOL (POOLID=id) can be a 1–4 character field used with the DBD statement to assign a given DL/I database to a specific shared pool. The three "FIX" options provide the ability to page-fix DL/I resources for performance.

The STRINGNM parameter specifies the maximum number of VSAM I/O requests that can be active to IMS at any time. This parameter can be used to override the MAXREGN parameter at IMS generation time or the PST value at EXEC, but should not exceed the maximum number of regions expected to execute concurrently.

VSRBF for Subpool Definition Each VSRBF statement defines the subpools within the shared resource pools (POOLID). The existing VSRBF statements (without the corresponding POOLID) continue to be supported for compatibility purposes but do not provide the enhanced subpool facilities. The syntax of the new VSRBF statement is

VSRBF=buf-size,num-bufs,type,HSO/HSR,HSN

Each statement defines one subpool, with the corresponding buffer size and number of buffers in the pool. The optional TYPE identifies whether the pool corresponds to an INDEX or DATA component. The last three options relate to Hiperspace support and the number of buffers for this subpool.

Enhancement to DBD Statement This statement has been enhanced to add Data Set Number and ID parameters that have previously not been applicable for VSAM databases. These parameters now apply to both OSAM and VSAM subpools. The DBD statement now assigns a given DL/I database to a specific shared resource pool with the corresponding POOLID and VSRBF statements.

RESVPOOL for New Subpool Control This new control statement can be used to restrict VSAM shared resource pools to address spaces other than IMS, such as CICS. If coded, IMS will not be allowed to use these pools. For example, if an installation wishes to restrict use of a shared pool in a CICS local DL/I environment, it can code

RESVPOOL=9,10
POOLID=ID1
VSRBF=1024,20,I
VSRBF=2048,20
DBD=DBD1(2,ID1)

to isolate SHRPOOLs 9 and 10 from IMS/ESA.

More information concerning this SPE can be located in a WSC (Washington System Center) FLASH 9027 or in GG66-3165, the IMS/ESA Version 3.1 Release Planning Notebook.

5.2 DL/I Structures

This section will attempt to define some of the resources and structures that are specific to DL/I in CICS. As in any database management system, proper specification of the data up front means efficient processing and full exploitation of the database facilities. These structures allow the application program to be autonomous of the way data is stored, concentrating on *what*, not *how* it is stored. There are two primary components of IMS/VS databases.

5.2.1 DBD — Database Description

The DBD is a control block that describes the physical structure of the data within the database. Within it are defined the fields or elements of the data and any relationships. Each record in a DBD is further divided into segments, the smallest addressable unit by a program. An analogy could be made that while most data in MVS is transferred in blocks or pages, DL/I data is transferred to the program in segments. Since IMS/VS is considered a hierarchical (rather than a relational) database, most relationships within the database are in a pyramid-like structure.

The highest level of the DBD is called the root segment, which is always unique. All other segments are "chained" from this segment and are dependent to it. This dependency is continued throughout the database and is designated by "parent" and "child" relationships. This is a simplistic arrangement to follow, with the child segment always below and therefore dependent on the parent segment. The following diagram illustrates a typical database structure.

> **Customer**
> Invoice   Order
> Payment   Shipment

In this example, the customer segment is the root segment (also a parent of the subsequent two). There are three parent segments: customer, invoice, and order. Since invoice and order are also child segments (to customer), four child segments exist in this example. These dependencies form the structures of DL/I databases and allow the program to view the data as logical relationships rather than physical records.

Figure 5-1 contains an actual DBD example. This database will be stored within a HIDAM/OSAM structure as specified in the ACCESS= parameter(1). While these structures are not CICS-dependent, the access method chosen may affect performance of the transaction. In addition, DL/I buffers are defined separately for OSAM databases. These buffers will be explained in greater detail in a subsequent section of this chapter.

```
          TITLE: ACCOUNT DATABASE PRIMARY
          DBD     NAME=DDACCAPR,ACCESS=(HIDAM,OSAM)    ①
DSG001    DATASET DD1=DDACCAPR,DEVICE=3380,SIZE=(23476),SCAN=001,      X
                  FRSPC=(,02)
          SEGM  NAME=DLACCT00,BYTES=00388,                    ID0445X
                PARENT=0,                                            X
                POINTER=(TB),                                        X
                COMPRTN=(DPKNCD,DATA,INIT)
          FIELD   NAME=(DLACCTSQ,SEQ,U),BYTES=009,START=00001,TYPE=C
          FIELD   NAME=DLBANKNO,BYTES=002,START=00001,TYPE=C    ID0429
          FIELD   NAME=DLAPPLID,BYTES=001,START=00003,TYPE=C    ID0429
          FIELD   NAME=DLACCTNO,BYTES=006,START=00004,TYPE=C    ID0429
          FIELD   NAME=DLPRGNUM,BYTES=002,START=00128,TYPE=C    ID0429
     ②   LCHILD  NAME=(DLACINDX,DDACCAIX),POINTER=INDX,RULES=LAST
          LCHILD  NAME=(DLACIND2,DDACCAI2),POINTER=INDX         ID0429
          XDFLD   NAME=DLPRTYSX,SEGMENT=DLACCT00,              ID0429 X
                  SRCH=(DLBANKNO,DLAPPLID,DLPRGNUM,DLACCTNO)    ID0429
          SEGM  NAME=DDBAL000,BYTES=00825,                    ID0428 X
                PARENT=((DLACCT00,SNGL)),                            X
                POINTER=(NT),                                        X
                COMPRTN=(DPKNCD,DATA,INIT)
          SEGM  NAME=DDFLOT00,BYTES=00150,                    IB0397X
                PARENT=((DDBAL000,SNGL)),                            X
                POINTER=(NT),                                        X
                COMPRTN=(DPKNCD,DATA,INIT)
          SEGM  NAME=DDPRA000,BYTES=00300,                    IB0389 X
                PARENT=((DLACCT00,SNGL)),                            X
                POINTER=(NT),                                        X
                COMPRTN=(DPKNCD,DATA,INIT)
          SEGM  NAME=DDPRAT00,BYTES=00050,                    IB0389 X
                PARENT=((DDPRA000,SNGL)),                            X
                POINTER=(T),                                         X
                COMPRTN=(DPKNCD,DATA,INIT)
          FIELD   NAME=(DDPRATSQ,SEQ,M),BYTES=006,START=00003,TYPE=C
          SEGM  NAME=DDSHDT00,BYTES=00016,                          X
                PARENT=((DLACCT00,SNGL)),                            X
                POINTER=(NT),                                        X
                COMPRTN=(DPKNCD,DATA,INIT)
          SEGM  NAME=DDSTOP00,BYTES=00141,                    DS5504X
                PARENT=((DDSHDT00,SNGL)),                            X
                POINTER=(T),                                         X
                COMPRTN=(DPKNCD,DATA,INIT)
          FIELD   NAME=(DDSTOPSQ,SEQ,M),BYTES=007,START=00004,TYPE=C
          FIELD   NAME=DDSTOPID,BYTES=003,START=00001,TYPE=P    DS5504
          SEGM  NAME=DDHOLD00,BYTES=00061,                          X
                PARENT=((DDSHDT00,SNGL)),                            X
                POINTER=(T),                                         X
                COMPRTN=(DPKNCD,DATA,INIT)
          SEGM  NAME=DDMSSC00,BYTES=00043,                          X
                PARENT=((DLACCT00,SNGL)),                            X
                POINTER=(T),                                         X
                COMPRTN=(DPKNCD,DATA,INIT)
          SEGM  NAME=DDUCF000,BYTES=00076,                    IB0390X
                PARENT=((DLACCT00,SNGL)),                            X
                POINTER=(NT),                                        X
                COMPRTN=(DPKNCD,DATA,INIT)
          SEGM  NAME=DLNAME00,BYTES=00370,                    D60000X
                PARENT=((DLACCT00,SNGL)),                            X
                POINTER=(T),                                         X
                COMPRTN=(DPKNCD,DATA,INIT)
```

Figure 5-1 DL/I data base definition.

```
TITLE: DEPOSIT PRIORITY GROUP SECONDARY INDEX DATABASE      00001000
DBD      NAME=(DDACCAI2),ACCESS=(INDEX,VSAM,PROT),           X00010000
         PASSWD=NO                                            00020000
DATASET DD1=DDACCAI2,DEVICE=3350,SIZE=(02048)                00030000
SEGM  NAME=DLACIND2,BYTES=00011,FREQ=00000000,               X00040000
         PARENT=0                                             00050000
FIELD    NAME=(DLPRTYSQ,SEQ,U),BYTES=011,START=00001,        X00060000
         TYPE=C                                               00061000
LCHILD  NAME=(DLACCT00,DDACCAPR),POINTER=SNGL,INDEX=DLPRTYSX  00070000
DBDGEN                                                        00080000
FINISH                                                        00090000
END                                                          00100000
```

Figure 5-2 DL/I data base definition of index.

Note that two logical child entries can be found in this DBD. The
LCHILD definitions(2) become the primary and secondary indexes
into the database as specified with the POINTER=INDX parameter.
These indexes must then be created as separate DBD definitions.
Figure 5-2 contains the index definitions to complete the account
database.

5.2.2 PSB — Program Specification Block

The PSB defines this logical view of the data for the application.
Since most programs require only a portion of the data from the
database, the PSB allows a subset to be defined. This "logical view"
of the data not only improves performance (fewer bytes processed)
but provides a form of security. If the program has access to only a
subset of the segments, it cannot update or modify segments of those
it does not have access to.

The PCB (within the PSB) not only defines the segments, but identifies the access allowed, read vs. update, for example.

After a PSB is defined, it is "genned," or generated as an executable module. This generation process is actually an assembly of the
macro, which is then link edited into a control block (PSB). These
control blocks are stored in a PSB library, much as a load module is
stored in a load library. Figure 5-3 contains a sample PSB that
would be used as input to the generation process. Note that while
the first PCB "points" to database BCBNKAPR and identifies nine
segments within that database, the actual DBD may contain many
more actual segments. This PCB definition limits the scope of access
to the database within this "communication block."

Each database defined in the PSB must be identified with the
TYPE=DB,NAME=xxxxxxxx parameters, with the subsequent seg-

```
PCB     TYPE=DB,NAME=BCBNKAPR,PROCOPT=GOTP,KEYLEN=24,      60000X
        POS=S                                              D60000
SENSEG NAME=BCBANK00
SENSEG NAME=BCDPDT00,PARENT=BCBANK00                       D60000
SENSEG NAME=BCDPD000,PARENT=BCDPDT00                       D60000
SENSEG NAME=BCDPA000,PARENT=BCDPDT00                       D60000
SENSEG NAME=BCDPIP00,PARENT=BCDPDT00                       D60000
SENSEG NAME=BCDPMS00,PARENT=BCDPDT00                       D60000
SENSEG NAME=BCDPCY00,PARENT=BCDPDT00                       D60000
SENSEG NAME=BCDPRE00,PARENT=BCDPDT00                       IC0420
SENSEG NAME=BCDPT000,PARENT=BCDPDT00                       D60000
SPACE 1
PCB     TYPE=DB,NAME=DDACCAPR,PROCOPT=RIP,KEYLEN=16,POS=S
SENSEG NAME=DLACCT00                                       D60000
SENSEG NAME=DDBAL000,PARENT=DLACCT00                       D60000
SENSEG NAME=DDFLOT00,PARENT=DDBAL000
SENSEG NAME=DDPRA000,PARENT=DLACCT00                       D60000
SENSEG NAME=DDPRAT00,PARENT=DDPRA000                       IB0389
SENSEG NAME=DDSHDT00,PARENT=DLACCT00                       D60000
SENSEG NAME=DDSTOP00,PARENT=DDSHDT00
SENSEG NAME=DDHOLD00,PARENT=DDSHDT00
SENSEG NAME=DDMSSC00,PARENT=DLACCT00,PROCOPT=GID           D60000
SENSEG NAME=DDPRYR00,PARENT=DLACCT00                       D60000
SENSEG NAME=DDTIME00,PARENT=DLACCT00                       D60000
SENSEG NAME=DDRET000,PARENT=DLACCT00                       D60064
SENSEG NAME=DDPSTI00,PARENT=DLACCT00,PROCOPT=GIRD          D00647
SPACE 1
PCB     TYPE=DB,NAME=DDLOGAPR,PROCOPT=I,KEYLEN=20,POS=S
SENSEG NAME=DDLOGR00,PROCOPT=GIR
SENSEG NAME=DDDCTR00,PARENT=DDLOGR00
SENSEG NAME=DDDBAC00,PARENT=DDLOGR00
SPACE 1
PCB     TYPE=DB,NAME=DPTRNAPR,PROCOPT=GOTP,KEYLEN=9,POS=S
SENSEG NAME=DPTRAN00
SENSEG NAME=DPACTR00,PARENT=DPTRAN00
SPACE 1
PCB     TYPE=DB,NAME=DPTELRPR,PROCOPT=RI,KEYLEN=9,POS=S
SENSEG NAME=DPTELR00                                       DS4041
SPACE 2
PSBGEN LANG=COBOL,PSBNAME=DDCHGA04
END
```

Figure 5-3 DL/I PCB definition.

ments. In this way, only the segments defined are "presented" to the application, although many more may actually exist in the database. In addition, the PROCOPT= parameter defines the processing options that are available for this database during this PSB. Some databases are defined PROCOPT=G (Get/Inquire only), while others have additional access.

The PROCOPT is extremely important to the CICS application, since it restricts the access allowed. If the request from CICS is not supported by the definition in the PSB, IMS rejects the request with a return code to the application. These definitions, therefore, delineate the scope of data and the processing capabilities that the CICS application can request.

Also important in this example are the entries with a PRO-COPT=GOTP. This value sets:

O   =   Read-only, do not enqueue to check availability.

T   =   Automatically retry once and then return "GG" to the application.

P   =   Path call: Read multiple segments with one GET.

The "O" processing option allows a program to access data that is being updated by other programs WITHOUT enqueueing to check for availability. This will reduce the amount of time required to get data but cannot be used to update data.

If the CICS application program reads data that is in the process of being updated by another address space, IMS may detect an "invalid pointer" and ABEND the program unless an "N" or "T" PRO-COPT is also used.

The "N" option will return a status code of "GG" to the program when IMS detects this situation, and the application may choose to attempt the CALL a second time. The "T" option is similar, but will cause IMS to attempt a second CALL before returning the "GG" status to the program, where additional attempts may be made.

Since the probability of reading a segment while IMS is updating pointers for other programs in the exact same location is minimal, the GOT and GON processing options are very useful for applications that require high performance. These options may also be used in nonshared environments as well as DBRC.

5.2.3 ACB — Access Control Block

After the first two "pieces" are created, the DBD and the PSB, a third process generates the logical path into the data for the application. This path is known as the ACB (Access Control Block) and is used by CICS applications to establish access to the data. The DBD and PSB control blocks are "merged" to create one common control block for CICS. (The ACB can be used by batch jobs, but is optional. It is REQUIRED for any access by CICS.) After the PSB is built, a job must be run to "BUILD" the PSB in the ACB library. This job creates or replaces the member, using input from both the DBD and the PSB. Since CICS has no native DL/I capability, the ACB serves as the bridge into the database when requested by an application.

```
          PROC  SOUT=W,COMP=,RGN=512K,SYS='SYS',LIB=IMS220            00000010
//G       EXEC  PGM=DFSRRC00,PARM='UPB,&COMP',REGION=&RGN             00000020
//SYSPRINT DD   SYSOUT=&SOUT                                          00000030
//STEPLIB  DD   DSN=&SYS..&LIB..RESLIB,DISP=SHR                       00000040
//DFSRESLB DD   DSN=&SYS..&LIB..RESLIB,DISP=SHR                       00000050
//IMS      DD   DSN=&SYS..&LIB..PSBLIB,DISP=SHR                       00000060
//         DD   DSN=&SYS..&LIB..DBDLIB,DISP=SHR                       00000070
//IMSACB   DD   DSN=&SYS..&LIB..ACBLIB,DISP=SHR                       00000080
//SYSUT3   DD   UNIT=SYSDA,SPACE=(80,(100,100))                       00000090
//SYSUT4   DD   UNIT=SYSDA,SPACE=(256,(100,100)),DCB=KEYLEN=8         00000100
//COMPCTL  DD   DSN=MVS.PROCLIB(DFSACBCP),DISP=SHR                    00000110


C997JVMG JOB (T,B,JDC,JVM),'ACBGEN         ',CLASS=T,NOTIFY=C997.  ., 00010000
//       MSGCLASS=X,MSGLEVEL=(1,1),USER=C997JVM,REGION=2048K          00020000
/*JOBPARM S=1CPU                                                      00030000
//*                                                                   00040000
//* SET THE 'SYS' SYMBOLIC AS FOLLOWS:                                00050000
//*                                                                   00060000
//*    LIB='IMS220'        PRODUCTION ACBGEN                          00070000
//*    LIB='IMS220.TEST'   TEST ACBGEN                                00080000
//*                                                                   00090000
//   EXEC ACBGEN,SOUT=X,LIB='IMS220.TEST'                             00100000
//G.SYSIN DD *                                                        00110000
   BUILD PSB=DDCHGA04                                                 00120000
//                                                                    00220000
```

Figure 5-4 Sample ACB generation.

Figure 5-4 contains a sample ACB generation. The first portion demonstrates the statements required to execute the PROC (procedure) with a single PSB as input. The second portion, with the contents of the PROC, contains the actual program executed — DFSRRC00 with the PARM=UPB. This IMS program "generates" the logical connection between the DBD and the PSB with input from the two concatentated IMS DD statements for the DBDLIB and PSBLIB. The output is then written to the IMSACB DD library.

Unfortunately, this ACBLIB is only read by CICS at initialization, so any updates to the ACBLIB require a recycle of CICS for use.

This can be a plus, however, in the stages of creating new PSBs for CICS. Some installations perform ACB "gens" to validate the syntax and relationships within the DBD and PSB structures. While a PSB generation may execute with zero condition codes, it does not validate any relationships within the segments, even if database names exist. The ACB generation process performs syntax and association checking and may identify incorrect or invalid entries in previously created DBD or PSB definitions.

This ACB control block data is used during the "schedule" process to build the thread between the application and the database. To provide that information, the ACB library exists as a JCL statement in the CICS region, such as

//ACBLIB DD DSN=IMSVS.ACBLIB,DISP=SHR

Of course, customers may have multiple ACB libraries for many reasons, and this statement would then have concatenated ACB libraries.

There have been restrictions in the past regarding PSB and, therefore, ACB sizes. Until recently, these control blocks could not exceed 64K. A recent enhancement, APAR PP21788, increases the maximum size of an ACB to 512K.

5.2.4 Scheduling a PSB

Online programs (CICS) must "schedule a PSB" before any DL/I calls can be made. This scheduling is actually the initialization of a connection between the program and the DL/I PSB (program specification block). In database terminology, the connection is called a "thread" and serves as the link between the two subsystems. This thread connection allows data to be passed between the two systems during the life of the application. In addition to the PSB name, the schedule must include the pointer to the UIB (user interface block) to establish addressability.

CICS programmers must realize that a PSB is scheduled for a task and is therefore associated with all processing during that task. While DB/2 contains "dynamic plan" selection and may modify resource connections during a task, DL/I has no comparable facility. The PSB, therefore, should be scheduled in the first program and cannot be changed in subsequent modules that are XCTL or LINKed to. If the PSB needs to be changed, the task must be terminated and reinitiated with a new PSB if necessary.

After all processing of DL/I resources by the application is complete, the application can terminate the PSB with the TERM command or call. Terminating the PSB causes all changes to be committed and the thread to be released. Of course, when the transaction is complete (via RETURN to CICS), this termination is automatic. For this reason, many programmers never use the TERM process.

At termination, CICS must synchronize all logging activity for the logical unit of work before the task can be terminated. This is accomplished via the ASRT function within IMS/VS. Consequently, many installations find CICS transactions waiting to terminate with a PSTFUNCT of ASRT when multiple DL/I applications terminate or the TERM is issued. This ASRT operation represents the functions of thread release and system log activity necessary at task termination before the CICS task can be fully terminated.

5.3 Data Sharing

Since IMS/VS contains the facilities to allow other subsystems access to databases, it is not only possible but probable that installations will require data access from multiple applications. This is especially true in an online environment, where both CICS and batch programs require concurrent access. IMS allows this process via several facilities. PI (Program Isolation) can be used within a single CICS address space to manage concurrent access by "locking" or preventing any subsequent request for update until the change is completed or "committed."

DBRC (Data Base Recovery Control) with IRLM (IMS Resource Lock Manager) supports sharing and is used to manage multiple access requests from multiple address spaces and authorize control over the data. Data sharing in IMS/VS can be performed at the database level or at the block level. Block level data sharing is controlled by IMS and occurs at the CI (control interval) level, as defined via the AMS (access method services) delineation of the data during creation. In block level data sharing, update requests are managed but only the CI containing the updated record is locked. This, of course, allows more concurrent requests and stabilizes the smallest portion of the database during the update.

Sharing of resources requires additional resources to ensure integrity. In some cases, data can be shared, but the facilities do not exist to guarantee integrity. Installations need to be aware of these dangers and the potential corruption of data if not protected.

This section will deal with data sharing and the issues that must be addressed in that environment.

5.3.1 Program Isolation Without IRLM

Prior to DBRC availability with data sharing, the only choice of technique for providing integrity of multiple update requests was via either PI (program isolation) or intent scheduling. Very few installations still use intent scheduling, since the protection applied to all segments of a given segment type. This produced slow scheduling, plus poor throughput and response times.

Program isolation can be used within a single CICS region to protect from multiple updates to specific occurrences of a segment type. Since true data sharing is not being used (DBRC), the recovery datasets (RECONs) are not necessary.

Use of program isolation requires specific design considerations:

- Transactions exposed to potential deadlocks as a result of program isolation must be defined with DTB (dynamic transaction backout) to provide removal of updates in case of failure.
- Resources should be accessed and especially updated in the same sequence to impose commit processing to changes and serialize the updates to avoid deadlock possibilities.

When a CICS task accesses a DL/I segment, it implicitly enqueues all segments in the same database record as the segment being accessed, the duration of the enqueue being a function of the access method utilized (direct or sequential). The application can override this process using a "Q" command in the argument or with the PROCOPT=E (exclusive) PCB macro to extend exclusive control over the period of update. Use of these techniques can extend the capabilities of program isolation, and provide some additional function to the installation not automatically provided with PI. As always, IBM recommends DBRC for any data sharing over PI, but the installation must decide whether the risks justify the additional costs of implementation.

Deadlock Detection in CICS   In a single CICS, several concurrent requests for the same resource may produce a "deadlock," or an extended wait until the data is available for update. This causes an ABEND in the CICS transaction, with the ABEND code of ADLD, indicating a DL/I program isolation deadlock. Without data sharing, and with no lock manager, deadlocks are the result of multiple concurrent update requests. Program isolation is the technique used to attempt data integrity within the multi-user CICS subsystem but cannot prevent deadlocks. If an application is experiencing excessive deadlocks, the logic of the program should be investigated for design defects.

Nonshared Manual Techniques for Data Integrity   DL/I resources (without DBRC) are similar to VSAM resources when multiple address spaces require concurrent access. When CICS owns the DL/I resource, batch jobs will either wait or, in most cases, authorization will fail. In some cases, these batch jobs require access for a short period of time, and installations must devise a way to temporarily provide that capability.

One technique to temporarily provide availability in a nonshared environment would be to remove the resource from CICS during the batch update, and then restore it to online status. DL/I databases can be stopped and deallocated to CICS, removing all access. The ADYN (allocate/deallocate) transaction in CICS must be used in IMS Version 1 to deallocate the database. IMS Version 2 databases are deallocated automatically when stopped. Of course, applications should accommodate this temporary unavailability with appropriate logic. Once stopped, the installation would use:

//DBD DD DSN=....,DISP=OLD

in the batch update programs to retain exclusive control during the update. Once authorization is provided to the batch job with exclusive control, any other requests (batch jobs or CICS) will wait until the initial job is complete. At that time, the database can be restored to CICS via the

CEMT SET DATABASE(xxx) STARTED

and ownership returns to CICS.

If the deadlock problem exists within CICS, rather than across multiple CICS/Batch address spaces, the technique for solving the problem is slightly more difficult. Multiple CICS transactions can concurrently execute, requesting update to the same resource, and produce a deadlock if the application design does not properly serialize updates. This situation is very similar to the type of deadlocks discussed in Chapter 3. See Section 3.3.3 for more detailed information concerning deadlocks.

5.3.2 Levels of Data Sharing

What is true data sharing? In DL/I, data sharing allows more than one CICS system to have concurrent access to a DL/I database. Of course, other address spaces are allowed the same access, and some facility must be in place to manage these requests.

Each database contains the specification for the permitted level of sharing. The SHARELVL operand of the INIT.DB command (when the database is initialized) defines the level for each specific database. The options or levels allowed in data sharing are:

EXCLUSIVE LEVEL (Sharelevel=0)
One subsystem or address space will be allowed access at any time. This level essentially eliminates the ability for sharing of this particular database.

DATABASE LEVEL (Sharelevel=1)
While multiple systems are allowed read access, only one is allowed to update. This value corresponds to the VSAM Shareoptions of (2,3) for native VSAM files.

This sharing at the database level allows only a single update request and, while providing integrity, can produce bottlenecks if multiple update requests are required concurrently.

INTRAHOST BLOCK LEVEL (Sharelevel=2)
Multiple subsystems are allowed either read or update access, but all requests must originate from the same host. Sharing is at the physical block level for ISAM or OSAM databases, and at the CI level for VSAM databases.

INTERHOST BLOCK LEVEL (Sharelevel=3)
This level extends the capabilities of Sharelevel=2 to one additional host processor. Data sharing is always limited to two hosts, whether virtual or physical. More explanation of this limitation will be provided in Section 5.3.3.

Since data sharing is implemented via DBRC facilities in each subsystem, such as CICS, the only additional facility required is the IRLM (IMS Resource Lock Manager). DBRC is a prerequisite to any level of data sharing, and the IRLM is required for block level sharing. IRLM controls the locks on specific blocks of data in a shared database.

5.3.3 DBRC with IRLM

Since data shared in this manner can be updated from multiple sources, what steps need to be taken to guarantee integrity? Following are several issues that must be understood in a shared CICS DL/I environment.

Buffer Invalidate When DBRC inserts records within data buffers, the buffers are not "externalized" to the actual database until a checkpoint or syncpoint is taken by IMS or CICS. At checkpoint, the buffer is written in its entirety, and the update is physically committed to DASD. Within the interval of read (for update) and physical commit to media, other requests for the same block may have been requested by other address spaces (batch or CICS). If the request was read, the data was presented to the requestor since no modifications were intended. When the block is updated by the initial requestor, all subsequent read operations contain invalid data, since a modification has since occurred.

DBRC attempts to resolve this problem with a "buffer invalidate" facility. When the update is committed, notification is sent to all other subsystems of the buffer invalidation. The other systems participating in the data sharing process must then handle this notification and reread the buffer if necessary.

Multiple CICS and IMS Systems Although data can be shared between multiple CICS and IMS systems, limitations exist in the combination of these address spaces. Installations may support both multiple IMS systems and multiple CICS systems. Multiple CICS systems can communicate (and therefore share DL/I data) with a single IMS address space via the DBCTL function. In reverse, however, a single CICS address space can communicate with one, and only one, IMS address space. If the installation supports multiple IMS systems, each can communicate with separate CICS systems. In other words, multiple CICSs can share (access) data but can communicate with only one database manager (IMS).

The only exception to this rule is via MRO (Multi Region Option) facilities. While some may consider multiple AORs (Application Owning Region) to exist within the same CICS system, they are actually separate and unique address spaces. With MRO, separate AORs may have access to different IMS systems. A transaction from one AOR may update data in one IMS system, while a transaction in a second AOR may access DL/I databases in another IMS system. IMS treats each AOR as a unique CICS access system.

Interhost (Multi-CPU) Sharing Many installations support not only multiple IMS systems, but multiple CPU configurations, with communication capabilities for network and data sharing. IMS supports interprocessor sharing, via either a CTC (channel-to-channel adapter) or a communications controller (e.g., IBM 37x5).

While this configuration can support any number of CPUs, and therefore copies of MVS, only two copies can participate in IMS Interhost Sharing. If XRF (Extended Recovery Facility) is used to provide backup and takeover in a multi-CPU CICS environment, the limitation remains. Only two MVS images are allowed to share, and a third operating system, even if only an alternate waiting for takeover, will violate the two-image limitation.

Version/Release Limitations of Sharing With so many versions and releases of CICS and IMS currently available, many customers are confused about compatibility, especially in sharing capabilities. Following is a chart of the existing IMS versions and the sharing allowed between each.

	IMS/VS 1.3	IMS/VS 2.2	IMS/ESA 3.1
IMS/VS 1.3	yes	no	no
IMS/VS 2.2	no	yes	yes
IMS/ESA 3.1	no	yes	yes

As shown, the only data sharing capable in IMS/VS 1.3 is within multiple systems of the same version. Sharing of data is possible within Version 2 systems, within Version 3 systems, and across the two versions.

Of course, to CICS, this is an IMS limitation and has nothing to do with the level of CICS. CICS/MVS 2.1 fully supports IMS/VS 1.3 as well as the newer versions and can, therefore, participate in all data sharing capable within the IMS restrictions.

Deadlocks in a Shared Environment While VSAM deadlocks can be diagnosed fairly easily via CICS trace facilities, DL/I deadlocks are more difficult since the resource is "external" to CICS. When CICS executes the call for DL/I data, the request is passed to the IMS subsystem for processing and then returned to CICS. The result is a large gap in the trace, without the resource name or other identifier required to detect the deadlock.

IMS provides an IRLM trace facility to capture this activity. The IRLM trace must be used and compared with the CICS trace entries for complete information from both sources. Until recently, however, these IRLM trace entries excluded information important during the diagnosis, such as the PSB name. Recent IMS maintenance adds a new data gathering capability for deadlocks within the IRLM. This report identifies the PSB name in contention at the time of the deadlock and can be used with the CICS trace for full analysis of these problems. See WSC (Washington System Center) Flash #8951, "IMS Service APAR for Deadlock Data Gathering," for full documentation of the enhancement.

In a shared environment, deadlocks can occur when batch jobs attempt to update DL/I resources held by CICS. The IRLM is the deadlock manager and attempts to resolve the deadlock whenever possible. Since IMS cannot detect individual tasks within CICS, the IRLM is unable to gain control over any specific task. If a "victim" needs to be selected, the batch job is the unfortunate casualty. The batch job is ABENDed if the deadlock cannot be resolved.

CI Reclaim/Reuse with Data Sharing   Since all VSAM DL/I databases are either KSDS (Key Sequenced) or ESDS (Entry Sequenced) VSAM datasets, they are initially built via the IDCAMS DEFINE command and then managed by IMS. Data records are recorded and managed within the CI (control interval) in much the same way as VSAM record processing. Data sharing may impact the manner in which these databases are maintained, however.

If the DL/I database is an ESDS, any empty CIs are eligible for reuse and are reclaimed for future space, whether data sharing is being utilized or not. Space is managed differently, however, for a KSDS in block level data sharing. CIs are not reclaimed, and a data CI that has been cleared (all records erased) is not returned to the pool of available CIs in the control area.

This may produce additional demands for space and potential performance problems for DL/I applications. The recommended solution to this problem is to monitor utilization of KSDS databases and, if extensive deletes are performed, reorganize or rebuild the database. Since the program contains the logic of potential record activity, system design of these applications should identify schedules for reorganization.

Multiple IRLM and CICS Combinations with Data Sharing   Many installations support multiple CICS systems, either within the same CPU or not. If these CICS systems are utilizing DBRC, with IRLM for data sharing, there may be a need for more than a single IRLM address space. During application test, separate and unique systems could provide the optimum environment. When a CICS test region requires test data, a separate IRLM for the test DL/I resources may be necessary. The test IRLM is identified to CICS via the

DLIRLM=YES,Subsystem Name

parameter in the SIT and can thereby connect the test CICS system to the test IRLM. The default subsystem name is "IRLM" but can be overridden for connection to an alternate name.

The IRLM subsystem identifies the specific CICS subsystem by the unique APPLID (VTAM Application ID) name as designated in the SIT parameter. In a data sharing environment, it is critical that every CICS system contains a unique APPLID name, since this name governs the access allowed by the IRLM. Without unique APPLID names, two CICS systems share the same SUBSYSTEM record in the RECOD data set, and data integrity can be comprised.

5.4 Logging and Recovery

Since most installations implement DL/I facilities to ensure integrity of the data, both logging and recovery are critical issues. These two functions of IMS/VS are used to guarantee integrity and fully backout any noncommitted resources in case of failure.

While DBRC (Data Base Recovery Control) has already been discussed within the data sharing section, DBRC is actually the IMS/VS feature providing recovery options for DL/I databases, whether the data is shared or not. DBRC "lives" in the CICS address space as an MVS subtask and records information about DL/I resource access in VSAM datasets called RECONs (REcovery CONtrol). CICS tasks CALL DBRC to update information in the RECONs.

5.4.1 RECON Data Set Initialization

After the RECON data sets have been created, they must be initialized to indicate the presence of recovery and/or data sharing control. Even if data sharing is not specifed, the database can be protected at some level via the initialization command SHARECTL. If the RECON is initialized with this level, and the database utilizes a data sharing level of "0" (exclusive control), DBRC prevents concurrent access by more than one CICS system.

If, however, the RECON is initialized with the RECOVCTL option, DBRC provides no protection from concurrent access, regardless of the data sharing level of the database. Programmers must ensure the proper combination in both places to guarantee total integrity and recovery capabilities.

When error conditions arise to indicate potential loss of integrity, either CICS or IMS intervene to attempt recovery. If the error is sufficiently serious, the transaction or the entire CICS system may be abended to provide data for analysis, such as dump or trace contents. In these cases, databases may be stopped, and backout processing may be initiated. If the installation has chosen

START=AUTO

in the startup options (the recommended value for any CICS system with database facilities), CICS then initiates an "Emergency" startup and takes specific actions for DL/I resources.

5.4.2 Emergency Restart

If the CICS region fails, the next initialization of CICS will detect the previous failure (via the CICS catalog) and begin an emergency restart of CICS. DL/I database updates that were "in flight" or uncommitted at the time of the failure will be backed out.

CICS reads the system journal (DFHJ01) forward to detect any Units of Recovery (UOR) for incomplete CICS tasks. If the UOR is incomplete, it is backed out by reading the journal backward and finding all changes during that interval. While the system journal contains information for all CICS recoverable resources, an additional extent, DFHJ01X, must be defined for DL/I support. During an emergency restart, if DL/I support is detected, system logging begins at the start of DFHJ01X. When the emergency restart is complete, logging continues at the beginning of DFHJ01A or DFHJ01B, depending on parameters defined.

IBM (SC33-0520 CICS Restart and Recovery Guide) advises customers to make an archive copy of this log following a successful emergency restart. If, however, this journal becomes full *during* an emergency restart, CICS initialization will fail with a U0116 abend. The journal must be deleted and reallocated with more space and the emergency restart repeated.

This allows the X journal to be expendable if the emergency restart is unsuccessful. Backout processing utilizes this journal for logging, then continues with the A and B journals, since they contain the status of the system at the point of the failure.

Archiving DFHJ01A/B and X with DFSUARC0 If the installation chooses to use DBRC for recovery control, a great deal of processing will be done using provided IMS/VS recovery utilities. One utility, DFSUARC0, is used to archive the DL/I system journals (DFHJ01A,B,X) after emergency restart. This utility copies both the IMS and the CICS log records from the CICS journal to an SLDS (system log datasets). This archive process must be done to notify DBRC that the appropriate records have been moved. If not archived, DBRC will attempt to create an additional PRILOG entry for the same dataset, and the GENJCL function will experience difficulty.

The utility, when executed, would be used with the following parameters:

//ARCHJRN EXEC PGM=DFSUARC0,PARM='CICS=Y,DBRC=Y'

to indicate that both CICS and data sharing are being used.

Some installations have experienced performance problems with the utility, especially if the log records are archived to tape media. IBM recommends extensive buffering on the input and output DD statements when using the utility to improve performance.

EEQE (Extended Error Queue Element) When I/O errors occur on a DL/I database, CICS provides error handling routines for recovery and diagnosis. In IMS/VS Version 2, CICS records data to describe the error into the CICS catalog (RSD). These error records are called EEQEs and contain information relating to the database experiencing the error.

Until the database is recovered, any applications that request access to the database (the segments affected by the error) will receive a status code of "AO" until the EEQE is deleted. These records, therefore, protect the database experiencing the error from further destruction.

When the database is recovered, specifically via the

CEMT SET DLIDATABASE (dbd) RECOVERDB

command, all EEQEs are deleted by CICS. After recovery is complete, the installation can provide access to the data via the

CEMT SET DLIDATABASE (dbd) STARTED

command. This permits recovery to be accomplished without disruption to any other CICS system or application.

Online Access to the RECON Data Sets Many installations use the DBRC recovery control facility, DSPURX00, to communicate with DBRC. Some commands can be submitted online to CICS using the CICS transaction CBRC. This transaction interrogates the RECON data sets for specific entries and utilization. Installations must take care, however, for CBRC requires 450K bytes of OSCOR storage to execute. This excessive OSCOR requirement must not exceed the amount of OSCOR free at the time of execution, or undesirable results will be experienced. The storage required may not outweigh the need for online access.

5.5 Application Issues

5.5.1 Call-Level Interface vs. Command-Level Interface

To communicate a processing request to DL/I, the application program can utilize either "CALLs" or "EXECs." The differences between these two techniques are as varied as the difference between macro and command-level COBOL. Following are just a few of the highlights.

With DL/I CALLs, the program contains the CALL from the host language (COBOL, PL/I, or assembler), including a list of parameters. These parameters provide input into the DL/I processing request as required by the application. A typical DL/I call might look like:

MOVE 'GU ' TO FUNCTION.
CALL 'CBLTDLI' USING FUNCTION PCB IOAREA SSA.

CBLTDLI is the "call to DL/I" interface, with the corresponding parameters for DL/I function, the name of the PCB, I/O area, and SSA (Segment Search Argument). These parameters are provided by the program to facilitate communication between the DL/I resources and the application.

While call-level techniques are still being used, some installations choose command-level DL/I. One reason is for debugging purposes. Any DL/I call, while imbedded within an existing command-level program, cannot be detected with typical diagnostic tools, such as EDF (execution diagnostic facility). Since EDF only "stops" at every

EXEC, the calls go unnoticed. Even CICS trace facilities do not display the CALL. For this reason, many installations embed application-created trace entries at the time of the CALL to record vital data values.

The command-level interface issues DL/I commands,

EXEC CICS DL/I function options

The syntax of commands is uncomplicated and appears very similar to typical CICS commands. The "function" in the command would compare to the values moved into the CALL, as described above. Any options could contain names, constants, or variables as used in the CALL.

An advantage of using commands is the debugging facility of EDF, and the entries that appear in CICS trace facilities. One disadvantage of the command facility, however, frustrates many programmers and causes them to continue coding with CALLs. The options available in an EXEC DLI command to retrieve segments are:

GN — Get Next
GNP — Get Next in Parent
GU — Get Unique

Experienced DL/I programmers will notice immediately that missing are the corresponding three functions of GHN, GHNP, and GHU, which are available via the CALL interface. Since the application is not given the granularity of either GN or GHN (with or without the HOLD option), the command-level facility forces the HOLD. CICS transactions written in DL/I commands, therefore, inherit the HOLD option in all GET requests and can produce locks when none are required.

The only alternative to explicit HOLD is to create an additional PCB within the original PSB that contains no update option. If the command GET is issued after "scheduling" a read-only PSB, the HOLD is not issued. Of course, this may require adding PCBs to the PSB, some with update and some without.

At this writing, it does not appear that the command facility will be enhanced to include the additional functions unless requirements are submitted to IBM.

The most helpful manual to use for any programming issues, either CALL or command, would be SC26-4177, IMS/VS Application Programming for CICS Users. This manual contains a chapter "Reference for Command-Level and Call-Level Programs," which attempts to summarize the differences between the two techniques.

In addition, IBM INFO items 3XHBB (for CALL) and 52RWJ (for EXEC) discuss the different interfaces. Specifically, they deal with the requirement for call-level programs to manage pointers to the PCB address list and the PCBs. The EXEC DL/I interface does not require (or allow) addressability to the control blocks.

5.5.2 CALL Interface with VS COBOL II

Until recently, COBOL II programs using the CALL interface to DL/I had to be link-edited with AMODE(24) RMODE(24) attributes. This caused execution (and storage utilization) below the 16-Mb line, diluting the benefits of COBOL II in CICS. COBOL II programs that used the EXEC DLI command can be linked with full 31-bit capabilities for virtual storage exploitation.

This restriction has now been removed via an enhancement, APAR PP55259. This service now allows COBOL II programs with DL/I CALLS to be linked with AMODE(31) RMODE(ANY), and therefore loaded above the 16-Mb line. The only existing restriction is that the CALL parameter list, and corresponding argument values including the I/O areas, must remain below the 16-Mb line.

CALL programs that are converted to VS COBOL II must also be changed to pass the address of a PCB list for a PSB. Since the BLL cells have been eliminated, the previous technique no longer works. The same results can be accomplished with a new technique.

When the PSB has been scheduled, the address of the UIB is returned to the program. Since the UIB contains the PCB address list, the CALL statement can now be coded:

CALL 'CBLTDLI' USING PCB-CALL PSB-NAME ADDRESS OF DLIUIB.

The DLIUIB field can then be used as a pointer and the PCB address established. A complete description of the process can be found in the IBM INFO item 7LJFP for CALL programs, item 52RWJ for command programs.

5.5.3 CICS/OS2 Access

In the recent release of CICS/OS2, Version 1.2, a new facility has been provided called DPL, Distributed Program Link. The application in CICS/OS2 can issue an

EXEC CICS LINK PROGRAM(program) COMMAREA(commarea)

to transfer control to another program, possibly a program residing on a host CICS system. This host program could access DL/I resources (via CALL or EXEC) and then return the results to the CICS/OS2 system. While the workstation application has no native access to DL/I, this technique can provide accessibility to the resources without physical distribution of the data. The DPL facility is only provided in the CICS/OS2 environment and (at this time) cannot be issued from the host program. It does, however, provide capabilities on a workstation not previously available, except in function shipping or transaction routing.

Since the DL/I resources are not native to the CICS/OS2 system, the request cannot be function shipped, and neither CALLs or EXEC CICS DLI statements can exist within the CICS/OS2 application. The DPL requested program is defined as a remote module, and the Communications Manager component of OS/2 transmits the request to the appropriate host system. DL/I resources, being host-based, will always exist externally to other operating systems but, via LU6.2 APPC interfaces, will be available for cooperative processing implementations.

5.6 DL/I Support in CICS

To properly utilize DL/I resources in CICS, definitions exist for the "connections" and unique local DL/I control blocks. Following are the most common definitions for DL/I resources and techniques for support specifications.

5.6.1 DL/I Dynamic Definitions

Figure 5-5 contains typical IMS libraries required for DL/I support in CICS. Note that while the IMS RESLIB must be defined in both the STEPLIB and in DFHRPL, an additional library exists in the STEPLIB called SYS.IMS220.CICSPP.DSN(1). This library provides

```
 CICSPP  PROC START=AUTO                                                  00010000
//CICSPP EXEC PGM=DFHSIP,REGION=10600K,TIME=1440,                         00020000
//         PERFORM=6,DPRTY=(15,14),DYNAMNBR=1,                            00030000
//         PARM=('START=&START,SI')                                      00040000
//STEPLIB  DD DSN=SYS2.CANDLE.OC450.LOAD,DISP=SHR                         00041000
//         DD DSN=SYS.CICS211.LOADLIB1,DISP=SHR                           00042000
//         DD DSN=SYS.IMS220.RESLIB,DISP=SHR,DCB=BLKSIZE=32760            00050000
//         DD DSN=SYS.IMS220.CICSPP.DSN,DISP=SHR                          00050100
//         DD DSN=MVS.CICS.ONLINE.LOADLIB,DISP=SHR                        00060000
//SYSIN    DD DSN=SYS.CICSPROD.PARMS(CICSPP),DISP=SHR                     00090002
//SYSPRINT DD SYSOUT=Z                                                    00100000
//****** THIS IS FOR XVSM OPTIMIZER                                       00110100
//SYSABEND DD SYSOUT=X                                                    00120000
//ABNLIGNR DD DUMMY                                                       00121000
//ABNLDUMP DD DUMMY                                                       00122000
//DFHRPL   DD DSN=SYS.CICS211.LOADLIB2,DISP=SHR                           00123000
//         DD DSN=SYS.CICS211.LOADLIB,DISP=SHR                            00124000
//         DD DSN=SYS2.CANDLE.OC450.RPL,DISP=SHR                          00125000
//         DD DSN=SYS.IMS220.RESLIB,DISP=SHR,DCB=BLKSIZE=32760            00150000
//         DD DSN=MVS.CICS.ONLINE.LOADLIB,DISP=SHR                        00160000
//         DD DSN=MVS.FSS.ONLINE.LINKLIB,DISP=SHR                         00210000
//         DD DSN=SYS.COPV13.LOADLIB,DISP=SHR                             00221006
//         DD DSN=SYS2.INTERTST.REL313.LOADLIB,DISP=SHR                   00230007
//         DD DSN=SYS.XARELO.V220.CICS21.LOADLIB,DISP=SHR                 00261000
//         DD DSN=SYS1.ETC30A.LOAD,DISP=SHR                               00261103
//PRNTOUT  DD DSN=SYS2.OMONSTRT.PRNTOUT,DISP=SHR                          00270000
//DFHDMPA  DD DSN=SYS.CICSPROD.CICSP.DUMPA,DISP=SHR                       00280000
//DFHDMPB  DD DSN=SYS.CICSPROD.CICSP.DUMPB,DISP=SHR                       00290000
//DFHSNAP  DD SYSOUT=V,OUTLIM=0                                           00300000
//DFHBUG   DD DSN=SYS2.CICS.CICSP.DEBUG,DISP=SHR                          00310000
//XVSM$OFF    DD DUMMY                                                    00311000
//*XVSMBOTH     DD DUMMY                                                  00312000
//DFHAUXT  DD DSN=SYS.CICSPROD.CICSP.AUXTRCE1,DISP=SHR                    00320000
//IMSACB   DD DSN=SYS.IMS220.ACBLIB,DISP=SHR                              00330000
//DFSVSAMP DD DSN=SYS.IMS220.DFSVSAMP(CICSLOCK),DISP=SHR                  00340000
//DFHJ01A  DD DSN=SYS.CICSPROD.CICSP.DFHJ01A,DISP=SHR                     00350000
//DFHJ01B  DD DSN=SYS.CICSPROD.CICSP.DFHJ01B,DISP=SHR                     00360000
//DFHJ01X  DD DSN=SYS.CICSPROD.CICSP.DFHJ01X,DISP=SHR                     00370000
//*DFHJ07A DD DSN=BCOL.COMLOAN.JRNL07A,DISP=SHR                           00371000
//*DFHJ07B DD DSN=BCOL.COMLOAN.JRNL07B,DISP=SHR                           00372000
//DFHRSD   DD DSN=SYS.CICSPROD.CICSP.DFHRSD,DISP=SHR,                     00380000
//     AMP='BUFND=9,BUFNI=9'                                             00381000
//DFHCSD   DD DSN=SYS.CICSPROD.DFHCSD,DISP=SHR                            00390000
//SYSTAT   DD DSN=SYS.CICSPROD.CICSP.SYSTAT,DISP=SHR                      00400000
//MSTPRT   DD DSN=SYS.CICSPROD.CICSP.MASTPRT,DISP=SHR                     00410000
//DFHTEMP  DD DSN=SYS.CICSPROD.CICSP.DFHTEMP,DISP=SHR                     00420000
//DFHINTRA DD DSN=SYS.CICSPROD.CICSP.DFHINTRA,DISP=SHR                    00430000
//AUTO     DD DSN=SYS.CICSP.AUTOINST.FILE,DISP=SHR                        00430100
//AUTOPATH DD DSN=SYS.CICSP.AUTOINST.PATH,DISP=SHR                        00430200
//**********    QUANTUM XARELO DATABASE                                   00430300
//XARLLIB  DD DSN=SYS.CICSPP.XARL.V220.XARLLIB,DISP=SHR                   00430400
//IPCPCDS  DD DSN=SYS.IPCP.COMMAND.DATASET,DISP=SHR                       00431000
//********************************************************************    00440000
//CICSDATE DD DSN=BTIS.TIS000.DATE,DISP=SHR                               00450000
//ATMVTAM  DD SYSOUT=(A,INTRDR),DCB=BLKSIZE=80                            00520000
//PCCSGET  DD DISP=SHR,DSN=BPCC.PCC000.GET                                00520100
//*SCREEN  DD DSN=BCOL.COL013.SCREEN,DISP=SHR                             00521000
//*TRAN    DD DSN=BCOL.COL013.TXFILE,DISP=SHR                             00522000
//*SWISSBR DD DSN=BCOL.COL180.SWISSBK,DISP=SHR                            00523000
//*OTCFILE DD DSN=BCOL.COL350.OTCFILE,DISP=SHR                            00524000
```

Figure 5-5 CICS JCL with IMS libraries.

```
JFSMDA TYPE=INITIAL
DFSMDA TYPE=DATABASE,DBNAME=DDACCAIX
DFSMDA TYPE=DATASET,DDNAME=DDACCAIX,DSNAME=C997JVM.DEP.DDACCAIX,     X
            DISP=SHR
DFSMDA TYPE=DATABASE,DBNAME=DDACCAI2
DFSMDA TYPE=DATASET,DDNAME=DDACCAI2,DSNAME=C997JVM.DEP.DDACCAI2,     X
            DISP=SHR
DFSMDA TYPE=DATABASE,DBNAME=DDACCAPR
DFSMDA TYPE=DATASET,DDNAME=DDACCAPR,DSNAME=C997JVM.DEP.DDACCAPR,     X
            DISP=SHR
DFSMDA TYPE=FINAL
       END
```

Figure 5-6 Dynamically defined DL/I databases.

support for a new facility in IMS Version 2 and 3, the "dynamic allocation" of IMS databases. Previous DD statements in CICS JCL can be removed, and databases can be dynamically allocated to any region when required. This facility provides both performance and usability improvements, since databases are only allocated when used and can be dynamically deallocated if necessary.

Figure 5-6 contains a typical example of dynamically defined databases. The DFSMDA macro contains an entry for every database, with the corresponding DSNAME= parameter for the fully qualified name. This macro is then linked into the library specified in the CICS STEPLIB. One drawback remains in this process. The library containing the dynamic definitions must be APF (authorized program facility) authorized.

Once created, however, the databases can be stopped via

CEMT SET DLIDATABASE(name) STOP

which also automatically deallocates it from the CICS region. In reverse, a database START will cause automatic allocation to occur. Installations with many databases can save both virtual storage and availability with this dynamic capability.

DL/I Pool Definitions in CICS   While several initialization options (SIT) must be specified for DL/I, probably the most important, especially to the application program, are:

DMBPOOL=

and

PSBPOOL=

```
CICSPP SYSTAT                                  ①              00018100

        PEAK NO. OF BYTES USED FROM DMB POOL         48,144   FROM A POOL SIZE OF    76,800
        PEAK NO. OF BYTES USED FROM PSB POOL        204,800   FROM A POOL SIZE OF   204,800
        PEAK NO. OF BYTES USED FROM ENQ POOL          1,024   FROM A POOL SIZE OF     8,192
        PEAK NO. OF DL/I THREADS USED CONCURRENTLY       19   FROM A MAXIMUM OF          21

        NUMBER OF WAITS FOR DMB POOL SPACE                0
        NUMBER OF WAITS FOR PSB POOL SPACE           20,166   ②
        NUMBER OF WAITS FOR A DL/I THREAD                 0

*******************************************ISC/IRC LINK STATISTICS*******************************************
```

Figure 5-7 CICS shutdown statistics of DL/I resources.

These values create the pools for DL/I resource allocation. Figure 5-7 shows the CICS shutdown statistics from an installation using a DMBPOOL=75 and PSBPOOL=200. Note that the peak utilization of the PSBPOOL exceeded the value of the pool size (1) and recorded a corresponding number of waits for that pool (2). This is not necessarily a problem, since the pool contents can be reused and the frequently used PSBs remain in the pool.

An extremely important value, however, is the size of the DMB pool, which holds the database management buffers. This value should *never* reach the maximum. If CICS is unable to load a database into the DMB pool, it will select a "victim" database, close the database to free up a slot for the request, and deallocate the database from the CICS system. This is a costly and slow process and should not be imposed on any CICS system unless performance will never be an issue. This is probably the most important DL/I statistic to monitor in any CICS system.

A normal rule to follow on pool sizes is: DMBPL (DMB Pool) should be large enough to contain all databases defined to the system. The output from the ACBGEN of each database provides these values. PSBPL (PSB Pool) should be large enough to contain the maximum number of PSBs that will be concurrently scheduled at any time. If PSBs are scheduled from batch jobs in addition to CICS transactions, they must be included in the calculation. Again, the ACBGEN output would contain the values to use in the calculation.

DL/I Content in CICS Journals   Since all DL/I requests are recorded in CICS journals for recovery, they can also be used for both problem determination and tuning. Some installations have written programs to format out the CICS system journal (01A,B, and X) to determine exactly what DL/I activity has occurred. The CICS/MVS Customization Guide documents the contents of journal records written on behalf of DL/I requests. These records can be used to determine *exactly* what DL/I requests were processed and by which CICS tasks.

In addition, specific data can be directed to either a CICS journal or the MVS SMF (System Management Facility) files. Use of the

```
  3618JTL7 JOB (T,B,JDC,JTL),'MRO MCTPP ',MSGCLASS=X,USER=B618J        00010004
//        CLASS=T,REGION=2048K,NOTIFY=B618JTL                         00020004
//TABLEASM EXEC DFHAUPLE,INDEX='SYS.CICS211',INDEX2='SYS.CICS211',    00031015
//    MTS='A.SMPMTS',NAME='LOADLIB'                                   00032011
//ASSEM.SYSUT1 DD *                                                   00050000
         PRINT GEN                                                    00060000
MCT      TITLE 'DFHMCTPP'                                             00070000
         DFHMCT TYPE=INITIAL,                                        X00080000
                EVENT=YES,                                           X00090000
                SUFFIX=PP                                             00100000
         DFHMCT TYPE=EMP,CLASS=PERFORM,                              X00101003
                ID=(PP,1),                                           X00102003
                COUNT=(1,GH,GN,GNP,GHU,GHN,GHNP,ISRT,DLET,REPL),     X00103003
                CLOCK=(1,SCHED,TERM,CALL,IWAIT),                     X00104003
                PERFORM=SCLOCK(3)                                     00105003
         DFHMCT TYPE=EMP,ID=(PP,2),CLASS=PERFORM,PERFORM=PCLOCK(3)    00106003
         DFHMCT TYPE=EMP,ID=(PP,3),CLASS=PERFORM,PERFORM=SCLOCK(1)    00107003
         DFHMCT TYPE=EMP,ID=(PP,4),CLASS=PERFORM,                    X00108003
                PERFORM=(PCLOCK(2))                                   00109003
         DFHMCT TYPE=EMP,CLASS=PERFORM,ID=(PP,5),                    X00109103
                PERFORM=(PCLOCK(2),MLTCNT(1,9))                       00109203
         DFHMCT TYPE=EMP,ID=(PP,6),CLASS=PERFORM,PERFORM=SCLOCK(4)    00109303
         DFHMCT TYPE=EMP,ID=(PP,7),CLASS=PERFORM,PERFORM=PCLOCK(4)    00109403
         DFHMCT TYPE=EMP,ID=(PP,8),CLASS=PERFORM,                    X00109503
                PERFORM=(PCLOCK(1),PCLOCK(2),PCLOCK(3),PCLOCK(4))     00109603
         DFHMCT TYPE=EMP,ID=(PP,9),CLASS=PERFORM,PERFORM=PCLOCK(1)    00109703
         DFHMCT TYPE=RECORD,                                         X00110000
                CLASS=ACCOUNT,                                       X00120000
                DATASET=5,                                           X00130000
                FREQ=900,                                            X00140000
                MAXBUF=1000                                           00150000
         DFHMCT TYPE=RECORD,                                         X00160000
                CLASS=EXCEPTION,                                     X00170000
                DATASET=5,                                           X00180000
                FREQ=900,                                            X00190000
                MAXBUF=1000                                           00200000
         DFHMCT TYPE=RECORD,                                         X00210000
                CLASS=PERFORM,                                       X00220000
                DATASET=5,                                           X00230000
                FREQ=900,                                            X00240000
                MAXBUF=2000,                                         X00250000
                CONV=YES,                                            X00260000
                CPU=MVS/XA                                            00270000
         DFHMCT TYPE=FINAL                                            00280000
         END                                                          00290000
```

Figure 5-8 Sample CICS MCT definitions.

MCT (Monitor Control Facility) can direct specific data to SMF records for subsequent processing by a performance tool or program.

Figure 5-8 contains a sample MCT definition to record DL/I resource utilization. Notice that specific DL/I request types can be specified and recorded. While this provides a great deal of performance information, the records contain the transaction name but not the DBD corresponding to the request. The performance information would be global, not specific to any database. A sample of MCT definitions can be found in the CICS/MVS Customization Guide, and a sample program (DFH$MOLS) can be found in the CICS.SAMPLIB library to process the records.

6

CICS with DB/2 Databases

A previous chapter dealt with IMS issues, specifically the use of DL/I databases within CICS. While many installations continue to use IMS as the database manager, other customers are choosing DB/2 and the CICS Attach Facility for their applications. The database managers are very different, both in structure and function. This chapter will deal with topics relevant to DB/2 utilization within a CICS system, and what additional requirements may be necessary for the application.

6.1 DB/2 Threads and the RCT

The core relationship between CICS and DB/2 is built by the assembly of a macro table, DSNCRCT. Since IBM is encouraging all customers to use RDO (Resource Definition Online), this table may appear in the online facility down the road. For the present, however, the table must be assembled and linked into a library defined to CICS in the STEPLIB DD, since these modules are MVS loaded and not typical programs.

This table establishes the relationships between CICS transactions and the DB/2 resources used by those transactions (DB/2 plans). These "connections" are also called "threads." Thread description will be completed later in this section.

RCT Parameters

TYPE=INIT

STRTWT	Option if DB/2 is not active
SUBID	DB/2 subsystem name
SNAP	SYSOUT class or NONE
SUFFIX	RCT suffix for CICS startup
THRDMAX	Maximum number of CICS attach threads

TYPE=ENTRY/POOL/COMD

AUTH	Authorization option
THRDM	Maximum number of threads
THRDA	Maximum Number of active threads
THRDS	Maximum Number of protected threads
TXID	CICS transaction ID
TWAIT	Action if no thread is available
DPMODE	Priority of thread TCB relative to CICS TCB
ROLBE	Action to be taken to deadlocks and timeouts

Figure 6-1 CICS RCT parameters.

6.1.1 DSNCRCT

The RCT (Resource Control Table) defines the connections that CICS and DB/2 will be required to establish for any application. Note that this module is not a CICS module (no DFH prefix), but a DB/2 module (DSNC prefix). Not only does it identify the connections, but the type and number of connections, such as:

- Type and number of threads per transaction
- Maximum number of threads from this CICS region
- Action that CICS should take if no available threads
- Plan name for thread allocation or name of dynamic plan exit (DB/2 V2.1 and up)

Figure 6-1 contains the principal parameters of the RCT that affect attachment between CICS and DB/2.

DPMODE This parameter seems to raise many questions from customers, since it affects CICS, DB/2, and MVS performance. The value of DPMODE sets the dispatching priority of the thread TCB compared to CICS. IBM recommends:

- Assign DPMODE=HIGH for a priority transaction with a high number of SQL calls
- Assign DPMODE=EQUAL or LOW for other transactions

If DPMODE=HIGH is specified, the thread TCB for that transaction will have a higher priority than the main CICS task corresponding to that transaction request. It has no effect on other CICS TCBs within the address space. It may, however, affect the ability for CICS to dispatch and should only be used for TRULY high priority requests.

If DBMODE=EQ is used, equal is attempted but not truly attained. Of course, two TCBs cannot be dispatched concurrently for the same unit of work. What happens, in fact, is that the DB/2 thread TCB is dispatched at a slightly lower priority than the CICS TCB. This is usually the recommended value, and the one that most customers use.

Another point to consider is that while the thread TCB is accessing the DB/2 table requested, CICS is free to dispatch other tasks. The CICS active chain may contain a dozen or more tasks awaiting dispatch, and the DB/2 thread affects only the requesting task, no others. The requesting task is placed into a WAIT state, yet remains on the active chain. A CICS application request for a complex process (such as a JOIN) affects the time of this WAIT state.

The CICS task must wait until the data requested via the DB/2 FETCH is available. This can be a short interval if indexes are used, or an excessively long interval if a tablespace scan is requested. While the CICS task is waiting (on the ACTIVE chain), other tasks (on the SUSPEND chain) cannot be selected for dispatch. A large number of DB/2 tasks in extended WAITs can impact the ACTIVE CICS chain, cause CICS to reach AMAX (active maximum tasks), and produce CICS performance problems.

6.1.2 DB/2 Threads — Unraveling the Mysteries

Probably one of the most mysterious topics of CICS–DB/2 attachment has to be the type, creation, and management of threads. While IBM has provided a great deal of autonomy in the specification of these resources, it places responsibility on the customer to properly define them. Once defined, they must also be continually monitored to ensure proper values. As applications grow and resource requirements increase, these resources must be "tuned" to complement the progress.

Compounding the process, IBM manuals were seldom clear and concise in their definition of thread specification to CICS. In addition, APARs have shipped for performance enhancements. These enhancements made significant changes to the thread allocation logic, not all of which were reflected in the manuals. Consequently, the confusion escalated. This section will attempt to discuss the major issues involved with DB/2 threads and their effect on the CICS environment.

Thread Types   The CICS Attach Facility provides for three types, or classes, of threads. These types are:

* COMD — command threads for the DSNC operator task
* POOL — pool threads for common tasks
* ENTRY — entry threads which can be protected or not

The COMD threads are automatically generated by the assembly of the RCT, since the DSNC task requires thread specification. If no explicit definition is made, the default values are

DPMODE=HIGH,TXID=DSNC,AUTH=(USER,TERM,*),THRDM=1,
THRDA=1,THRDS=1,ROLBE=NO,TWAIT=POOL

Customers may wish to make changes to the authorization parameters to suit specific needs, rather than allowing the default values. Since this thread type affects only the DSNC task, it has minimal impact on threads used by normal applications. It *does*, however, affect the performance of DSNC, and some installations choose to "protect" this thread. If the default of THRDS=1 is used, the thread is attached at startup or at DB/2 connection and is "protected."

If the value is changed to THRDS=0, the thread is not protected from inactivity. If insufficient command activity continues and the thread is not "protected," the thread is terminated after the purge cycle interval (usually 30–45 seconds).

POOL threads are specified for tasks that the installation does not wish to explicitly connect to an ENTRY thread. With only one TYPE=POOL entry in the RCT, all transactions that are not satisfied with an ENTRY thread use POOL threads. These threads, therefore, become the pool that applications use that do not require specific or "protected" threads.

The differences between POOL threads and ENTRY threads become most significant when the application issues intermediate SYNCPOINTs during the course of the task. If no explicit SYNC-POINT is issued, the LUW (logical unit of work) ends at task termination, and the thread is terminated. This occurs similarly for either POOL or ENTRY threads. If the application uses explicit SYNC-

POINTing, POOL threads are terminated at the time of SYNC-POINT. Applications that use explicit SYNCPOINTs need to realize this difference.

There are, of course, exceptions to this rule for POOL threads. The thread will not be terminated if:

• Another task requesting identical resources is waiting for a thread (same plan and user-id)

or

• The task is not terminal-initiated (as in a STARTed task)

POOL threads may also be used by ENTRY threads that have been "diverted." In the thread specification,

TYPE=ENTRY,THRDA=n,TWAIT=POOL,...

requests that are queued may be shifted to POOL threads.

The normal recommendation is to use POOL threads for low volume tasks, those that will not be continually generating requests for recreation of these threads.

ENTRY threads come in two "flavors": protected and unprotected (or nonprotected). The choice of selection should be based on resources consumed and the objective required at termination.

Unprotected ENTRY threads are terminated at task termination, unless another transaction with the same plan is waiting for that thread. Realize that thread termination *does not* mean TCB termination and the subsequent release of storage. A TCB is not "detached" from CICS until the specified limit is exceeded (THRDMAX). More explanation concerning TCB vs. thread assignment can be found later in this section. When an unprotected ENTRY thread is terminated, the next request must consume necessary resources to identify the plan and establish the path back into DB/2.

Why specify unprotected threads? These are truly efficient type threads for high volume transactions, since the probability of another task with the same plan would be significant. Applications with low CICS activity would release the thread for another requestor, providing optimum utilization of resources. Unprotected ENTRY threads are specified via:

TYPE=ENTRY,THRDS=0,....

Protected ENTRY threads are *not* terminated at either SYNC-POINT or task termination. These threads remain until the second DB/2 purge cycle detects no activity. Since the purge cycle occurs every 30 seconds, the average termination time is 45 seconds.

Many installations support extremely active CICS systems and have transaction rates of 20–40 transactions per second. If a protected ENTRY thread remains unavailable for 45 seconds, literally thousands of tasks could have been executed during that interval. Resources that could have been available are unused and wasted. For that reason, protected threads should be used with great care. Overspecified protected threads consume resources that may be needed elsewhere.

CICS Thread Display (DSNC DISPLAY THREAD)   To fully understand the results of the display request within CICS, a fuller explanation may be required of connections within the CICS-DB/2 Attachment Facility. This understanding includes the "states" of a thread during the creation and termination process. This process can best be defined via three states documented in various IBM publications. Some sources actually define a "three phase connection process" to fully establish the thread creation. In the most simplistic terms, the original request from CICS proceeds via:

- IDENTIFY
- SIGNON
- CREATE THREAD

Until the completion of the last phase, connection has been requested, but is incomplete and unavailable for CICS dispatch. A more complete explanation of these three phases follows.

IDENTIFY: This request is initiated by CICS and is transmitted to DB/2 via the MVS subsystem interface facility. This process is required for authorization, ensures validation of the requestor via the SAF facility (System Authorization Facility), and establishes the TCB for transfer of data. Although both address spaces (CICS and DB/2) have established communication, access to data is not yet allowed.

These connections can be found in the DISPLAY output with a value of "0" in the "REQ" field. The status (ST) column will contain "N."

SIGNON: The second phase of the connection process identifies the userid of the requestor (CICS) for future authorization of DB/2 resource access. Since CICS is a MUSASS (multiple user address space), it establishes the authorization IDs to be used with the CICS requestor's connection.

These connections will contain a nonzero value in the "REQ" field, a status (ST) value of "N," and the PLAN column blank. The columns "ID" and "AUTHID" will contain the values as identified during the SIGNON process from CICS.

THREAD CREATED: This last phase of thread construction can and will identify the PLAN from the requestor as specified in the RCT. The path into the required resource can be established, and the connection can be built. When the PLAN is allocated to the thread, DB/2 initiates a lock on the PLAN to indicate that it is allocated and in use.

These connections appear with the status (ST) value of "T," a nonzero value in the "REQ" field, and valid entries in the "ID," "AUTHID," and "PLAN" fields. In addition, if the thread is currently active with a CICS task, the active "A" field will display an asterisk, "*." A protected thread waiting to be reused or terminated will display a blank value in this field.

The most important item to remember is that the DISPLAY command will present ALL TCBs, regardless of the phase in which the thread currently exists. The values of each field identify the phase. Another important field, "ACT-IND," indicates if the thread is active in DB/2 or is "inflight" between SQL calls.

Since the DISPLAY command is so powerful, it can provide a great deal of information not only during CICS execution, but during problem diagnosis. Figure 6-2 contains an explanation of the command with a corresponding sample output. Note that although the report identifies many threads that have completed SIGNON (ST value of "N"), only five have connections (ST value of "T") and four are active (A value of "*").

Miscellaneous Thread Issues

Plan Section   The CICS Attach Facility allows an application to be designed and implemented with Dynamic SQL statements. Since a dynamic SQL call is actually bound and validated at runtime, some programmers conclude that the RCT entry must be unique. This is not so. In fact, a transaction with both static and dynamic SQL can use the same ENTRY thread. The dynamic bind has no effect on the type of thread. If the program has static and dynamic SQL in the same plan, the dynamic bind does not generate a new thread. As long as authorization succeeds, the execution is successful.

For each active thread, the following information is displayed when issuing the DSNC-DISPLAY THREAD TYPE(ACTIVE) command:

NAME
: A variable that represents the "connection name" used to establish the thread.

STATUS
: A connection status code having one of the following values:

N
: The thread is in either IDENTIFY or SIGNON status.

QT
: The CREATE THREAD request has been queued.

T
: An allied, non-distributed thread has been established (plan allocated).

TR
: An allied, distributed thread has been established and is requesting data from another location.

RA
: The thread is performing a remote access on behalf of a request from another location.

QD
: The thread is queued for termination as a result of the termination of the associated allied task.

D
: The thread is in the process of termination as a result of the termination of the associated allied task.

ACT-IND
: An asterisk if the thread is active within DB2, otherwise blank.

REQ-CT
: A wraparound counter to show the number of DB2 requests.

CORR-ID
: A variable representing the recovery "correlation-ID" associated with the thread.

AUTHORIZATION ID
: The authorization ID associated with a signed-on connection.

PNAME
: A variable representing the plan name associated with the thread.

ASID
: A hexadecimal number representing the ASID of the home address space.

Figure 6-2a Sample DB/2 DISPLAY THREAD command and resulting output.

```
DSNV402I - ACTIVE THREADS -
DSNV401I - DISPLAY THREAD REPORT FOLLOWS -
DSNV402I - ACTIVE THREADS -
NAME    ST    A           REQ ID        AUTHID   PLAN       ASID
PSICLF  N                   3           DPTSOCS             0039
PSIADM  N                   3           DPTSOCS             0044
PSIADM  T     *             3 GCOODSNC  PCC                 0044
PSIADM  N               30304 GTOONAMO  V20                 0044
PSIADM  N                 437 GTO1NAMO  F19                 0044
PSIADM  N                8229 GTOOMCS3  P43                 0044
PSIADM  N               12873 PTOOUMG1  H73                 0044
PSIADM  N                2185 GTO1MCS3  465                 0044
PSIADM  N                3147 GTOONAR1  F05                 0044
PSIADM  N               11631 PTO1UMG1  B64                 0044
PSIADM  N               20233 GTOONAB1  154                 0044
PSIADM  N               16736 GTO1NAB1  V20                 0044
PSIADM  N                8009 GTOOICS1  E15                 0044
PSIADM  N                6398 PTO2PHBD  Y52                 0044
PSIADM  N                1925 GTO1ICS1  G62                 0044
PSIADM  N               13549 GTO1NAR1  J90                 0044
PSIADM  N               11567 PTO3EPU1  L86                 0044
PSIADM  N               14679 PTO4STI1  H37                 0044
PSIADM  N                4994 GTO2NAB1  366                 0044
PSIADM  N                4729 PTO5STI9  G34                 0044
PSIADM  N                4783 PTO5NAIO  E60                 0044
PSIADM  N                3638 PTO6AM07  H66                 0044
PSIADM  N                1377 PTO7AM26  H58                 0044
PSIADM  N                7708 GTOONAUO  126                 0044
PSIADM  N                  60 GTO2NAMO  P43                 0044
PSIADM  N                 994 GTO2NAR1  884                 0044
PSIADM  N                 110 GTO2ICS1  H60                 0044
PSIADM  N                 164 PTO8AM06  YLH                 0044
PSIADM  N                  48 PTO9UMG1  966                 0044
PSIADM  N                  77 GTO1NAUO  154                 0044
PSIADM  N                  10 PT10AM04  030                 0044
DB2CALL T     *         11009 TDMDMLB   DPATDMD  DB2450AC  0041
DB2CALL T     *             8 TJSUVIK2  DPATJSU  DB2450AC  0030
DB2CALL T               26462 NOMAD     NOMAD    DB2450AC  004B
TSO     T     *             3 DPADPCP   DPADPCP            004E
DISPLAY ACTIVE REPORT COMPLETE

DSNV412I - DSNVDT NO INDOUBT THREADS FOUND FOR NAME = TSO
DSNV412I - DSNVDT NO INDOUBT THREADS FOUND FOR NAME = DB2CALL
DSNV412I - DSNVDT NO INDOUBT THREADS FOUND FOR NAME = PSIADM
DSNV412I - DSNVDT NO INDOUBT THREADS FOUND FOR NAME = PSICLF
DSN9022I - DSNVDT '-DISPLAY THREAD' NORMAL COMPLETION
```

Figure 6-2b Sample DB/2 DISPLAY THREAD command and resulting output.

A new feature of DB/2 V2.2 changes the recommendation for authorization of these type of plans. Previously, installations coded the AUTH parameter in the RCT to bypass authorization checking because of the performance impact to check at each access. In V2.2, PUBLIC plans are "cached," therefore checked only at first pass, then stored in the EDMPOOL for each subsequent iteration. With this new feature, IBM now recommends that the installation grant authorization of the plans to PUBLIC and not bypass authorization checking.

In addition to performance improvements, the new authorization checking will force the application to reissue SIGNON. This will produce an additional DB/2 accounting record and allow each CICS transaction to have a corresponding DB/2 accounting record.

THRDMAX, THRDA, and THRDM   There are some misconceptions concerning these thread specifications. THRDMAX affects all thread TCBs built by the CICS Attach Facility, the connections between the CICS address space and DB/2. This value is the maximum number of active threads allowed, plus 2 for CICS command processing (DSNC). The value is actually a "throttle," since the number will limit the total number of DB/2 calls that CICS can process.

Remember from the previous thread discussion that when a thread terminates, the subtask does not. This avoids the excessive unnecessary overhead of "attaching" the new subtask for every new thread. The only time that CICS detaches these subtasks is when the attachment facility itself is stopped (or when CICS comes down). An exception to this rule is when the number of active thread TCBs exceeds THRDMAX-2. If this value is met, CICS will detach at least one thread TCB (subtask) until the correct number is established (THRDMAX-2).

THRDA and THRDM, on the other hand, relate to specific transactions or transaction groups. They correspond to the same plan and specify the maximum active and maximum total (active + inactive) threads for that category.

There are several techniques used in the calculation of THRDMAX. Some IBM publications use

THRDMAX = THRDM + 3

or

THRDMAX = THRDS = 4

Many customers believe that the thread maximum should actually correspond to the number of all active threads, and use

THRDMAX = +THRDA from all RCT TYPE=ENTRY and POOL

The best advice would be to use one of these techniques, closely monitor the results, and tune each system differently. Each mix of applications will produce different results and must be tailored to the specific needs. The maximum number of concurrent threads to a

DB/2 system (Version 2) is 200. These can come from a single or multiple CICS systems, but cannot exceed this value.

OSCOR Requirements for DB/2 Threads   Threads are created via the MVS ATTACH macro, which creates the thread TCB. Since CICS is issuing an MVS command, the storage required to satisfy this request and create the thread must be "gotten" from OSCOR. This type of storage is limited and must be specified at CICS initialization in CICS/MVS. If the installation is already constrained in OSCOR utilization, the value must be increased for DB/2 attach. How much? Since the value of THRDMAX defines the total number of threads, this number will be used in the calculation.

IBM made significant enhancements to this requirement in Version 2. While DB/2 Version 1 required 1500 bytes for each thread, Version 2 now requires only 400. The calculation, therefore, would be

CICS OSCOR increase = THRDMAX * 400

Of course, this OSCOR is only used for each connected thread, but if the activity ever reaches or approaches the maximum, then the full amount will be required.

An ENTRY thread may exist, especially if protected, much longer than a POOL thread. They will require, therefore, more concurrent OSCOR for longer periods of time. All threads, regardless of type, use the same amount (400 bytes). The type of thread will determine the length of this use.

6.2 DB/2 Attachment to CICS

Before a CICS application can retrieve data from DB/2, the attachment must be made between the two subsystems. This connection establishes the "link" and allows the imbedded EXEC CICS SQL statements to be processed. The attachment can be made automatically when CICS initializes via a CICS PLT (Program List Table) program. Alternately, the installation can choose to manually execute the

DSNC STRT x

command from CICS after initialization. The x parameter corresponds to the RCT suffix previously assembled.

Another technique is to utilize the DSNCRCT override parameter in the CICS initialization step, such as

//CICSINIT EXEC PGM=DFHSIP,PARM=(SIT=4$,DSNCRCTx...)

In any case, when the connection has been completed, a message will appear in the CICS log indicating

DSNC023I THE ATTACHMENT FACILITY HAS CONNECTED TO 'DSN' USING 'DSNCRCTx'

Until this message appears, applications will be unable to issue any SQL statements. Any attempt will produce a CICS ABEND code of AEY9, indicating that the attachment is not active. This is probably one of the most common ABEND codes in CICS-DB/2 systems, especially if the attachment is not started automatically.

6.2.1 Attachment Statistics Display: DSNC DISPLAY STAT

After the attachment is complete, statistics can be displayed concerning activity between the subsystems. These statistics can be very helpful to programmers when monitoring their applications. The information provided can assist in the analysis of COMMITs, total number of CALLs, etc. Figure 6-3 contains a complete explanation of the output fields of a DSNC DISPLAY STATISTICS command and sample output. This report can also be extensive, yet can be invaluable for monitoring and tuning of DB/2 applications.

Note that this information is not automatically created by CICS, and must be produced with the appropriate DB/2 command if required. It can, however, provide a programmer with actual activity of plans, including the number of thread waits and/or overflow to pool.

6.2.2 DB/2 Unavailability During Attachment

While the attachment can be automated within CICS (via PLT program), it is the responsibility of CICS, not DB/2, to connect. In other words, the CICS subsystem requests attachment to DB/2, but not the reverse. If DB/2 is not active during CICS initialization, options can be set to specify alternatives.

The STRTWT option in the RCT directs CICS connection in case DB/2 is not available. The options are:

For each RCT entry, the following information is displayed when issuing the DSNC DISPLAY STATISTICS command:

TRANSACTION NAME

PLAN	
CALLS	(total number of SQL calls in this connection)
COMMITS	(total number of units of recovery committed)
ABORTS	(total number of units of recovery rolled back)
AUTHS	(total number of sign-ons (new authorizations))
W/P	(number of times the transaction waited for a thread or overflowed to the pool of threads)
HIGH	(the highest number of threads requested for the transaction)
R-ONLY	(total number of read-only commits)

Figure 6-3a Sample DB/2 DISPLAY STATISTICS command and resulting output.

- YES — CICS should wait for DB/2 to initialize and then complete the connection when possible.
- NO — CICS should not wait and should terminate the connection request immediately. The connection must then be requested via the manual DSNC STRT command.

Note that if YES is used, the connection will be completed when possible. This does *not* mean that CICS will continually check for DB/2. In fact, MVS contains internal control blocks for DB/2 and records the attempt by CICS to establish connection. When DB/2 finally becomes active, the notification is shipped to the CICS system and the attachment process continues.

6.2.3 Avoiding AEY9 ABENDS Before Attachment

As previously noted, if the attachment has not completed, any SQL request will return an AEY9 ABEND to the program. Most installa-

```
DSNC014I   STATISTICS REPORT FOR `DSNCRCTA` FOLLOWS
```

TRAN	PLAN	CALLS	COMMITS	ABORTS	AUTHS	W/P	HIGH	R-ONLY
DSNC		3	0	0	1	0	1	0
POOL	DEFAULT	0	0	0	0	0	11	0
AML1	IS200	0	0	0	0	0	0	0
AMQ1	IS211	1193	0	0	41	41	2	41
ACSU	IS543U	209	48	0	51	51	2	3
UCS3	IS547	112	0	0	8	8	1	8
AM00	BR350X	34	2	0	4	4	1	2
AM01	IS201X	4005	356	4	1160	1169	2	809
AM02	IS202X	20885	364	0	1812	1858	3	1494
AM03	IS203X	10041	345	1	950	971	2	625
AM04	IS204X	16327	468	0	2256	2327	2	1859
BRIO	BR310	1347	0	0	449	449	2	449
BRA0	BR320	346	49	0	51	51	1	2
BRU0	BR330	72	8	0	21	21	1	13
BRB0	BR340	7858	0	0	801	801	2	801
BRD0	BR350	0	0	0	0	0	0	0
NAR1	NA201	83593	0	2	24392	17	8	25603
NAM0	NA300	6565	0	0	5159	1	4	6541
NAM1	NA301	194	0	0	194	194	1	194
NAB1	NA311	153845	0	0	5355	40	12	5496
NAIO	NA320	2409	0	0	804	804	2	804
NAA0	NA330	1868	467	0	467	467	2	0
NAU0	NA340	4107	328	0	677	0	2	563
NAC0	NA345	6100	116	0	380	397	2	281
NAB2	NA350	482	0	0	43	43	1	43
STI1	ST310	1172	0	0	394	394	2	394
STI2	ST320	9	0	0	3	3	1	3
STI3	ST330	7608	0	0	349	349	2	349
STI6	ST335	0	0	0	0	0	0	0
STI4	ST340	25903	763	0	4346	4401	3	3638
STA1	ST350	10873	837	0	1746	1746	3	908
STI5	ST360	18494	104	0	2079	2091	3	1987
STA3	ST365	227	0	0	51	51	1	51
STI7	ST370	19209	799	0	2274	2291	4	1492
STI8	ST380	849	0	0	168	168	2	168
STI9	ST390	4403	1082	0	1108	1108	4	26
ICS1	IS548	28026	0	0	3691	0	3	3937
ICS2	IS551	537	0	0	53	53	1	53
AMG1	MG001	5610	0	0	1411	1411	2	1411
UMG1	MG003	38217	0	0	9532	9555	4	9555
AMG3	MG005	2681	0	0	383	383	2	383
PMG1	MG020	7908	0	0	1939	1977	2	1977
PCS1	IS402100	1813	0	0	239	259	2	259
BEM1	IS521	0	0	0	0	0	0	0
MEM1	IS522	530	0	0	266	266	2	266
MCS3	IS540A	27872	0	0	3971	23	4	3994
BCS1	IS549	2004	0	0	278	278	1	278
HCS1	IS550	14723	0	0	2386	2390	2	2390
BCS2	IS553	19927	0	0	2835	2835	3	2835
TU01	TU001	283	0	0	41	41	1	41
ECO1	EC100	8289	1316	1	2431	2432	3	1115
ECQ1	EC310	174	0	0	36	36	1	36
ECB1	EC320	127	0	0	22	22	1	22
EPI1	KP210	83	0	0	32	32	1	32
EPU1	KP220	665	74	0	207	207	1	133
EPA1	KP230	378	61	0	63	63	1	2
DSI1	DS200	139213	0	0	79	79	2	79

```
DSNC020I   THE DISPLAY COMMAND IS COMPLETE
```

Figure 6-3b Sample DB/2 DISPLAY STATISTICS command and resulting output.

tions would prefer to avoid these failures and "handle" the condition instead. At the current time, no HANDLE CONDITION exists via standard programming interfaces to avoid the ABEND. Other techniques can be used, however.

The recommended method for avoiding AEY9 ABENDs would be to code a routine to "extract" the status from the DB/2 module built during the attachment process. This module is DSNCEXT1 and can be interrogated via

```
EXEC CICS EXTRACT EXIT
PROGRAM ('DSNCEXT1')
ENTRYNAME ('DSNCSQL')
....
IF OK, the connection is up
Else send a message ... 'DB/2 Not Available'
```

Perhaps future releases of the subsystems will provide a more straightforward method.

6.3 DB/2 Deadlocks in CICS

In some cases, CICS applications will attempt to access DB/2 resources, and a deadlock condition will result. This can happen in native VSAM as well as databases, but additional conditions may need to be handled by the program (see Section 3.3.3).

6.3.1 CICS FORCEPURGE Results

If the deadlock cannot be resolved by the application and prior to the DB/2 timeout value, the transaction can be terminated with the FORCEPURGE option. Since this command is initiated by CICS, and not by DB/2, this is mainly a CICS issue. The problem arises in the integrity of the database being accessed.

The CICS command CEMT FORCE PURGE causes the currently executing transaction to be flagged for removal from the CICS active chain and deleted from the system. If the task was actively executing an SQL request, it has been placed in a CICS WAIT during the I/O (or wait for I/O). Until it can be dispatched, it cannot be purged, since the task purge logic is found within KCP (task control program). In other words, CICS cannot terminate something until it is running. As soon as the SQL request completes or the timeout value is reached, CICS will regain control and can purge the task if requested.

Of course, if the task completes abnormally, DB/2 will be notified and will roll back all updates within the LUW (logical unit of work).

6.3.2 Deadlocks in CICS with DB/2 and IMS

Some CICS applications access both DB/2 and IMS data (DL/I). It is possible to create deadlocks across database managers. For example, one task can lock a DB/2 resource and wait for the lock on a DL/I resource. Another task could have the lock on the DL/I resource and be waiting for the lock on the DB/2 resource. Of course, this is unlikely, but not impossible. Since both products use the IRLM, the deadlock detection is similar. In most cases, however, the two subsystems use different IRLMs (the recommended technique). A DB/2 IRLM can tell the difference between a timeout and a deadlock within two tasks competing for DB/2 resources. Two IRLMs cannot correlate information between DB/2 locks and IMS locks.

In this example, the lock managers will not detect and manage the deadlocks; timeouts will administer control over the problem. The IRLMWAIT parameter can be used to purge the deadlock. In addition, the CICS DTIMEOUT parameter can be used to detect inactivity and force the task to terminate if the task is suspended. In CICS/ESA V3, the DTIMEOUT parameter for the transaction can be used to force termination of either suspended or active tasks. This could be valuable for CICS applications that want to terminate in less time than the IRLMWAIT value. Since most CICS-DB/2 tasks remain on the active chain during thread use, DTIMEOUT has little value in CICS/MVS 2.1.1.

6.3.3 -911 Return Code Processing

If DB/2 detects either a deadlock or a timeout, a return code of -911 is passed back to the application. The program then has the ability to test for these values and "handle" the condition. Some alternatives would be to terminate the transaction "cleanly" with some appropriate message to the terminal or to retry the update from the last commit point following the -911.

If the application is experiencing excessive timeouts and the time required for the request is appropriate, the IRLMRWT value can be increased (from the default 60 seconds).

If the -911 is the result of a deadlock, DB/2 has chosen this transaction as the victim in the attempt to resolve the stalemate. When the application receives the return code, it must be designed to consider the ROLBI and ROLBE parameters in the RCT. These options choose whether to COMMIT or ROLLBACK the updates completed since the last COMMIT. If ROLBE=YES was chosen, the application has no choice or control, and the ROLLBACK is performed. If the value is NO, the application can take control and make the decision to ROLLBACK or COMMIT. For this reason, the application should always check for the -911 return code and take appropriate action.

6.4 CICS Application Issues with DB/2

When a CICS application contains calls to DB/2, via the EXEC SQL command, additional steps need to be taken for database management functions. These steps are described in Figure 6-4 and illustrate the phases that must be added to program preparation for DB/2. While normal CICS programs must use the CICS translator and then language compiler, additional steps must be added for the DB/2 precompiler and BIND process.

After precompile, the DB/2 commands remain within the CICS program and are linked with the SQL language interface stub, DSNCLI. Output from the precompiler also produces a DBRM (database resource module), which is then input to the DB/2 BIND. This "binding" procedure creates a DB/2 PLAN. The PLAN is allocated to the DB/2 thread as explained in the previous section. The connection, therefore, can be made between the program and the DB/2 resources requested, and data can flow between the two subsystems.

6.4.1 Syncronization of the Program and the PLAN

These two components *must* be available at execution time, and *must* be "in sync." If the program module (from the precompiler) and the PLAN (from the DBRM that was "bound") do not have synchronous date/time stamps, an error condition is raised and execution terminates. DB/2 makes every attempt to ensure proper coordination between these two components. Installations must establish standard procedures for this link-edit=BIND process to guarantee synchronization.

If an application experiences this problem, a return code of -811 will result. The program can then take any action required to notify the user or display an appropriate message. Before successful execution can take place, the two components will require action to "resync."

The timestamp is inserted into the program module and the DBRM by the DB/2 precompiler. If no SQL statements are added,

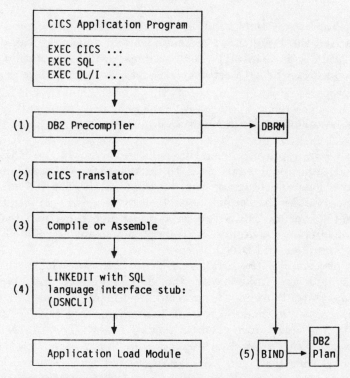

Figure 6-4 CICS/DB2 application program preparation.

changed, or inserted into the source program when other changes are made, the precompiler need not be invoked. Program changes can be made to the precompiler-generated output, which already has the matching timestamp with the previously bound PLAN. This technique can be used to avoid unnecessary BINDs and excessive activity to the DB/2 Catalog and Directory. The only time a re-BIND should be necessary is when changes are made to SQL-affected resources, requiring the precompile and two resulting output files (program source and DBRM).

6.4.2 CICS-DB/2 Trace Entries

Since CICS programs with DB/2 calls contain additional commands, the trace entries produced will (as expected) contain additional entries to display a trail of these commands. What programmers may *not* expect, however, is the method DB/2 uses during this trace process.

Remember that DB/2 is an external database manager, and that the data and the DB/2 code are "outside" the CICS address space. A call for DB/2 resources will establish a thread and connect the two subsystems together. The thread allows the data to pass to CICS, but all processing of the database will be performed by DB/2, not by CICS. The trace records, therefore, document this "external" resource manager request. DB/2 was written to use the TRUE (Task Related User Exit) facilites and operate as an external resource manager. The trace records, therefore, substantiate this process.

Figure 6-5 contains a sample trace entry from a CICS program call to DB/2. Notice the first trace entry created by the EXEC SQL (1). This trace entry is a type E7, which CICS documents as a type DFHERM, from the task-related user exit interface. The two other critical entries for these trace record types are:

Field A	**Field B**
First 4 characters	Bytes 12–14
of resource	next 3 characters
manager name	of the name
	Byte 15
	X'00' — Entry to RM
	X'0F' — Exit to RM
	X'F0' — Return from RM
	X'FF' — Exit from DFHERM
	. . .

As indicated in the first trace entry, the resource manager's name is "DSNCSQL" (2), and the application is entering (X"00"). A few trace records further, the next E7 can be found (3) "Passing control to RM." At this point, control is delivered to DB/2, and the application remains "active," yet in a wait for return from DB/2.

Also associated with the DB/2 Attach is a C0 entry trace record (4) from the resource manager. The format for these records is:

Field A	**Bytes 8–10**
	X'00' — UR not in doubt
	X'01' — Request made by SQL call
	X'02' — PREPARE
	X'03' — COMMIT2
	X'04' — ABORT
	X'05' — DB/2 command
	X'08' — UR cannot be resolved
	X'80' — The last CALL was the first request to fail
	...

CUSTOMER INFORMATION CONTROL SYSTEM - TRACE UTILITY PROGRAM   PAGE 9

TIME OF DAY	ID	REG 14	REQD	TASK	FIELD A	FIELD B	CHARS	RESOURCE	TRACE TYPE	INTERVAL
15:14:08.117184	FA	4074856A	0005	02320	00000000	00000000	....		BMS RETN	00.00003
15:14:08.117184	F1	807C46EE	4004	02320	01081EB4	01081EB4	....		SCP FREEMAIN	00.00003
15:14:08.117216	C9	50777810	00F4	02320	00044BE0	85000028	....		SCP RELEASED TERMINAL STORAGE	00.00003
15:14:08.117216	E1	800DD2A6	00F4	02320	00044BE0	00001802	....		EIP RECEIVE-MAP RESPONSE	00.00000
15:14:08.140416	C3	70527A74	0002	02320	000B8434	E4E2F0F4	....US04	....	USER 195	*00.02320
15:14:08.140448	E7	800DD2A6	0004	02320	00000306	E2D8D304	DSNCSQL.	②	ERM ENTRY	00.00003
15:14:08.140480	F1	807C46EE	CC04	02320	000D0690	01081EB4	....		SCP GETMAIN INITIMG	00.00003
15:14:08.140512	C8	50777810	8904	02320	000D0078	8C000318	...O....		SCP ACQUIRED USER STORAGE	00.00003
15:14:08.140544	C8	807B83CE	0004	02320	000AAF30	89000088	....		SCP GETMAIN	00.00006
15:14:08.140640	E7	800DD2A6	CC04	02320	C4E2D5C3	E2D8D300	DSNCSQL		SCP ACQUIRED RSA STORAGE	00.00003
15:14:08.140640	F1	800DD2A6	0004	02320	000AAF30	01081EB4	....		ERM PASSING CONTROL TO RM	00.00003
15:14:08.140672	C8	507777D4	CC04	02320	00000134	01081EB4	....		SCP GETMAIN INITIMG	00.00003
15:14:08.140704	E1	504996B8	0004	02320	000DAAD0	C000148	....		SCP ACQUIRED USER STORAGE	00.00003
15:14:08.140704	F1	007C46EE	0004	02320	000000B6	01081EB4	....		EIP HANDLE-CONDITION ENTRY	00.00003
15:14:08.140736	C8	507777D4	CC04	02320	000D9B0	8C0000C8	.R......		SCP GETMAIN INITIMG	00.00003
15:14:08.140736	E1	504996DE	0004	02320	000DAAE0	8C0000C8	.R...H		SCP ACQUIRED USER STORAGE	00.00003
15:14:08.140768	E1	504996B8	00F4	02320	00000208	00000208	....		EIP HANDLE-CONDITION RESPONSE	00.00003
15:14:08.140800	E1	504996DE	0004	02320	00000000	00000208	....		EIP ASSIGN ENTRY	00.00003
15:14:08.140800	E1	504996DE	00F4	02320	00000000	00000208	....		EIP ASSIGN RESPONSE	00.00003
15:14:08.140832	E1	50499DAC	0004	02320	00000000	00000208	....		EIP ASSIGN ENTRY	00.00003
15:14:08.140864	E1	504996DE	00F4	02320	00000000	00001202	....		EIP ASSIGN RESPONSE	00.00003
15:14:08.140928	E1	50499762	0004	02320	00000000	00001202	....		EIP WAIT-EVENT ENTRY	00.00006
15:14:08.141344	D0	007C2F78	0504	02320	80000000	00001A04	.R.		KCP WAIT DCI=SINGLE	00.00041
15:14:08.148352	F0	50499DAC	4004	02320	01000006	00000000		BR330	KCP DISPATCH	00.00700
15:14:08.148384	E1	50499DAC	00F4	02320	000DAAE0	00001A04	....		EIP WAIT-EVENT RESPONSE	00.00003
15:14:08.148416	E1	50499DAC	0004	02320	000DAAE0	00001A04	....		EIP ENTER ENTRY	00.00001
15:14:08.148448	C0	5049A004	0002	02320	01000006	00001A04		BR330	USER 192	00.00003
15:14:08.148448	E1	5049A004	00F4	02320	000DAAD0	000D01A04	....		EIP ENTER RESPONSE	00.00003
15:14:08.148480	F1	807C3D62	4004	02320	000DAAD0	01081EB4	....		SCP FREEMAIN	00.00003
15:14:08.148512	C9	50777810	0004	02320	000DAAD0	8C000148	....		SCP RELEASED USER STORAGE	00.00003
15:14:08.148512	E7	50148576	4004	02320	C4E2D5C3	E2DBD3F0	DSNCSQL0		ERM REGAINING CONTROL FROM RM	00.00006
15:14:08.148576	F1	5077B558	0004	02320	000AAF30	01081EB4	....		SCP FREEMAIN	00.00003
15:14:08.148576	C9	50777810	4004	02320	000DD9B0	89000088	....		SCP RELEASED RSA STORAGE	00.00003
15:14:08.148608	F1	807C46EE	0004	02320	01081EB4	01081EB4	....		SCP RELEASED USER STORAGE	00.00003
15:14:08.148640	E7	800DD2A6	4004	02320	C4E2D5C3	8C0000C8	.R..H		ERM RESPONSE	00.00096
15:14:08.148672	C3	70527A74	0002	02320	000B48E8	E4E2F0F4	....US04	....	USER 195	00.00003
15:14:08.149632	E7	800DD2A6	0004	02320	000AAF30	E2DBD300	DSNCSQL.	⑥	ERM ENTRY	00.00003
15:14:08.149664	F1	807B83CE	8904	02320	000D0078	01081EB4	....		SCP GETMAIN	00.00003
15:14:08.149696	C8	800DDA76	0004	02320	000D0134	89000088	....		SCP ACQUIRED RSA STORAGE	00.00003
15:14:08.149728	E7	800DDA76	CC04	02320	C4E2D5C3	E2DBD300	DSNCSQL.		ERM PASSING CONTROL TO RM	00.00003
15:14:08.149760	C8	507C3CAE	0004	02320	00000134	01081EB4	....		SCP GETMAIN INITIMG	00.00003
15:14:08.149760	E7	50499DAC	0004	02320	000DAAE0	8C000148	....		SCP ACQUIRED USER STORAGE	00.00006
15:14:08.149792	C8	50499DAC	00F4	02320	000DAAE0	00001202	....		EIP WAIT-EVENT ENTRY	00.00003
15:14:08.149856	F0	007C2F78	0504	02320	00000000	00000938	.R.		KCP WAIT DCI=SINGLE	00.00064
15:14:08.151904	D0	507C2CD6	00F4	02320	000DD938	00001202		BR330	KCP DISPATCH	00.02048
15:14:08.151968	E1	50499DAC	0004	02320	000DAAE0	00001A04	....		EIP WAIT-EVENT RESPONSE	00.00064
15:14:08.152000	C0	5049A004	0002	02320	01010006	00001A04		BR330	USER 192	00.00032
15:14:08.152032	C0	5049A004	0002	02320	00000000	00001A04			EIP ENTER ENTRY	00.00033
15:14:08.152064	E1	5049A004	00F4	02320	00000000	00001A04			EIP ENTER RESPONSE	00.00000

Figure 6-5   CICS trace with DB/2 CALL.

Byte 11
X'01' — Last call for this transaction
X'02' — Request overflowed to pool thread
X'04' — Trans. connected to a terminal
X'08' — Message is from a subtask
X'10' — Last UR for RESYNC processing

As noted in this C0 trace record, bytes 8–10 contain x"01000006" and indicate that this was an SQL call (no obvious problems), the task is connected to a terminal, and the request overflowed to a pool thread. Any potential problem would be recorded in this field and in Field B. Although in this example Field B is zeros, a request that could not be processed would record a reason code from the request in this field. For example, if the request failed, and Field B contained x"00F30040," the programmer could assume that the plan requested was unavailable.

When DB/2 has completed the request and "taps" CICS with the results, another E7 trace entry can be found (5). DB/2 is returning control, as indicated via "Regaining control from RM," followed by the final trace record (6) "ERM Response" with an X"FF" in byte 15 of Field B. This would indicate a final exit from the resource manager and full control back in CICS.

Since all database processing is accomplished in the DB/2 address space, the trace merely records the transfer of control and return. Any problems are returned by the resource manager as a return code (a negative number) that must be handled by the program. Of course, DB/2 records trace entries within its own subsystem. Any analysis of database problems must be done with the DB/2 trace. More information concerning DB/2 trace can be found in Section 6.5.

6.4.3 CICS-DB/2 Recovery — The Two-Phase Commit

The two subsystems (CICS and DB/2) participate in a type of recovery called a two-phase commit. This coordinated recovery allows true integrity of data, even though it is managed in one address space (DB/2) and processed in another (CICS). Both subsystems record necessary data in their own logs, and communicate any abnormal conditions to the other.

The coordination of commit begins from the moment the two systems begin communicating. The CICS Attach Facility initiates the connection to DB/2 and obtains information from DB/2 of any "indoubt" (incomplete) units of recovery from the DB/2 log. CICS then determines from its own log if any transactions terminated abnormally and how the in-doubt DB/2 units of recovery (UR) should be resolved.

The two-phase process, in normal execution of a CICS task, occurs as follows:

Phase 1 — each subsystem attempts to complete the request successfully and record sufficient recovery information in its own respective log to COMMIT the update. If successful, the two systems communicate a positive reply.

Phase 2 — since each subsystem received a positive indication, data is actually changed, or updated. If either subsystem should terminate during the update, both logs contain adequate information for recovery during restart of the subsystem.

In any "coordinated" process, one entity must be dominant and, therefore, initiate the operation. CICS performs the initial request for the attach and is also the "coordinator" of all SYNCPOINT/ROLLBACK processing. CICS tasks, therefore, are responsible for originating SYNCPOINT requests.

In any recovery scenario, although CICS has originated the request, *both* parties must participate for full implementation. If either DB/2 or CICS fails, and *both* logs are not available, recovery is not possible. Requests may remain "in doubt," even after both subsystems are reinstated. If the CICS log becomes unusable or a COLD start rebuilds the log before attach to DB/2, the two phases are not possible. CICS systems that attach to DB/2 should ALWAYS use START=AUTO to ensure recovery.

6.4.4 CICS SYNCPOINTing

A CICS SYNCPOINT can originate via the following techniques:

Implicitly — at task termination when the program RETURNs control to CICS. An LUW (logical unit of work) or UR (unit of recovery) cannot, therefore, extend beyond a single transaction.

Explicity — when the EXEC CICS SYNCPOINT command is issued by the program prior to task termination.

Either occurrence of SYNCPOINT will initiate the first phase of two-phase commit processing.

6.4.4.1 Effects of SYNCPOINT on DB/2 CURSOR Position   When either type of SYNCPOINT is detected (implicit or explicit), the DB/2 CURSOR will be closed, since all open CURSORs are automatically closed at the termination of a UR.

When a CURSOR is opened by an application, it is positioned before the first row of the table. The SELECT statement within the DECLARE CURSOR statement identifies the rows requested by the program, but does not actually retrieve the data. Data must be FETCHed by the program for processing.

If (before FETCH) the CURSOR is closed, the current position within the table is lost. The position of the CURSOR can be saved and restored, but this process must be overtly taken BEFORE the COMMIT is detected. More complete information on retention of CURSOR position can be found in SC26-4376, DB/2 SQL User's Guide. The section "A Unit of Recovery and Open Cursors" details the required process.

6.4.4.2 Reasons to Explicitly SYNCPOINT   As previously stated, SYNC-POINTS are implicitly issued at task termination. In some cases, programs may wish to mandate a COMMIT of resources via the explicit SYNCPOINT command. The issues involved in the decision are primarily resources consumed vs. concurrency. DB/2 will release all locks and allow these resources to be available to other applications when committed. The two-phase COMMIT, however, uses CPU cycles to perform the requested work.

The decision by the programmer to explicitly SYNCPOINT, therefore, should be made with the awareness of resource consumption. In some cases, however, it would be genuinely appropriate to use explicit SYNCPOINTs.

Is concurrency required? If the resources are highly active and need to be released as soon as possible for multiple concurrent requests, then explicit SYNCPOINTs will facilitate the process.

Is the resource being accessed with SELECT only? If no UPDATE, DELETE, or INSERTs are being used, the locks are "shared" with other concurrent SELECT requests. If excessive nonshared requests must be performed within the application, use of SYNCPOINTs may be necessary.

Is the interval of the UR (unit of recovery) extended? If the duration of access within DB/2 is extensive or numerous accesses of DB/2 resources are necessary before task termination, SYNCPOINTs may be used to release these resources.

Is the application using the Dynamic Plan Exit? A SYNCPOINT must be done prior to the next SQL statement to properly destroy the thread and drive the exit for new thread creation with the new PLAN.

6.4.5 CICS LINK and XCTL Issues with DB/2

Many CICS customers use standard I/O routines to structure their applications. These routines contain support for all transfer of data from any application and, therefore, do not have to be rewritten by each program. While this technique avoids redundancy of coding, it requires additional attention if DB/2 is used.

The CICS-DB/2 Attach Facility is limited by the architecture of CICS task control. All CICS tasks are transaction-based, not program based. Note that DFHEIB, the interface block for all programs, contains task information, but no program identification. The TRANSID is the key to all CICS work. This becomes a factor in design of DB/2 applications within CICS.

If a CICS transaction LINKs or XCTLs to a routine that uses SQL, the program name changes but not the TRANSID. Since the task is not terminated, neither is the thread or the plan. All DBRMs must be bound into a single plan, since the transaction that originates the LINK requires the DBRM of the target routine. This approach can produce a *very* large plan, since it must contain all DBRMs. Prior to DB/2 Version 2, many customers chose to avoid LINK and XCTL, redesigning the program to initiate a new transaction instead.

In DB/2 Version 2 (any release), IBM introduced a new facility, "Dynamic Plan Selection." This facility is actually an exit that can be used by the installation to avoid the LINK and XCTL problem. Dynamic Plan Selection allows the application to change the plan within the same transaction, allowing DB/2 to select the correct plan. A more complete description of the facility follows in the next section.

Without dynamic plans, a program issuing XCTL or LINK may receive the SQL return code:

-805 (Program Name Not Found in PLAN)

The PLAN for the sending transaction does not contain the DBRM for the receiving transaction.

This problem does not apply to programs that use START or RE-TURN (transid). These commands can change the PLAN since they actually terminate the current task and begin a new transaction to CICS.

6.4.6 DSNCLI — the CICS Attach Interface Module

While all CICS COBOL programs are link-edited with DFHECI (the command level language interface module), CICS-DB/2 applications must also be linked with DSNCLI, the CICS Attach Interface Module. In fact, CICS requires that the CICS command module (DFHECI) be ordered as the first control section (CSECT) in the target load module.

In addition, while linking these required modules into the load module, care must be taken to ensure the correct CSECT is included for the correct environment. If the installation is using both DB/2 and IMS, common modules exist in the interfaces, and the concatenation of libraries is critical. If both subsystems exist, the installation contains both an IMSRESLIB for IMS support and DSNLOAD for DB/2 support. Problems arise when applications are link-edited and the proper language interface modules must be included in the resulting load modules.

DSNHLI is an entry point to the TSO attach (DSNELI), the IMS/VS attach (DFSLI000), and the CICS attach (DSNCLI) code. While the attach language interface for CICS and TSO are provided by DB/2, the IMS attach language interface is provided by IMS. Application programs that execute in a mutual IMS-DB/2 environment must be link-edited with the IMS language interface module (DFSLI000). It can then access one DB/2 subsystem, in addition to DL/I resources from CICS. DB/2 application programs that issue SQL calls use this common interface module (DSNHLI) regardless of which environment or attachment facility used. When the DB/2 pre-compiler converts the SQL statements into source, the CALLs convert to

CALL 'DSNHLI' USING

with external references that are resolved at link-edit time. For this reason, at link time, all program INCLUDEs must utilize the proper interface module for the environment in which the application will execute.

The SYSLIB concatenation will resolve these "included" interface modules and is critical in a combination IMS-DB/2 environment. The sequence of these libraries (IMSRESLIB and DSNLOAD) will determine which environment is allowed during execution. If the application will request DB/2 resources, the DSNLOAD library must precede IMSRESLIB. If a DB/2 program is linked with the incorrect attach interface module, the program will ABEND at execution.

6.4.7 Dynamic Plan Selection Exit

When DB/2 Version 2 Release 1 was announced, it contained a new facility called Dynamic Plan Selection. Any CICS transaction could now dynamically select any DB/2 plan at execution time. Prior to Version 2, RCT plans were associated with specific transactions. A second plan could not be requested within the same transaction. In addition, the previously discussed problem with LINK and XCTL (Section 4.5) restricted many CICS applications. The new facility is provided as an exit, DSNCUEXT is shipped as a sample, and can be modified to fit any specific customer needs.

6.4.7.1 Implementation Steps and Utilization Installation of DSNCUEXT can be performed in three steps:

1. Use the sample DSNCUEXT or write a "tailored" one
2. Identify the program to CICS via RDO DEFINE PROGRAM
3. Update and reassemble the RCT with the new plan parameters

Additional information can be found in SC26-4376, DB/2 System and Database Administration Guide Appendix E. IBM has also created a Washington Systems Center FLASH #8950 to further document the process.

This exit is invoked and a plan is selected when the first SQL statement is detected within an LUW (Logical Unit of Work). Since a single transaction can contain multiple LUWs (and multiple programs), a single DB/2 plan seldom works for the entire transaction. The exit provides a facility to "break" a single transaction into multiple plans and, therefore, DBRMs.

The exit is driven by the CICS Attachment Facility, not by the CICS commands (LINK, XTCL, or even SYNCPOINT). When CICS detects (via the RCT parameters) that the exit is active, it executes additional logic AT EVERY INITIAL occurence of

EXEC SQL ....

for the LUW. The initial occurrence is driven by task initiation *or* the termination of the previous LUW via explicit SYNCPOINT by the program. For this reason, explicit SYNCPOINTing is mandated to terminate the LUW and destroy the existing thread.

Normally, an SQL statement will drive the CICS Attachment Facility to create (or reuse) a thread via the RCT entry for the TRANSID, PLAN=planname. If, however, no PLAN= parameter is coded, and PLNEXIT=YES with the PLNPGME= parameter is found instead, the exit program selected determines the name of the plan to associate with the new thread.

For this reason, use of the exit requires:

```
DSNCRCT TYPE=INIT,
     PLNPGMI=name of the default dynamic exit program
     TYPE=ENTRY or POOL,
     PLNEXIT=YES,
     PLNPGME=name of tailored exit program for this
     RCT entry if the default is not adequate
```

If no PLNPGME entry is coded in the RCT, the default is taken from the PLNPGMI entry of TYPE=INIT. In the default provided by IBM, the exit will use the DBRM of the first SQL statement as the default PLAN name selected. If the installation has designed a single correlation between the DBRM name (program name) and the PLAN name to execute, the default exit provided by IBM is adequate and can be used without modification. If the installation must correlate unique DBRMs with different PLANs, then the exit will require additional logic to accommodate this correlation.

The most important things to remember about this dynamic exit are:

- The exit is *not* driven by any CICS command: LINK, XCTL, RETURN, or SYNCPOINT. The exit will only be driven by the FIRST SQL statement in any new LUW.
- The PLAN name will be determined by the DBRM used by the SQL statement, default is DBRM name = PLAN name.
- The default for PLNEXIT is NO and must be changed to YES to drive the dynamic exit, and no PLAN=planname can be coded.
- The program *must* issue an explicit EXEC CICS SYNCPOINT prior to the exit to terminate the previous thread and the corresponding LUW. This would normally be done prior to the RETURN from the LINK or CALL. The work must therefore be committed prior to the new PLAN being executed.

Thread Allocation Implications   There are also thread implications with these dynamic plans. Since the plan name can change during a single transaction, the thread must be released and recreated for every invocation of the new plan. Only POOL and ENTRY type threads are allowed with Dynamic Plan Selection, and dedicated threads are not advised since they cannot be reused.

In addition, IBM advises that TYPE=ENTRY threads use the options:

THRDM=0,THRDA=0,
TWAIT=POOL

to avoid task queueing when a plan switch requires a new thread.

6.4.7.2 Performance Issues   As previously mentioned, Dynamic Plan Selection cannot reuse threads, since new plans will be required at every execution. Since the exit routine is driven at every initial EXEC SQL statement, the resource consumption could be excessive for applications that utilize the exit excessively. Any high-volume transactions may not be good candidates for this facility, since they would be penalized by the continual thread termination/creation process.

Installations must analyze their own specific needs to determine if this dynamic facility would be an advantage. The decision would be made based on performance vs. application development flexibility. In most cases, a good rule would be:

• Use Dynamic Plan Selection for low-volume applications that are XCTLed or LINKed to often. A good example would be a menu screen with one LUW (logical unit of work) that would select a specific plan based on operator selection.
• Do not use Dynamic Plan Selection for high-volume applications that require thread reuse for performance or applications that issue excessive explicit SYNCPOINTs.

6.4.8 DB/2 Data Exception ABENDS

Some CICS applications use SQL facilities that can produce data exceptions. One example would be a DB/2 SELECT statement with a WHERE option comparing a packed numeric decimal DB/2 field to a COBOL variable containing low values. DB/2 cannot detect that type of data exception (host variable does not belong to DB/2).

The problem not only produces a DB/2 DSNC ABEND, but it causes a SNAP dump of the CICS region. Depending on the type of dump options chosen in the SIT, this can produce a formatted dump in the CICS dump dataset or a complete unformatted region dump into a SYS1.DUMPxx dataset. This is not only unnecessary (especially for a mere data exception) but also resource-consuming, since CICS must process an entire SNAP dump of the address space.

The only way to avoid this problem is to use the XPCABND global user exit (the standard exit from CICS Program Control, DFHPCP). When the exit is invoked, these abends can be intercepted and the dump can be suppressed.

6.4.9 Pseudoconversational Browse Issues

As previously stated in the first chapter, most installations require, if not recommend, that all CICS applications be designed as pseudoconversational. This technique frees resources during the life of the task for other CICS processing.

CICS applications that access DB/2 databases require additional design considerations. Some of the problems that arise may be:

- Cursor Positioning
  EXEC CICS RETURN TRANSID(xxxx) closes all cursors
  Position is lost and must be manually maintained
- Browse Operations
  SQL SELECT does not retrieve the records
  FETCH is required to produce data and:
  . . . cannot scroll backward
  . . . can only produce one row at a time
- Thread Allocation Overhead
  Each new task requires another thread
  (unless the thread is protected)

These are only a few of the issues that must be considered during design. Many programmers use a combination of techniques to circumvent these problems, including saving cursor position, data contents, and many other pieces of data between executions. While the COMMAREA is used very frequently for pseudoconversational programming, it may be inadequate for many applications.

Programmers should remember that other CICS storage is available when needed, especially CICS Temporary Storage. TS MAIN provides an easy-to-use storage area for small amounts of data that require high performance. TS AUX provides a large area to store data between task executions for subsequent retrieval. Some programmers FETCH large numbers of rows, write them into TS AUX, and then scroll temporary storage. Additional problems of concurrency could arise, however, since updates can be made to the data after being written to temporary storage.

Programmers must weigh performance, concurrency, and availability issues and then choose the optimal technique.

6.5 Recording DB/2 Activity in CICS

As discussed in Section 4.2, any CICS applications that contain SQL calls record trace entries in both the CICS and DB/2 traces. These traces are primarily used for debugging any application problems within the two subsystems.

The two subsystems also record activity in "system" journals that can be used for both accounting and performance monitoring. Installations have been using CICS CMF (monitoring facility) records for many years, since they contain data for both charging systems and performance. With DB/2, additional records need to be used to thoroughly account for all CICS activity.

6.5.1 Using CMF and SMF Records for CPU Utilization

When CICS detects the SQL call, it transfers control to the DB/2 subsystem for processing. The DB/2 subsystem records this activity in SMF (MVS System Management Facility) as type 101 records. These records, therefore, must be used in addition to the CMF records for complete accounting of the application.

The CICS CMF records contain the CPU utilization for the CICS ASCB (address space control block) and the CICS main task. The ASCB CPU time would include utilization by the CICS main task plus all subtasks. Subtask activity would include DB/2 threads; VSAM subtasks; and OPEN/CLOSE for journals, DL/I, and VSAM files. The CPU time for the CICS main task does not include any subtask activity and would be used for CPU time directly attributed to each transaction.

The CPU time recorded in the DB/2 records does not contain any CICS CPU time, merely "in DB/2" thread CPU time. To calculate the total CPU time for a CICS application with SQL calls:

CMF records: USRCPUT (CPU use for CICS main task)
SMF records: QWACEJST — QWACBST (DB/2 Thread CPU use)

6.5.2 Correlating CMF and SMF Records

Since data is recorded in two locations, they must be coordinated to produce one "logical" view of any CICS task. Unfortunately, there is no supported technique to correlate the CICS CMF performance records with the DB/2 SMF accounting records. Two reasons why this is not only difficult but impossible are:

1. There are no fields in the DB/2 accounting records that can be used to match the corresponding CICS CMF records. While the SMF records contain the transaction name, there is no field for the unique task number, which would differentiate one record from another.
2. There is no one-to-one relationship between single records in the two facilites (CMF and SMF). Since DB/2 does not create an SMF type 101 record if the thread is reused, a single record can correspond to one CICS task or multiple CICS tasks. With Dynamic Plan Selection, multiple plans (and, therefore, threads) are used, and many SMF 101 records can be produced by a single CICS transaction.

IBM recommends that installations use the DB/2 signon exit routine (DSN3SSGN) to add the CICS task number into the SMF records. With this field, multiple CMF and/or SMF records could be correlated into one group. Additional information can be found in GG24-3202, CICS/DB2 Interface Guide, for methods of linking the two record types.

6.5.3 Using SMF Records for CICS-DB/2 Performance

When using SMF type 101 records to analyze performance of a CICS program with SQL calls, remember that elapsed time for the DB/2 processing *does not* include the time consumed in the creation or termination of the thread. The time value includes the interval:

• When DB/2 begins to execute the first SQL instruction
• Until the point directly preceding thread termination or reuse

DB/2 records two classes of SMF type 101 records. These two types contain elapsed times for the application (Class 1) and for the DB/2 "system" (Class 2). Again, neither of these records contains time consumed in thread creation/termination. While the elapsed time of the

Class 1 records corresponds to the life of a thread within the application, Class 2 records are more accurate, since they more correctly correspond to the life of the transaction "in DB/2." Both, however, underestimate the elapsed time of any application, since they do not include time spent between any SYNCPOINT and the creation of new threads.

In summary, the CICS-DB/2 Attach Facility has provided a supported and easily used transaction processor for DB/2 databases. The facility will, no doubt, continue to evolve and be enhanced by IBM as the command-interface to DB/2.

7

Storage Control

7.1 Application Program Storage

CICS applications have many options available for control over storage required to complete a task. Programs can request storage to be used during the life of the transaction. Of course, in CICS, when the task terminates, all storage related to that task is released, since the base control block (the TCA Task Control Area) is deleted. If a task wishes to retain any of those storage areas or perhaps pass them to another task which may initiate and require the same data, the storage must be placed into an area that can be managed by CICS and made available to a subsequent task.

Several techniques are available to manage storage, both within and across transactions within a CICS system. This section will attempt to cover many of these techniques and the issues that are raised when utilizing CICS task storage or storage that is created by, and therefore associated with, an application.

7.1.1 GETMAIN/FREEMAIN

The GETMAIN/FREEMAIN commands in CICS applications are used to provide temporary work areas for the task that are not normally provided by CICS (such as COMMAREA, EIB, etc.). This storage is released by the application (FREEMAIN) or by CICS automatically when the task terminates (normally or abnormally).

CICS treats this storage like other task storage, in that the storage area is "chained" to the task and, therefore, managed as storage related to a specific task. A complete explanation of the characteristics of task storage will be included in a following section. In CICS macro-level programming, this technique was very common to produce a type of reentrancy for the program. CICS command-level facilities provide this feature automatically and also provide many "supported" and managed storage areas for the application to use. For these reasons, GETMAIN and FREEMAIN functions are now used much more rarely. In addition, management of storage by the application can be very dangerous and produce storage corruption, also called storage violations. A complete section is dedicated to these problems and ways to avoid them.

Programmers who use GETMAIN/FREEMAIN should be aware of the issues dealing with the storage request to ensure that the facility is used efficiently and wisely.

Actual Storage Allocated   Whatever the request, CICS will allocate all storage requested with GETMAIN in a double word (16 bytes). In addition, since CICS must "chain" the storage from the task's anchor (TCA), 8 bytes in the front and back of the storage must be used for the SAA (storage accounting area). These SAAs are CICS's way of tying the storage together within the application's storage.

In other words, CICS takes the GETMAIN, adds 16 bytes (2 SAAs), and then rounds the request to the next double word boundary (a multiple of 16 bytes). CICS requires this additional storage to place the control information necessary for storage management. The customer would see a block of user storage (type X"8C") in task storage as a result of this request.

Shared Option   In CICS macro-level programming, an option existed for GETMAIN to allow the "shared" option. Since CICS/MVS 2.1 is the last version of CICS to support macro-level, this function would require a comparable facility in command-level for compatibility. IBM has released an APAR, PL39566 (for CICS/MVS 2.1), to provide this facility via commands. With these APARs, storage is allocated from the Shared subpool when requested via the GETMAIN command. This enables task-to-task common storage which is *not* released at the end of the first task (and, therefore, "shared" between tasks). Since this storage is not automatically freed, it must be FREEMAINed by the program to release the resources.

Storage Initialization and Release   In some instances, storage needs to be initialized by a new task or cleared by the previous task to ensure that no residual values are left and therefore available to the new task. A global user exit, XSCREQ, is available, which is invoked at every entry to CICS storage control program (SCP). This exit could be used by the customer to clear any storage areas of residual data. Of course, in every instance, releasing of storage by the application must be done with extreme care to avoid corruption.

While the GETMAIN command is used with the SET(ptf-ref) option, the FREEMAIN command contains no such option and, if used, will result in a translation error. The FREEMAIN command (and subsequent release of storage) must be used with the DATA option of the command to specify the address of the storage to be freed. While the CICS APRM (Application Programmer's Reference Manual) provides the syntax of FREEMAIN, it does not provide an example of the technique to use.

Programmers could use either a DATA area previously defined in the linkage section to specify in the GETMAIN SET and subsequent FREEMAIN DATA(data-area) within the COBOL program or a register previously defined and then utilized in the Assembler program as FREEMAIN DATA (0(Rx)).

Since more applications are using storage areas provided and managed by CICS, the use of GETMAIN and FREEMAIN will continue to diminish in COBOL programs.

7.1.2 COMMAREA

The communications area (COMMAREA) is available only to command-level programs and can transfer data between two programs within the same transaction or two transactions from the same terminal. In the second case, the technique is called "pseudoconversational" programming and will be covered more fully in the programming section.

The COMMAREA can be used when the program issues a LINK or an XCTL, but the results are slightly different. Use of the COMM-AREA by CICS programs is very prevalent and is generally the preferred technique for communication of data from one program to another. It is also the fully supported and advised method of data transfer within applications. The length of the area passed can be found in the EIB, from field EIBCALEN. Other than the length, the content, size and format are nonstandard and, therefore, not specifically defined in any supported location.

Issues dealing with COMMAREA utilization normally center on differences between passing data within the same transaction and across multiple transactions.

COMMAREA within a Transaction Data can be transferred between two programs within the same transaction via the COMMAREA facility. The data passed may have been defined within the Working-Storage section of the program or any other area to which the program has access. Control can be transferred (and data passed) to another program by either a LINK or an XCTL (transfer control). These two techniques are covered more completely in the programming section of this book; however, the COMMAREA is handled differently for the two commands.

While the XCTL is more efficient programmatically (CICS does not have to worry about RETURNing to the original program), use of a COMMAREA can dilute the efficiency. With XCTL, CICS copies the area passed into temporary storage first before transferring the data. This is necessary since the transferring program (and its control blocks) is no longer available after the transfer and the "link" is gone. While the write and subsequent read to temporary storage (MAIN) may be small, it produces I/O requirements during the XCTL and subsequent overhead.

Use of a COMMAREA with the LINK does not produce any requirements of temporary storage and is, therefore, a more efficient way to pass data. Of course, the LINK itself is more overhead than the XCTL, so performance may need to be considered.

Different Size COMMAREAs In some situations, data may be passed via a LINK or XCTL with a COMMAREA more than a single time. For example, a program(1) may LINK to another program(2), which XCTLs to another program(3). If the COMMAREA has been passed each time, then program(3) has been passed addressability to the COMMAREA originally created by program(1). If the COMMAREA created by program(1) is not the same size as received by program(3), CICS tests both the address and the length. If either is different, another COMMAREA is acquired by CICS and the old one is deleted, along with any changes made along the way. For this reason, care needs to be taken to ensure that the COMMAREAs passed have the same address and length so that any changes made during the transfer are still available when control is returned to the original program.

COMMAREA Between Transactions This utilization of COMMAREA is designed to pass data between multiple transactions in a pseudoconversational environment. CICS transactions are normally designed for efficiency, both in program cycles and storage. Use of pseudoconversational programming provides optimum utilization of all resources and is normally accomplished via the RETURN of the task to CICS, with a COMMAREA that retains adequate data to reinitiate the execution environment. The COMMAREA (and its related storage) is then released as soon as the new task begins.

This use of COMMAREA can be efficient, yet must be used properly. Since CICS must manage the COMMAREA storage (the program has RETURNed control to CICS and terminated), this storage is in CICS's subpools and, therefore, takes resources from within the DSA (see CICS/MVS 2.1.1 enhancement information below). In addition, CICS must retain this storage for the length of time necessary to initiate the next transaction (TRANID). Until the next task is started from that specific terminal, CICS cannot transfer (and delete) the data.

In addition, CICS/MVS 2.1.1 contains an enhancement to move the COMMAREA of a RETURN TRANID above the 16-Mb line. If the receiving program is running in AMODE 31 (such as COBOL II), only the address will need to be passed. If the receiving program is AMODE 24 (below the 16MB line), CICS will copy the COMMAREA to main storage and update the calling program's COMMAREA upon RETURNing to the program.

Upon initiation of the next transaction (TRANID), the COMMAREA saved by CICS from the previous task is made available to the new task via the DFHCOMMAREA. While many programmers use the Working-Storage section of their program to define COMMAREA, other techniques can be used. In the program statement:

EXEC CICS RETURN TRANSID(xxxx) COMMAREA(data-area)

"data-area" can be specified in the linkage section. This can produce a more efficient utilization of program storage within an application, since the COMMAREA is not in working-storage and, therefore, does not increase the size of the load module. A large load module can place increased requirements upon CICS both to load the program and store the module within the CICS DSA during execution. Use of this technique can reduce storage requirements for the program.

It can, however, produce addressability problems and is dangerous if not used properly. For a complete description of this process, see Section 1.5.1.

COMMAREA Issues Use of COMMAREA can also produce problems for both the application and for CICS if not used properly. Of course, with any storage that can be managed by the application, care must be taken to ensure lengths are validated and correct. Invalid passing of COMMAREAs and incorrect specifications can produce storage violations that impact the application and the entire CICS address space.

Installations should establish standards for COMMAREAs and ensure that sizes are standardized between programs that share data. Copybook sizes and COMMAREA sizes should be managed carefully. Lengths of COMMAREAs can always be validated by the program via an EIB field (EIBCALEN), and programs can take advantage of this technique to avoid using an incorrect length.

Remember that a COMMAREA is just another block of user storage to CICS, and if passed within a transaction, is always "chained" off the task's TCA control block. CICS produces the SAA (storage accounting area) around the storage and additional address pointers to keep track of the COMMAREAs. The length requested for the COMMAREA will always be smaller than the actual storage allocated, since CICS must build its own control areas and also attempts to align this storage within the address space.

The COMMAREA is, and will no doubt continue to be, the preferred vehicle for transfer of data within CICS applications. Little definition is required from the program, and IBM will continue to support (via command-level programming) this facility. Additional material on DFHCOMMAREA is contained in another chapter of this book, "COBOL Programming Issues." See Chapter 1 for specific programming issues relating to program storage.

7.1.3 Other Program Storage — TWA, CWA, TCTUA, EIB, etc.

In addition to using COMMAREAs, temporary storage and transient data for passing data within CICS applications, there are additional areas that can be utilized. Some of these storage areas are specific to the task, some are specific to the terminal, and some are global to all tasks within the same CICS system. Each has advantages within certain conditions and the ultimate goal of retaining the data. Use of these storage areas and adherence to the CICS protocols when using them produces the best (and most desirable) results.

TWA — Transaction Work Area   The TWA is automatically built at task (transaction) initiation and the size is fixed, based on the value from the transaction definition, whether PCT (Program Control Table) or RDO (Resource Definition Online) is defined. The PCT macro or RDO transaction definition would contain

TWASIZE=nnnnn

where nnnnn is the number of bytes to allocate for the TWA, not
exceeding 32K bytes. Since this value exists in the transaction definition, the size is static for all executions of any programs within the
task and is not released until the transaction terminates.

This block of storage, unlike the COMMAREA, is not "chained" as
a separate piece of storage from the TCA, but actually exists as an
extension of the TCA. Task storage will be discussed more completely in the next section of this chapter. Although the TWA is actually part of the TCA control block, it is more addressable (and, therefore, accessible) than the TCA (which cannot be accessed by an application). It is another way to utilize storage as a "scratch pad" during
the life of the transaction.

Since COMMAREAs are not available to macro-level programs, the
TWA has become the viable alternative for macro programmers. Of
course, since macro-level programs are not supported after
CICS/MVS 2.1, TWAs may be replaced with COMMAREAs when the
programs are converted to command-level. TWAs have the disadvantage of being fixed in size for the entire transaction, whether the
storage is utilized by subsequent programs or not. It is also not
available across transactions, as the COMMAREA is, since all storage is released at task termination. For this reason, many macro
programmers use temporary storage instead of TWA storage if data
needs to be retained after task termination.

CWA — Common Work Area   The CWA is similar to the TWA in that
the storage exists as an extension to an existing CICS system control
block. The CWA is appended to the CSA, the Common System Area
of CICS. The CSA is the anchor control block to CICS, since it is
built during initialization and exists for the life of the address space.
Since the CWA extends the CSA, it is also built during initialization
and is a fixed size based on the SIT (system initialization table) parameter

WORKAREA=nnn

where nnn is the number of bytes to be allocated for the CWA, not
exceeding 3584. The default size, if not coded, is 512.

Since the CWA is an extension of a global control block, the data
stored within the CWA is accessible to all tasks at any time. For this
reason, it is often used for small amounts of data that must be available to any transactions in the installation. The danger, however, is

that the data cannot be secured, is not recoverable, and is not managed by CICS to ensure content. If applications that record or retrieve from the CWA do not "play by the same rules," undesirable results can be expected. In addition, the area is only available to tasks executing in a single CICS address space. Any use of transaction routing would make the data stored in the CWA unavailable to the task routed to another CICS. IBM discourages use of the CWA whenever a viable alternative is available. Installations that utilize CWA storage normally establish standards and "copybooks" for all programs to use for storage mapping.

CWA Disadvantages   Additional disadvantages of using CWA storage are that applications must use the

EXEC CICS ADDRESS TWA(twaptr)

to obtain the address of the CWA. Programs can also load addresses into the CWA (for future pointers to storage areas) but must do so with care. Programs passing data by means of a CWA area must follow restrictions that apply to the mode of execution. If the program is executing in AMODE(31), the address passed must be 31 bits. Addresses passed as data to an AMODE(24) program must be 24 bits (less than 16 Mb) to produce correct interpretation by the called program.

Since the CWA is a global control block to the specific CICS address space, it is limited to tasks executing within that CICS system. If the installation is using MRO (multi-region option) or ISC (intersystem communication), data cannot be passed to other CICS "regions." A transaction that has been routed to another AOR (application owning region) or FOR (file owning region) may not have accessibility to the data stored in another CICS's CWA. In these cases, the COMMAREA could be utilized or the TCTUA; both will be passed along with the task to the target CICS region.

TCTUA — Terminal Control Table User Area   The TCTUA is also a block of storage built as an extension to an existing CICS control block. The TCTUA is appended to the TCTTE (Terminal Control Table Terminal Extension) and exists for the life of that terminal control block. The storage is a fixed size, based on the TCT or RDO definition:

TCTUAL=nnn

where nnn = 0 - 255 bytes. This value should be made as small as possible, since the storage is appended to each and every terminal in session with CICS. Installations with large networks could place significant virtual storage requirements upon CICS by creating large TCTUAs for each terminal.

Unlike previous storage areas, the data stored within the TCTUA is only available to tasks executing from the specific terminal. Data that must be available to all tasks would need to be written to each TCTUA. A common technique to fulfill this requirement is to utilize a CICS "sign-on exit" that is driven each time the terminal is signed on to "load" the data into the TCTUA.

In addition, as with any application-managed storage, care must be taken to ensure that the data stored does not exceed the length of the storage area defined in the TCT. Since this area is an extension of the TCTTE, data written beyond the designated limit will often corrupt other CICS storage. A storage violation could result in the loss of the entire CICS system. For this reason, use of TCTUA storage is usually restricted and managed by technical or systems personnel to guarantee integrity.

Auto-Install Issues of TCTUA Storage   A new facility was introduced in CICS/OS 1.7 that allowed installations to "auto-install" terminals. This process allows the installation to selectively build the control blocks relating to terminals (and subsequent storage) only if the terminal has overtly requested that a session be established with that CICS system. In other words, the terminals eligible for auto-install are not known to CICS until they sign on and establish that session. In the past, all terminals were defined in the TCT and the storage (control blocks) were built for them during CICS initialization. If terminals never signed on to the region, the storage was still allocated and, therefore, unavailable to other applications. Large networks required a great deal of storage merely to build terminal entries (TCTTEs) that may never have been used.

With auto-install, CICS builds the TCTTEs (and consequently the TCTUA) at sign-on time. An additional feature of auto-install deletes the TCTTE (with the TCTUA) as soon as the operator signs off. This saves storage but raises additional issues for any data stored within the TCTUA. If the TCTUA was built at sign-on and modified during the course of operation of the terminal by any application, those changes are deleted with the TCTUA at sign-off. The TCTUA is rebuilt at sign-on, but with the original data as loaded from the sign-on program, without the modifications made during the interim.

Installations that utilize the TCTUA for data storage and modification will need to rethink the process with the auto-install facility. This feature provides a great deal of flexibility and VSCR (virtual storage constraint relief) for customers with large networks. The use of TCTUA storage may need to be analyzed and possibly modified to accommodate these new issues.

EIB (Execute Interface Block)   Although some programmers would argue that the EIB is not truly a storage area for an application, since the program can only read, not write, to the area, this CICS control block contains a great deal of data that the program can access and use during execution. The EIB is also the accepted and IBM-recommended storage area to retrieve many valuable fields within the CICS environment.

Since any application can reference data within the EIB by field name, the fields do not need to be defined within the program. They are completely documented (by IBM) in several places, including the CICS Application Programmer's Reference Manual. Whenever IBM enhances the product or produces a new version or release, the EIB remains intact, and any programs that utilize EIB fields require no changes. This fact alone provides good reason to use data stored within the EIB.

The EIB is, in fact, a storage area used to communicate information from CICS to the application program. It exists within the program (whether used or not) since the translator (during translation and compile) inserts the control block into the linkage section of the program. At that point, the EIB exists as a storage area, addressable at field level to the program for any available data.

Contents of the EIB   The contents of the EIB are constantly changing during execution of the application, since CICS "loads" values into the fields based on the transaction environment. For example, fields such as EIBFN, EIBRESP, and EIBRCODE are "set" or stored with data based on conditions that have been raised as a result of processing. The contents may be (and usually are) changed constantly during execution, and are, therefore, interrogated by the application (via the HANDLE instruction) when necessary.

Other fields change only when "triggered" by specific conditions or at specific CICS management functions. The field EIBRSRCE contains the identifier of the resource being accessed by the latest executed command. This is not *always* set, however, by *any* executed command, and is only available after file control, temporary storage, transient data, or terminal control commands. If the prior request, for example, was for interval control, the EIBRSRCE field would not be updated.

Another example of "triggered" EIB fields is EIBTIME. This field can be utilized during execution to provide the time at which the task was started. It is updated at task terminated, but not updated any other time during the life of the transaction. CICS can be triggered to update this field via the

EXEC CICS ASKTIME

command to provide the current time. The application can then ensure that the time stored within this EIB field is current rather than reflective of the initial value.

EIB fields contain data based on "triggers" within CICS and on the environment within which the task exists. The field EIBTRMID can be valuable to the application to determine the terminal ID of the device and logically process the task accordingly. Different "branches" could be taken based on the source of the request. Realize, however, that although most CICS tasks originate from terminals, not all of them do. ATI (automatic transaction initiation) tasks and ICE (interval control element) tasks are "started" based on conditions, or time values. Since a physical terminal device did not initiate these tasks, a terminal identifier cannot be located to store within this EIB field. In cases where specific devices cannot be associated with the task, CICS stores hexadecimal zeros (X"0") within EIBTRMID. The application would have to accommodate these environmental conditions.

Intercommunication Issues with EIB   When an installation utilizes multiple CICS systems and establishes the ability for these CICS systems to communicate with each other via MRO (multi-region option) or ISC (intersystem communication), additional EIB issues are raised. CICS creates EIB fields specifically for this purpose, and, therefore, provides the means for CICS to communicate with an application "across" CICS systems. Based on the values in these fields, the application can control the flow of execution between CICSs. This environment is also known as DTP (Distributed Transaction Processing) when applications "share" data or process in more than a single CICS region (or system).

One very important EIB field during DTP is EIBRECV, which contains X"00" (off) if the transaction is in the SEND state or X"FF" (on) if in the RECEIVE state. With this field, the application can determine the communication state and manage the flow during execution. This field is available in either MRO or ISC environments, but some are not.

EIBSYNC and EIBFREE are only valid in ISC processing, since they deal with APPC or LU6.2 processing. These fields deal with sharing resources and both syncpoint and release of the resources within multiple CICS systems. Since sessions are established between multiple CICS systems, applications must manage (and FREE) the sessions when necessary. EIBFREE is one field that can be used to detect the status of the session and when it must be terminated. Others are available, especially for abnormal condition handling, and can be found in EIB documentation.

7.1.4 Task Storage

Most of the storage areas previously discussed are created by the application or are created by CICS and managed by the application. The EIB exists within the program, but is created and managed by CICS. Applications may also create areas of storage that are not actually part of the program, but are data areas "corresponding" to the task.

The TCA, Task Control Area   When a task is first "dispatched" by CICS, a block of storage called the TCA (task control area) is created by CICS for that task. The TCA is the "anchor" of the task, and then either contains, or points to, any storage requested by that task. When the task is dispatched, a TCA is acquired and built for that specific task. The TCA contains both a system area (for system–related data) and a user area (for application program–related data). In addition, when the TCA is acquired, CICS determines if (via the transaction definition) a TWA should be appended to the TCA. The creation and size of the TWA is specified in the PCT or RDO transaction definition.

The TCA exists for the length of the task and is deleted at task termination (normal or abnormal). During the life of the task, however, CICS uses this control block anchor for a pointer to any additional storage acquired for the task. When the application requests storage, the CICS storage control program (DFHSCP) analyzes the type of storage requested, determines what CICS subpool should be utilized, and locates the proper amount of storage in that subpool. A page allocation map (PAM) is used to control allocation within the subpools and manage the storage. Figure 7-1 identifies each subpool that CICS uses to satisfy requests for task storage.

Application Storage Classes   When an application request is received by DFHSCP, the request contains not only the amount of storage

Subpool Number	Subpool Name
01	Control
02	TP (Teleprocessing)
04	Task
05	Shared
06	RPL (Request Parameter List)
08	Program

Figure 7-1 CICS subpools.

required but also the storage type. The type of storage is determined by the type of request made by the application. This storage type, along with the size, becomes part of the block of storage allocated. The type also determines the subpool that DFHSCP will use to satisfy the request. Figure 7-2 contains a portion of the table that DFHSCP would use to select the subpool. It also identifies many of the common storage classes that a programmer may find as part of the task storage created by the application.

These storage classes are stored within the first section of the data acquired for storage. This area is called the SAA (storage CICS subpools accounting area) and is CICS's way of "chaining" the storage together within the task. Note that the TCA itself is a block of storage, with the storage class of X"8A." It then also contains this SAA as the first area within the control block.

Storage Class	Storage Name	Subpool Selected
85	TIOA	02
86	ICE	01
87	AID	01
88	Program	08
8A	TCA	04
8C	User	04
8F	File (VSAM)	04
90	RPL	06
99	Map	05
9F	DL/1	05

Figure 7-2 Common CICS storage classes.

The format of an SAA is:

Byte	Description
0	Storage Class Code (X"8A" for a TCA)
1	Subpool Code if a TCA
	INITIMG value if the area is initialized
2+3	Length in bytes of the storage area
4-7	Address of the next SAA on the chain
	(points back to the TCA at the end of the chain)

Consequently, the TCA points to the next storage area built for the task, and the second one points to the third, etc. The SAA for each storage area shows, therefore, the type and the length of the storage. An SAA is also built at the end of the storage, and serves to "enclose" the block of storage and ensure integrity when freed. This trailing SAA becomes extremely important when the storage is released. If either SAA has been "corrupted" and is, therefore, unavailable or invalid, a storage violation results (see Section 7.2).

At task termination, any task storage that has not yet been freed is released along with the TCA. CICS then returns the pages of storage to the appropriate subpool for reuse by other tasks. Understanding task storage and identifying these types of storage can enhance diagnosis of problems and allow the programmer to analyze the application for optimum performance.

7.1.5 CICS ADDRESS and ASSIGN

These commands allow applications to access data in CICS system storage areas, such as have been previously covered, and also to access information "outside" the application in other external areas. Since they provide access to privileged fields, i.e., CICS internal control blocks, these commands will lose capability as the product evolves to object code support.

ADDRESS This command provides access (and addressability) to CICS system areas such as the CSA, CWA, EIB, TCTUA, and TWA. Use of the command establishes addresses to the control block, and the application can then reference fields within the control block via field structure. Since IBM now publishes the layout of these control blocks (CICS Data Areas), the application can define this layout within a "01" level structure and then reference fields within the storage area. In the case of the EIB, most fields are automatically "reference-able." This command can be used to obtain addressability after first invocation.

Once used, the application must execute a SERVICE RELOAD command to rebuild the BLL cell for each storage area. If the application program is written in COBOL II, SERVICE RELOAD is no longer required.

CICS/MVS 2.1 continues to provide ADDRESS capability for all the above CICS system storage areas. Since CICS/ESA 3.1 is the first version to ship (at least partially) as object code (no source code) for some CICS components, the ADDRESS command has been limited. In the announcement of CICS/ESA 3.1, IBM states:

. . . CICS/ESA Version 3 Release 1 is the last release to support direct addressing of CICS control blocks other than the EIB and user areas (CWA, TCTUA) . . . The EXEC CICS ADDRESS CSA command will not be supported after CICS/ESA Version 3.1 . . .

IBM goes on to suggest that applications should begin migration to the EXEC CICS SET/INQUIRE facilities, which will continue to be supported and will be the facility that provides access to system information. It is logical to assume that SET/INQUIRE will continue to be enhanced to provide access that is currently available via ADDRESS.

ASSIGN This command is used to access values outside local environment of the application program. Common uses of the ASSIGN command are to:

• access lengths of user storage areas (CWA, TWA, TCTUA)
• access values required for BMS maps
• access values relating to terminals, such as features
• access values relating to abends, such as abend code

A complete list of ASSIGN command options can be found in the CICS Application Programmer's Reference Manual.

7.2 CICS Storage

CICS applications do not, typically, have control or requirements to manage CICS system storage. The applications can, however, significantly affect storage availability or lack of availability. Knowledge of how CICS manages storage can lead to more productive applications, better response time, and efficiently utilized CICS systems. Applications can impact performance of other tasks and the entire CICS region. This section will discuss techniques that can be used to properly request and utilize CICS facilities, including CICS dynamic storage. Also covered will be CICS storage and how the version and/or release of CICS and other IBM components may change some of the issues.

7.2.1 DSA (Dynamic Storage Area) Issues

The DSA provides storage to CICS transactions as requested. If insufficient DSA is available, CICS must manage the storage very closely and reuse areas as soon as possible. This process, called "program compression," will be discussed at great length within this section. The specification and utilization of DSA within a CICS region can significantly impact performance of tasks and should, therefore, be carefully calculated and subsequently monitored. CICS/ESA Version 3 now provides E-DSA, or extended ESA to accommodate 31-bit programs. This new facility also manages the storage more efficiently, and practically eliminates the need for excessive program compression.

Earlier in this chapter, storage classes were identified for many different types of program storage. In addition, these storage classes were grouped into the appropriate subpool from which the storage was allocated. These subpools are actually the components of the CICS DSA, and comprise the groupings from which CICS selects the storage on behalf of the application request. How is the DSA specified? It isn't, actually. The DSA is built during CICS initialization, but becomes a block of storage that is left AFTER many other areas are built. In other words, the DSA is the storage left and available for programs after most of the other areas have been created.

This process has changed slightly in CICS/ESA Version 3. Since DSA issues have decreased significantly in Version 3, most of the following material deals with remaining issues in CICS/MVS Version 2.

Storage Cushion　The DSA does have one specification available, the storage cushion. In the SIT (system initialization table), the parameter

SCS = xxxxx

where xxxxx = the number of bytes to reserve for the storage cushion. CICS will take this number, round it to a multiple of PGSIZE (also from the SIT) and make this storage available when the DSA is exhausted. These pages are used when CICS is unable, via program compression or other means, to satisfy requests for program storage. It is used to purge tasks when CICS reaches SOS, or short on storage, to attempt to free adequate storage to continue processing.

The amount of storage cushion to allocate depends on the CICS environment in the installation. It should be large enough to accommodate the largest program request, since this cushion is CICS's last attempt to respond to the task's request. Also, the four CICS pages (PGSIZE) are reserved by CICS from the cushion to purge tasks when the SOS condition occurs. If CICS cannot purge any tasks, and attempt to free storage, no new work will be dispatched. Therefore, depending on PGSIZE,

If PGSIZE = 2048, 4 × 2048 = 8192 (8K)
If PGSIZE = 4096, 4 × 4096 = 16,384 (16K)

If the storage cushion is less than 8192 (PGSIZE = 2048), or 16,384 (PGSIZE = 4096), the storage cushion is inadequate to accommodate even the smallest request. A typical storage cushion would be 16K–32K, depending on the environment.

DSA Calculation Since the DSA cannot be calculated, other parameters must be adjusted to create the proper DSA size. CICS attempts to assist the installation in the calculation by providing messages during initialization. These messages are prefixed by DFH1500, appear during CICS initialization, and identify the amount of storage available during different phases. The three messages are:

DFH1500 SUBPOOL SIZE BEFORE LOADING RESIDENT PROGRAMS XXXXX

DFH1500 SUBPOOL SIZE AFTER LOADING RESIDENT PROGRAMS XXXXX

DFH1500 AVAILABLE STORAGE IN THE SUBPOOL XXXXX

During initialization, CICS loads system nucleus modules (sometimes called "static storage"), CICS macro tables, and other system areas such as the CICS trace and formatted dump. It then, prior to DSA creation, must load any programs defined resident (by either the Application Load Table, ALT, or program definition in the PPT or RDO entry). The first message (above) identifies how much storage is available at this point. The second message provides the result of loading the resident programs and, therefore, could be used to calculate how much storage is being used by those programs.

The third message indicates exactly how much storage is left after all processing and is the actual size of the DSA. The reason that the values may be different between messages 2 and 3 is a result of CICS utilization of some areas of the DSA prior to any program storage requests. Remember that the DSA consists of multiple subpools, such as TP (02), RPL (06), etc. CICS allocates some part of these subpools for itself. Examples of this would be RDO entries for programs and transactions, table manager storage, and some areas for terminal auto-install.

The third message provides, however, an exact accounting of the DSA and what is available for program storage requests. If the DSA is too large, then storage is allocated that may not be required. It also means the total region size (REGION= on the JOBCARD or STEP) is too high and the total MVS system may experience paging based on overallocation. If the DSA is too small, CICS will experience frequent program compressions, tasks being purged to attempt storage recovery, and a possible SOS (short on storage). This value should be monitored on a regular basis to ensure that the DSA is being created at a proper size.

Program Compressions If an application is experiencing poor response time, but only at irregular intervals, the reason may be that CICS is undergoing frequent program compressions. This phenomenon occurs when:

A GETMAIN cannot be satisfied from available free storage

A successful request for storage leaves fewer pages than are specified in the storage cushion

Even though CICS "frees" all program storage used by the task at task termination, the pages are not reclaimed until CICS performs program compression. This process is very similar to MVS PDS management (partition datasets). When a member is deleted from the PDS, the space is not reclaimed until the PDS is compressed. The CICS DSA must be compressed to reclaim program storage; however, the process is much more significant.

When CICS performs program compression, it interrogates every page and frees the storage of all programs that are not currently in use (active). This process is VERY CPU-intensive and can take several seconds, depending on DSA size and CICS activity. In addition, no new programs can be loaded until compression is complete. When complete, active or frequently used programs must be reloaded into the DSA before the task can be dispatched again. The only way to keep the programs from being continually reloaded is to define them RESIDENT. Of course, resident programs are loaded prior to DSA creation (as covered earlier), so all resident programs decrease the size of available DSA. This Catch-22 situation is a constant dilemma for installations trying to properly calculate their DSA.

Calculating the Frequency of Program Compressions Although there are no CICS statistics provided (in the shutdown stats) on the frequency of program compressions, vendor packages that monitor CICS can be purchased and usually contain this information. If the installation has not purchased a CICS monitor, some calculations can be performed with other CICS shutdown statistics to determine the frequency of program compressions. In the CICS shutdown, program statistics are provided, and one heading contains

'NUMBER OF TIME FETCHED'

Since a program must be fetched (and reloaded) every time CICS compresses the DSA, frequently used programs will have a fetch count that closely parallels the compression rate. The programs with the highest number of fetches (excluding those RELOAD=YES or USAGE=MAP) were probably fetched every compression. This value is *at least* the number of program compressions experienced during the life of that CICS system.

Although CICS does not report compressions, the number is accumulated and recorded in exception-class monitoring data. The installation could process these records for field PCOMPRTM to determine compression frequency. The documentation for this facility can be found in the CICS Customization Guide.

Program compressions will always occur, since the DSA should never be too large for normal activity. If, however, the compression rate is so high that CICS is constantly struggling to reclaim space, more CPU cycles are being spent to manage storage than to perform productive work. One or two program compressions per hour would be acceptable. Ten or more would be counterproductive.

As previously stated, CICS/ESA has changed the management of program storage. Program compression problems are minimal in the new version.

7.2.2 CICS Initialization Issues

During CICS initialization, many storage areas are built, some of which will remain intact for the life of the region. Others will be dynamically increased and decreased as resources are requested. In the previous section of this chapter, the initialization messages were explained which indicate DSA subpool sizes. These messages can be used to determine availability of program storage during CICS execution. Some installations note a difference in this value based on the START= value, depending upon whether the startup is COLD or AUTO. This may be possible for several reasons.

The third DFH1500 message is produced without regard to programs executed during initialization (PLT programs). These programs would remain in the DSA (and affect the calculated value) but would have a use count of zero, therefore being deleted at first program compression. If these programs are impacted by the startup type, they may impact the value in the third message.

In addition, the primary difference in a COLD vs. AUTO startup is the recreation of many terminal storage areas. Realize that a WARM start reuses many control areas from the RSD (restart data set), while a COLD start rebuilds them all and may produce fragmentation. This is especially true if terminal auto-install is being used extensively.

If an installation is experiencing this situation, the best analysis of the problem should come from the actual storage layout after initialization. After CICS initialization, both COLD and WARM, take a SDUMP of the region (via CEMT or the OS DUMP command) and analyze the programs actually remaining in storage. The SDUMP can be processed with DFHPDX, and the module map at the end of the report will display all storage areas at the time of the dump. If the installation uses CICS formatted dump, an index at the end of the dump would also display both programs and control blocks in existence after initialization.

CICS startup has been substantially enhanced in CICS/MVS 2.1 and even further in CICS/ESA Version 3 and provides many options not previously available. The new parm in the SIT for auto-install provides a means to delay the rebuilding of terminal control blocks and, therefore, reuse the storage areas within the specified period of time. There are fewer reasons to COLD start CICS, and START=AUTO is now recommended in most situations.

7.2.3 VTAM Issues

As previously mentioned, many storage issues in CICS are related to other components, such as VTAM. Installations have a great deal of control over utilization of CICS storage, such as the choice to use terminal auto-install, and can control and manage CICS storage as these choices are taken. This section will cover many storage issues that specifically deal with VTAM facilities.

ITLIM vs. OPNDLIM The ITLIM parameter was introduced into VTAM to attempt to control all applications "communicating" to VTAM. In the early days of VTAM, large networks placed heavy loads on the product, and it did not recover well at all from storage problems. If resources, such as storage buffers, were depleted, it was not uncommon for the entire network to fail or require the installation to IPL MVS. This parameter (ITLIM) was introduced to "throttle" network requests for resources. CICS also introduced the OPNDLIM parameter to control the flood of OPNDST requests to VTAM. Most installations, however, chose to use ITLIM since it could restrict not only CICS requests, but any application requests from other products.

When IBM began shipping VTAM 3.2, the ITLIM parameter was discontinued. It was assumed that this release controlled the resource consumption in a more natural way and that the parameter was no longer needed.

Installations must now decide if the CICS requests to VTAM remain to be limited. IBM states that this parameter is useful only when large quantities of users would log on or log off all at the same time. Other applications would be the use of CONNECT=AUTO, where all terminals would be logged on at CICS startup time, therefore utilizing large quantities of storage during the mass log on. The value of OPNDLIM specifies the number of concurrent requests available to process and would limit the number of requests that CICS would have to process concurrently.

Since installations are moving away from automatic connection to CICS at initialization, this parameter is losing value in priority of terminal specification. More installations are turning to auto-install for terminals, since many terminals sign on infrequently or for short periods of time. This new facility builds storage for terminals only when requested and releases it after log off. The new parameter in the SIT for auto-install is becoming much more valid to control terminal storage creation.

VTAM Use of CSA   While the use of CSA does not directly affect CICS, any storage required in the Common System Area is storage unavailable to any other application's private area size. MVS builds the CSA at IPL time, and this amount of storage will detract from the amount of free private below the 16-Mb line. Installations that are experiencing VSCR (virtual storage constraint) find that the size of their CICS private area is limited by the other areas, such as a large CSA.

Even though CICS does not use CSA, this is not true with VTAM, but the amount varies with the version and release currently installed. Prior to Version 3.1, VTAM required large amounts of storage in the CSA for buffer management. In VTAM 3.1, a great deal of that storage was moved into extended CSA (above the 16-Mb line), but the I/O buffers (IOBUF) remained in the CSA. If installations required large sizes and numbers of I/O buffers, CSA utilization stayed high.

In VTAM V3.2, all VTAM buffers are satisfied from E-CSA. If an installation is experiencing virtual storage constraint and needs a larger region for CICS, the most current release of VTAM will provide some relief.

CICS Terminal Auto-install   Since CICS/OS/VS 1.7, installations can choose to use a facility that builds storage for VTAM terminals only when the device requests to log on to the CICS region. This process is called auto-install and was further enhanced in CICS/MVS 2.1. CICS/ESA Version 3.2 will take the facility even further with removal of definition requirements in CICS, using the VTAM definitions instead. While the entire facility is well documented in a publication, GG66-0288 CICS 1.7 Terminal Definitions with Auto-install, this section will deal with some of the auto-install issues as they affect CICS storage utilization.

When a terminal is available for auto-install, no explicit definition is required for the device, as was previously necessary via the TCT (terminal control table). CICS builds the definition (the TCTTE) dynamically at log on time, and deletes the storage when the terminal logs off. In addition to the time saved by not having to maintain a table for each terminal in the network, considerable CICS storage can be saved from terminals that never log on. Granted, additional processing is required to create and delete these entries, but the savings can be well worth the cycles.

A terminal definition is usually at least 500 bytes of CICS storage and can be significantly larger based on the size of the TCTUA. Since the TCTUA appends the TCTTE, it adds to the amount of storage required for each device definition. With auto-install, therefore, an installation can save over 1K of storage for every two terminals that do not log on or log off after short periods of processing. Reports of 500K–700K storage savings are not uncommon in large networks when the installation moves to auto-install. This saving is immediately available to the DSA and, therefore, program storage.

Limiting Auto-install Storage   While the amount of storage for each auto-installed device is fixed (TCTTE + TCTUA), the amount of storage to support the log on at any given time can be limited. In the SIT, the parameter

AUTOINST=(xxx,DFHZATDX,hhmmss,hhmmss)

can be used to limit the number and duration of definitions.

xxx = the maximum number of devices allowed to concurrently auto-install (default 100)

DFHZATDX = the name of the auto-install program, if customized from the IBM-supplied version

hhmmss = the delay period to allow before definitions are deleted during an emergency restart (default 700 or 7 minutes)

hhmmss = the delay period to allow before definitions are deleted after a session is ended with CICS (default 0 meaning delete at session end)

CICS provides a great deal of flexibility with this parameter and allows the installation to specify concurrent auto-installs and the length of time to retain the terminal definition at two different scenarios. These parameters were not available in the early versions of auto-install and have been added by the customers who used the facility in its early phases and submitted requirements to IBM for these enhancements.

When CICS detects the number of concurrent log ons equal to the AUTOINST value, it sends a message to VTAM to hold any additional logons (SETLOGON=HOLD). Any further attempts to log on to CICS will be queued, and storage consumption will be "throttled."

The time values in the parameter allow the installation to give CICS users a chance to log back on (in case of device or system failure) without incurring the additional overhead of rebuilding the definition. This can save both storage and cycles, since the definition is retained and reused if the terminal requests log on during the specified interval.

These enhancements to auto-install give the customer an opportunity to use this facility and limit the resources as needed. Again, a complete explanation of CICS auto-install is documented in the previously specified publication.

7.2.4 OSCOR Issues

One of the most controversial storage issues in CICS is the specification of OSCOR — how large to make it, how it is used, where to find it, how to tune it. While all issues can hardly be covered at great length in a single section of this chapter, OSCOR will be defined, and many of the most important issues will be covered. A detailed view of storage including all types can be found in a publication, G320-0597 Virtual Storage Tuning Cookbook. While this manual has been available for some time and may not cover all of the most recent issues dealing with storage, it contains a great deal of relevant information. Any installation with storage issues should locate this publication and use many of the hints and techniques contained within.

The amount of OSCOR available to CICS is specified by the installation in the SIT parameter:

OSCOR=xxxxx

where xxxxx = the number of bytes of storage to reserve for OS GETMAIN requests from access methods within CICS. The default, if no value is specified, is 8192, and is guaranteed to be inadequate for any installation. How does an installation calculate a "reasonable" value for OSCOR? It depends especially upon the release of CICS and other components, since the utilization varies within these releases. For the most part, specification of OSCOR is mainly dependent upon how many of the resources that use OSCOR will be required. Demand for OSCOR comes from various sources:

- All files defined in the FCT, when OPENED
- The RSD (restart data set)

- BDAM IOBs (input/output blocks)
- DB/2 threads
- Temporary storage and transient data
- IMS DBRC (database recovery control)

to name just a few. Probably the most significant user of OSCOR is FCP (file control program), since OSCOR is required for every file opened. The amount of OSCOR is dependent upon the release of DFP (Data Facilities Product) that exists in the MVS/XA or MVS/ESA system. In the calculation, therefore, storage would be required for EVERY file that was opened for the duration of the open. If files are opened, and never closed, OSCOR would be allocated for the duration of the CICS system.

80A ABENDs If an open is requested, and insufficient OSCOR remains for the request, one of two results will be experienced:

- The open will fail, returning a message of the failure
- CICS will terminate with an 80A ABEND

While the first result would certainly be preferable, a complete system failure may be experienced. OSCOR is certainly a resource to be monitored and tuned, since it can have significant impact on the availability of CICS to all users.

Locating and Tuning OSCOR Unfortunately, OSCOR utilization is not provided by default either within CICS during execution or in the statistics at shutdown. Monitors (IBM and other vendors) can be purchased which locate and display OSCOR utilization while CICS is executing. Unfortunately, most of them display allocated storage, but not who, or what, is using it.

OSCOR is also unavailable in any CICS dumps. Use of either CICS formatted dump or SDUMP (with DFHPDX to format) will not produce OSCOR displays, since OSCOR is actually free storage within the region and cannot be tied to any task or module.

IBM supplies one facility, a replacement for CSFU, that can be used to detect OSCOR utilization during file open. Two programs, DFHFCOS and DFHFCST, can be run during a test for OSCOR and will produce some input into the calculation. These should not be used on a regular basis, since they replace the usual CICS file open utility programs, but can be run in test. Use of these programs will produce a message at CICS shutdown with the statistic:

OSCOR USED FOR FILE OPENS: xxxx (DEC) BYTES

Since the opening of files accounts for a great deal of OSCOR utilization, this number can be used as a starting value and increased to accommodate additional requests. For complete documentation on this facility, see CICS/MVS Installation Guide. As previously stated, the value will fluctuate based on the version and release of CICS and other components. For example, the initialization sequence was changed from CICS/OS/VS 1.7 to CICS/MVS 2.1. This change moved storage requirements from CICS areas to OSCOR, so while the overall net effect is no additional storage, the value of OSCOR must be increased for 2.1.

The version and release of DFP (Data Facility Product) also affects OSCOR. DFP 2.3 decreased the demand for OSCOR since it moved many of the control blocks previously built in OSCOR to areas above the 16-Mb line. DFP 3.1, since it is an ESA-only version, will require CICS/ESA 3.1 and will significantly change all OSCOR issues. These topics will be covered in the next section.

In summary, OSCOR calculation is much more important than other storage calculations, since it can affect the availability of the entire CICS system. Further information on this topic can be found in the publication CICS/MVS 2.1 Performance Guide, Appendix D: How to Estimate the OSCOR Parameter.

7.2.5 Release Dependencies

Utilization of CICS storage changes based on the release and version of both CICS and other IBM components used by CICS. Installations should locate and analyze IBM documentation prior to installation of new releases to make themselves aware of these changes. This section will discuss a few of the release dependencies relating to program and CICS storage issues.

CICS/MVS 2.1   Since CICS/OS/VS 1.7 is now removed from marketing, and not a current version of the product, customers should be advised to move to Version 2. This version will continue to be supported, and enhanced, and will provide continued VSCR (virtual storage constraint relief).

Storage enhancements in CICS/MVS Version 2 are, at the time of this publication, still evolving. Some enhancements provided in the first phase of Version 2 were:

- Terminal log-off time to reclaim storage at time-out
- DFP V2.3 moved control blocks above the line, and reduced the requirements for OSCOR

With the newly released modification level, CICS/MVS 2.1.1, additional enhancements to storage control were:

- Further reductions in storage requirements including:
  — COMMAREA moved above the 16-Mb line
  — RSD (restart dataset) buffers
  — TMP (table manager program) storage areas
- Use of CICS/MVS 2.1.1 with DFP V3.1 reduces storage of:
  — VSAM strings
  — Remaining VSAM control blocks above the 16-Mb line

Again, CICS/MVS 2.1 will continue to be supported, and perhaps enhanced. Further changes to storage management may have been announced since this material was produced.

CICS/ESA Version 3 As of this writing, CICS/ESA 3.1 has begun to ship, and CICS/ESA 3.2 has been announced. From the Release Guide, and other materials made available, it is clear that this new version is *substantially* different. Reductions in storage requirements are apparent, especially since the new code base (object only) now allows CICS to execute many of its management functions in 31-bit mode.

Another major change is the removal of OSCOR functions entirely and the addition of DSA and EDSA parameters in the SIT. The entire problem of calculating OSCOR, and potential 80A ABENDS is eliminated. In addition, program storage can be requested from EDSA, a seemingly inexhaustable area. These new and exciting functions will completely change the way installations build and tune their CICS systems for storage utilization.

Customers with IMS/ESA 3.1 installed can take advantage of the new DBCTL (database control) facilities provided in CICS/ESA 3.1. Use of the DBCTL feature moves DL/I code and its associated control blocks outside of the CICS address space. Depending on usage, this can remove a large amount of storage requirement from CICS. Storage that was previously required to contain local DL/I resources within CICS can now reside in the DBCTL address space.

As CICS/ESA 3.2 is shipped and installed at customer sites, additional information will become known about this new version. Version 3.2 moves even more virtual storage above the 16-Mb line, including additional CICS nucleus modules and TCTTEs (Terminal Control Table Terminal Entries). While this may not directly impact programmers, it will have repercussions on any programming techniques that accessed these storage areas. In addition, transactions will be more efficient since this storage "placement" will free more CICS storage for program loading and execution. It is certain that all major enhancements to the product will be contained within Version 3.

7.3 Storage Violations

Storage violations are often the most frustrating and difficult problems to avoid and diagnose when detected. The new architecture in CICS/ESA 3.1 attempts to isolate task storage via the new "domain" facility and will hopefully remove many of the storage corruption problems that CICS customers currently face. This section, however, will deal with CICS/MVS 2.1 issues — how storage violations occur, how they can be avoided, and how they can be debugged when necessary.

Storage violations occur when a task (or CICS) modifies storage incorrectly, corrupting the original value of that portion of storage. The amount of corruption may be a single byte or a large portion. The size is irrelevant; the location is much more relevant to the detection, or lack of detection, of the violation. In fact, many CICS systems experience storage corruption, but never detect the violation. How can that occur? The key is in the characteristics of CICS storage, especially task-related storage, and the process that CICS uses to manage it. As CICS manages storage, via DFHSCP (storage control program), the areas are built and released at task termination. DFHSCP controls this program storage via SAAs (storage accounting areas), creating an SAA at the beginning and at the end of each block of allocated storage. The SAA contains the necessary information to "chain" all allocated storage for one task together. At task termination, CICS releases all related storage areas via the pointers within the SAA. If the logical connections cannot be made (the chain is broken), the storage areas cannot be found.

Storage Recovery Decisions CICS provides a mechanism for the installation to decide whether to attempt storage recovery if corruption is detected. In the SIT, the storage recovery parameter is

SVD=YES/NO/nn

where NO indicates that no storage recovery is to be attempted, while nn= indicates the number of storage violations for which a dump will be produced. If YES is coded, a dump will be produced for each and every storage violation detected.

Many installations choose not to allow any storage recovery attempt, since storage has been corrupted and the integrity of all tasks has been jeopardized. If SVD=NO has been coded, and a storage violation is detected, the message

DFH0501 CICS ABEND: STORAGE ERROR DETECTED ... RECOVERY NOT SPECIFIED

appears in the CICS log, and CICS will be ABENDed with a 501 ABEND code. A dump will be produced to assist in the diagnosis of the problem.

If storage recovery has been requested, CICS will produce a dump (the type specified in the SIT, DUMP= parameter) and attempt to recover. If possible, the CICS system remains operational, and processing continues. Storage may remain in program subpools, however, since CICS was not able to release all areas. Of course, since recovery may be successful, the entire CICS system is not lost. In some cases, however, even if recovery is attempted, the process is unsuccessful. CICS produces the DFH0501 message with

RECOVERY NOT POSSIBLE

and the same 501 ABEND results.

To avoid or diagnose storage violations, programmers must be aware of the process that CICS uses to manage program storage. The characteristics of these storage areas are critical to the understanding of CICS storage management.

7.3.1 Task Related Storage Characteristics

A previous section of this chapter dealing with the TCA (task control area) contained the format of an SAA. That section highlighted application storage classes and how different types of program storage produced the value for the class contained within the SAA. In addition to storage class, the SAA contains the value of the length, or size, of this piece of storage PLUS an address to the next piece of storage on the chain. For review, the SAA format contained in that section is repeated below.

SAA Format

Byte	Description
0	Storage class code (X"8A" for a TCA)
1	Subpool code if a TCA
	INITIMG value if the area is initialized
2+3	Length in bytes of the storage area
4–7	Address of the next SAA on the chain
	(points back to the TCA at the end of the chain)

Note that the first 8 bytes of any storage area are allocated and managed by CICS, the actual storage allocated to the program AFTER the SAA.

In addition to the SAA at the beginning of the storage area, CICS creates a "trailing" SAA at the end. This second SAA is an exact duplicate of the first 8-byte SAA, and serves to "wrap" the allocated storage area with the SAA pair. When storage is freed, CICS compares these two SAAs, matching all 8 bytes. If they are not identical, they have been corrupted by some task and have been illegally modified.

Since storage is not freed until task termination, the request to release the storage and subsequent detection of the storage violation does not occur until the end of the task. In addition, if the SAA has been overwritten, the offending task may not be the owner of the corrupted storage. In many storage violations, by the time storage is freed and the violation is detected, the task causing the problem has long since terminated. The dump containing the storage violation contains the victim of the corruption, not the criminal.

Figure 7-3 contains a section of program storage from a typical CICS transaction. As specified, the first (and last) 8 bytes of storage contain the SAA pair, with the trailing SAA pointing back to the address of the beginning SAA. This example shows program storage that has not been corrupted. The last section of this chapter contains material dealing with storage that has been incorrectly modified, creating a storage violation.

```
TASK STORAGE 0001BB20

0000  8C000258  0001B000  0001BCB8  00000000  00000000  00000000  40404040   .........
0020  00021D04  00021D04  00000000  000CB000  00000000  00199E54  00000000   .........
0040  00000000  00000000  00165E18  00000000  B01A0D44  A01F482C  801A0B1A   .........
0060  0001BCE0  005D0000  0001BE50  0001B000  00060000  A01A0D44  A01A1D4A   .........
0080  0801D330  00000000  00000008  40100001  00093076  0001BCB8  00000000   ....L....
00A0  00000000  01000008  00000000  00000000  001F34A4  0001BCB8  80059008   .....M...
00C0  00000000  001F6A00  00169AB8  0001D330  001F34A4  00092030  00169AB8   ....N..NQ
00E0  001A3370  001F6A00  00169AA0  001A4258  0001B000  001F6600  001F316C   .........
0100  00058784  0001BB20  0001B190  0001B000  32200000  00000000  001F6A00   .....L...
0120  0001BBD4  8001B8D8  00000000  001U0000  00000000  00000000  001D5DB    .M..Q..L.
0140  00000000  00000000  0001BCB8  0001D394  00000000  00000000  FF000000   .N..NQ...
0160  40C4C6C8  C5C9C240  01502310  00901937  C3C5C3C9  0000033C  D3F1C4F7   DFHEIB..CECI.L1D7
0180  00007004  06000000  000000C6  C903C5C1  40404000  00000000  001U0003   FILEA.L1D7
01A0  40404000  00000000  00000000  00000000  00000000  00000000  F1C4F740   .........
01C0  00000000  00000000  00000000  00000000  00000000  00000000  00000000   .........
01E0  00000000  00000000  00000000  00000000  00000000  00000000  00000000   .........
0200  00000000  00000000  00000000  00000000  00000000  00000000  00000000   .........
0220  00000000  00000000  00000000  00000000  00000000  00000000  00000000   .........
0240  00000000  00000000  00000000  00000000  00000000  8C000258  0001B000   .........
```

Figure 7-3   CICS COBOL program storage.

7.3.2 Normal Causes of Storage Violations

Since the event that triggers a storage violation is the comparison of the two SAAs, storage can be corrupted and not be detected by CICS. CICS compares the SAAs only when a request is made to free storage. If the task corrupts storage (its own or another task's) and the scope of the corruption does not affect the beginning or ending SAA, CICS is unable to detect the violation. The task completes normally and may then produce data areas that are invalid and without true data integrity.

Programs written in COBOL can produce storage violations in a number of different ways, but the most common are:

Subscripting or indexing incorrectly — using the wrong values and thereby continuing past the logical end of the table

Incorrect or inappropriate copybook — using the wrong one or a copybook with an incorrect (and probably too large) length

Addressability error — failure to establish addressability to a program or CICS area before using the contents of the area

These errors can cause storage violations, and subsequent CICS failures, if the corrupted storage is extensive. If the overwritten storage is a CICS system area (CSA, TCA, etc.), recovery is seldom possible. This can be caused by user areas (such as the CWA or TWA) extending their previously defined size and modifying the following storage area.

If copybooks are included and extend beyond the length of the actual storage area, they may overlay the trailing SAA and the beginning SAA of the next storage area. In this situation, the storage violation can affect the offending task PLUS storage owned by another task.

Addressability problems can be realized by failure to issue a Service Reload when necessary or the correct setting of a BLL (Base Locator Linkage) cell. Since COBOL II removes this requirement, the occurrences of storage corruption should decrease.

Additionally, use of COMMAREAs can cause storage violations when sizes are not standardized and adhered to. The COMMAREA length can be validated via the EIB and should be checked to ensure that the data (or copybook) being moved never exceeds the COMMAREA size.

In summary, any CICS storage areas should be used with care, and all standards should be kept. Storage violations are extremely disruptive to CICS operations and cause extensive downtime.

7.3.3 Diagnosing Storage Violations

As previously stated, storage violations are detected at task termination, when storage areas are released. For this reason, diagnosis is difficult, and must be done with the knowledge that the storage corruption is probably not recent. Programmers diagnosing storage violations must attempt to locate previous activity in CICS and hope to find the offending task.

A previous publication by this author, *CICS Debugging, Dump Reading, and Problem Determination,* presents an entire chapter of storage violation debugging techniques. Those materials should be consulted for an in-depth review of diagnosis.

For an introductory review of storage violation debugging, programmers should review the previous "Normal Causes of Storage Violations." No doubt one or more of those standards were not followed closely enough. Perhaps a copybook size was changed, a SERVICE RELOAD was not done, or a user portion of storage was exceeded.

The most common technique for storage violation dump debugging is to use two sources within the dump:

- The block of program storage with the corrupted SAA
- The CICS trace entries during the interval

The piece of storage that was corrupted may or may not have been corrupted by the task at the time of the *detection* of the violation. In either case, it may be possible to review the contents of the storage and identify the data. Many times, when the SAA has been overlaid, the data can be identified and traced back to a particular task or application. Once the programmer recognizes the contents of the data, it may be a simple task to locate the program code that produced the overlay.

In addition, CICS dumps always contain a portion of the trace during a predefined interval. The trace contains the exact instructions when CICS detected the violation. In the trace entry, one field will identify the address of the storage as it was being freed. It may be possible to scan the trace (backward) to locate the creation of that storage and detect any time that task, or another task, modified that range of storage. This is a very difficult technique, especially if the trace contains many other transactions in a high-volume CICS system. The trace may not contain adequate entries to locate the original creation of the storage, since many CICS regions support dozens of transactions per second. It is one technique, however, that may produce some insight into the problem. If neither of these techniques is successful in diagnosing the violation, further investigation will be required.

BMS — Basic Mapping Services

Since the advent of online systems, programs have been processing data and producing results on terminal screens rather than the former punched card/printed report media. As batch processing decreased, and terminal networks grew, the need for increased support of screen input/output became more obvious.

8.1 Introduction to Basic Mapping Support

BMS is the bridge between the application program and the CICS system. It provides the ability to receive data and route output displays to terminals based on preprepared "maps." BMS supports three levels of mapping, each level providing additional function. Customers choose which level of BMS via SIT options, in addition to another BMS parameter that should be coded. The SIT options for BMS are as follows:

```
BMS=MIMIMUM,STANDARD,FULL,
    UNALIGN,ALIGN,
    DDS,NODDS
```

The first group of choices (MINIMUM, STANDARD, FULL) allows the selection for minimum to full function of BMS. The default is FULL and provides the highest level of BMS functions. The chart below includes the BMS functions as supported by each level.

BMS Function	BMS Level Required
SEND MAP	MINIMUM
RECEIVE MAP	
SEND CONTROL	
Default/Alternate Screens	
Extended Attributes	
Map Set Suffixes	
Null Maps	
Block Data	

****

Outboard Formats	STANDARD
Map Partitions	
Magnetic Slot Reader	
MLEOM Printer Mode	
SEND TEXT	
Subsystem LDC	

****

Operator Paging	FULL
Cumulative Maps	
Page Overflow	
Cumulative Texts	
Routing	
Message Switching	
Return BMS-generated Data	

As shown, each level supports each previous level's functions plus additions. The advantage of these options applies to customers who only need minimum or standard features. CICS will only need to support those features and will, therefore, provide a smaller subset of modules (and overhead) during BMS processing. In other words, customers should not request full function BMS unless the features will be used.

The second group of choices (UNALIGN, ALIGN) became necessary with CICS/OS/VS 1.6. This was the first release of CICS to allow maps of different alignments to coexist. Prior to CICS/OS/VS 1.6, all BMS maps were assembled as unaligned. CICS required that *all* maps have the same alignment option and could not be mixed. With CICS/OS/VS 1.6, maps contain indicators to identify alignment or not, set during the assembly.

Specification of UNALIGN (which is the default) may result in unpredictable results if the stated alignment does not agree with the actual alignment.

The last parameter (DDS, NODDS) refers to suffixed versions maps and map sets. The default, DDS, instructs CICS to search for suffixed versions when loading maps. This may be necessary when the same transaction executes on terminals with different characteristics (such as screen sizes). In this case, different maps would be necessary to accommodate the larger (or smaller) screen size.

If, however, this is not the case, use of DDS (device dependent suffixing) forces CICS to search for a suffixed map at EVERY MAP LOAD. This can extend the response time of the transaction and waste processor cycles. This option (if not turned off) appears very obvious in CICS traces, since every map request is followed by an unsuccessful suffix search before the successful map locate. Don't use the default in this parameter.

8.1.2 Physical and Symbolic Maps

Each BMS map has two forms or styles that must be created. These are called the symbolic map and the physical map. While both physically exist, they exist in different locations and serve different functions.

The symbolic map remains in source language form, much like a copybook or a DSECT, and contains definitions that are used by the application to resolve field references. For this reason, it is usually created by the map assembly and placed into a COPYLIB or COPYBOOK for later input into the program compile process.

The physical map, however, is assembled and link-edited into a LOADLIB much the same way that an assembler program would be. This load module (while not actually executable) must exist in a library known to CICS (via the DFHRPL), be defined to CICS via an RDO or PPT entry, and be loaded in much the same way as an application program module. This physical map provides the definitions the BMS must use to embed control characters in the data stream. More information pertaining to data streams will be provided in the next section.

A typical sequence of events is listed below to identify the steps necessary to create both physical and logical form of a map.

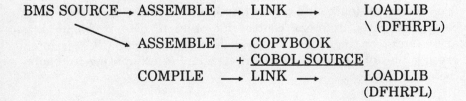

```
BMS SOURCE → ASSEMBLE → LINK →        LOADLIB
                                      \ (DFHRPL)
          → ASSEMBLE → COPYBOOK
                     + COBOL SOURCE
    COMPILE → LINK →        LOADLIB
                            (DFHRPL)
```

8.1.3 SDF for Map Creation

Rather than coding the source BMS statements, products can be purchased which will generate the statements from screen definitions. The IBM products available are SDF/CICS and SDF II. SDF (Screen Definition Facility) can be used as an application within CICS and is available as SDF/CICS 1.5. This is the last release of SDF to be supported within CICS, since IBM has announced withdrawal from support after CICS/MVS Version 2.

The recommended version is SDF II, which runs within TSO/ISPF. It will continue to be supported in existing and future releases of CICS.

With either version, BMS macros can be generated from within the product. These macros can then be assembled into an object map for future link-edit into a LOADLIB. SDF can also generate the symbolic map to include as a COPYBOOK into the program compile process. Why would the source instructions be necessary? If the installation distributed processing and needed to transmit the maps to another target system, the load module cannot be shipped. The BMS source or object map can be shipped, however, and can be reconstructed on the target system (or operating system). Additional material on this topic is included later in this chapter.

SDF is not the only product that can be used as an alternative to generating native BMS code. Other vendors provide similar facilities, with comparable features. Many installations are finding that the products free programmers from the tedious task of BMS coding and save a great deal of time in the development process of the application.

8.2 Inbound vs. Outbound Data Streams

Since CICS is in the business of transferring data back and forth between interactive terminals, data streams serve that purpose. Most of the contents (other than the actual data) of the data stream contain similar components, since they are created by terminal control. Inbound data streams (inbound to CICS) are slightly different from outbound (outbound to the terminal), however, since they must contain slightly different control information. The problems that arise center on these architectural differences, since CICS is interpreting the inbound data, and the terminal is attempting to display the outbound data.

Outbound Data Streams Terminal control sends outbound data streams to the terminal much differently than the operator actually observes it on the screen. The data is sent with control information to identify the contents and the position within the screen. Each of these control fields can be thought of as a command, since it executes the control over the location and structure of the data. Some typical data stream commands are:

SBA	Set Buffer Address
SF	Start Field
PT	Program Tab
RA	Repeat to Address
EUA	Erase Unprotected Field
SFE	Start Field Extended
MF	Modify Field
SA	Set Attribute

The SBA (Set Buffer Address), for example, identifies the position of the data within the screen. It allows the data to be placed exactly at a row/column position. This technique eliminates the need for "spacing" to a particular location and reduces the size of the data stream necessary to transmit. If, then, an SBA of

x'114040'

was detected, CICS would recognize the hexadecimal command of x"11" as SBA and place the cursor at location Row 1, Column 1.

The other data stream commands operate similarly, as the first byte of the control field identifies the command, and then contain additional bytes for descriptor data. Complete documentation concerning data stream transmissions can be found in the CICS/MVS Application Programmers Reference Manual.

Inbound Data Streams These data streams are similar, since they also contain SBA and other control fields with attribute bytes. Inbound data streams, however, contain an AID byte (attention identifier). The AID byte is always sent to CICS when a 3270 input operation is performed and contains the cause or the function requested. Some examples of AID commands are:

PF keys	PA keys
CLEAR	ENTER

Once the data stream is created, the program has access to the AID via two sources, EIBAID (in the EIB) and TCTTEAID (in the TCTTE). The program can then interrogate this field to determine the direction of the branch in logic. Many programmers use this AID information to correlate PF or PA keys to specific functions or transactions.

Since the program has control when the inbound data is created, most programmers use this control to "edit" the data, screening any invalid contents. If the edit is not successful, most programs return error messages to the screen, ensuring accuracy before passing the data back to CICS to be processed.

Since outbound data streams have less control over this editing process, most terminal problems are caused by invalid contents in the outbound transmissions. The most common, ATNI abends, are usually a result of corrupted or incorrect data being sent to the terminal.

8.3 Extended Data Streams

While, for many years, most 3270 terminals were MFI (mainframe interactive) devices, with minimal color, highlighting, etc., newer devices are now available including extended features. These terminals may be used to "enhance" the previously dull and monotonous displays that installations have used for so long.

CICS applications now have the ability to use these extended functions, but must assume the responsibility of detecting their presence. For example, an application may execute within a CICS system containing thousands of terminals. Some of these terminals may be old, standard 3270, but some may be new devices with all the features. The application must check for the ability to use these extended features, since the data streams that must contain additional control fields. Where is the information found? In the terminal definition, of course! When the terminal is defined to CICS, either by RDO definition, auto-install model, or TCT macro, the contents identify the attributes and capability of the device. In this way, CICS is made aware of the level of support to provide for the device. In the terminal definition, the FEATURE parameter identifies terminal characteristics.

FEATURE=(feature,feature...)

In the TCT, this syntax will define applicable features for the 3270 device. If features are coded that the device cannot support, data streams can be created that the terminal is unable to execute. This becomes a significant issue in the auto-install of terminals. Since CICS selects a "best fit" model, the fit may not be suitable. Installations that implement auto-install must accommodate *all* types of 3270 terminals that may be utilized. The best manuals to utilize for auto-install issues are CICS/OS/VS IBM 3270 Data Stream Device Guide (this manual was not reshipped with CICS/MVS 2.1) and GG66-0288 CICS/OS/VS Terminal Definitions with Auto-install Considerations.

8.3.1 Extended Data Stream Checking

While CICS builds a terminal definition to identify terminal capabilities, the application must check these values to determine the environment during execution. For example, the program can examine what type of terminal is supporting the execution, and then use appropriate features. The vehicle for this interrogation is the ASSIGN command.

Using ASSIGN, the program can obtain values from the terminal definition and execute accordingly. The process would check for any number of values, including:

IF			
	EXTDS	=	extended data stream capability
	BTRANS	=	background transparency
	COLOR	=	extended color
	GCHARS	=	graphic characters
	HILIGHT	=	highlighting
	OUTLINE	=	outlining
	PS	=	programmed symbols

An important note to remember is that EXTDS does *not* automatically include all other values. If highlighting is required, that specific value must be tested for, even if EXTDS is turned on.

8.3.2 Extended Data Stream for File Transfer

In order to transfer data from a mainframe to a PC (personal computer), the IBM file transfer program can be used. This transfer program requires that extended data stream be utilized by the PC during the transfer. If this workstation is also used by CICS, BMS will check all EDS options for incorporation into the final data stream. If EDS was specified in the terminal definition for file transfer, it will also be detected by BMS when the device is used by CICS.

One mistake that many installations make is the addition to other options in the terminal definition beyond EDS. Remember, BMS detects and checks for each option individually. While the PC contains color support, it does *not* support Extended Color (7-color support). If the terminal definition specifies

FEATURE(EXTDS,COLOR,feature...)

the data stream will contain the appropriate control characters. Since most 3270 PC emulators contain only four-color support, the COLOR feature cannot be used in the terminal definition. Make sure that the extended features in the device definition truly match the capabilities of the device.

8.3.3 QUERY Feature

Many customers discovered this feature when implementing CICS auto-install for the first time, since this feature is turned on in the default DFHLU2 model. While a complete description of the SNA QUERY function is contained within the CICS/MVS Resource Definition Online Manual, a few items will be discussed here.

As previously stated, any BMS application has the ability to interrogate the device and receive information concerning the features supported. This interrogation is also called a "query" and can be performed by the application or by CICS at the time the terminal is identified to CICS. Since many installations are now automating the creation of terminal control blocks with the auto-install feature, a "model" is used during install rather than single, explicit definitions for each device. This not only saves extensive time necessary to code definitions for each terminal, it saves a great deal of virtual storage that was previously allocated whether the terminal was ever used or not.

Within the model (which *must* be defined via RDO), all features are specified that will be used to create the terminal definition. The TERMTYPE definition becomes the auto-install model via the specification:

AUTOINSTALL (YES/NO/ONLY)

where ONLY mandates that this TERMTYPE will be used for no other purpose than as a model. In addition, a number of other parameters must be chosen to customize this TERMTYPE appropriately for the terminal control blocks that will be created. Of course, all the EDS options are available and can be specified. One definition that must be analyzed is:

QUERY (ALL/COLD/NO)

where

ALL   =   CICS determines the features each time the terminal is
            connected

COLD =   CICS determines the features when the terminal
            is connected for the first time after a cold start

NO   =   CICS does not query the device at all, since the
            terminal probably does not support any EDS

In the IBM-delivered TERMTYPE model for DFHLU2 (most 3270-SNA devices), the query parameter is set to QUERY=ALL. This is inappropriate for many 3270 devices, since they do not support any EDS features. In fact, if a nonquery device attempts to install with this model, the install will fail. While the model does not have to match *exactly* for a successful install, the QUERY bit *must* match the VTAM logmode for EDS support. Watch this "gotcha," and if the device does not support EDS, create a new LU2 TYPETERM model with QUERY=NO.

If, however, the device contains EDS or any extended feature support, QUERY should be turned on. This QUERY bit also needs to be included if any underscore displays will be used in the maps.

8.3.4 BMS Advantages with EDS

BMS is actually an interface between the application program and Terminal Control (DFHTCP). The format of the data flowing between the terminal and CICS is not altered when BMS is used. BMS simply assumes the responsibility of formatting the screen for each type of device that may be used. This can be a significant advantage to an application, since it has no way of knowing (and shouldn't care) what type of terminal is being used. Of course, in some cases, the program can QUERY the device for extended attributes to use, if necessary.

If, on the other hand, the application was designed to use extended attributes, can it then run on a device that does not support these functions? Yes, and, in fact, the programs do not even require any modification or recompilation. BMS, as the interface, will recognize the limitations of the non-EDS device from the terminal definition provided. The non-EDS device will not be presented to the extended attributes, since BMS will automatically omit them. The terminal operator will see the extended functions (such as color) if the device is capable and will not if the terminal does not have the capacity.

For this reason, among others, BMS is widely accepted as the standard terminal interface facility within CICS. Of course, as CICS/OS2 grows in acceptance, this may change for the OS/2 environment. Since CICS/OS2 supports Presentation Manager Services, applications may call PM for the extended features available within OS/2. PM contains may facilities, especially "windowing," which far exceed BMS functions. Until these PM features are available within MVS, however, BMS will continue to be the standard.

8.4 CICS/OS2 Mapping Services

As previously stated, CICS/OS2 provides additional facilities for terminal displays, primarily via OS/2 functions. Customers who wish to use CICS/OS2 need to be aware of both the enhancements that are available and the level of BMS support within the product.

In the first release of the product, CICS/OS2 Release 1, applications were not able to issue PM (Presentation Manager) calls. CICS applications could execute within a "window" and could, therefore, be supported as another task within OS/2.

CICS/OS2 Version 1.2 now allows PM calls from within the application. In other words, CICS is transferring the interface from BMS to the OS/2 PM facility for screen handling. This will enable CICS to perform all processing and pass the responsibility for screen handling to another source, PM. It will, hopefully, allow both parts to perform at their optimum, doing what they do best. Of course, this may produce an application that is not portable, since these PM calls are not supported in other CICS environments.

8.4.1 CICS/OS2 Support of 3270 Data Streams

CICS/OS2 supports data streams via BMS, but is restricted to the limited BMS definitions as specified in the APRM. The CICS/OS2 support would correspond to the Minimum Function BMS as described in the manual.

In addition, the product supports native 3270 data streams via terminal control commands if the application chooses not to use BMS. The applications are then dependent upon the data formatting requirements of the specific device and are much more difficult to write. For example, CICS/OS2 can support native data streams but not:

Structured fields
Extended attributes beyond field boundaries

8.4.2 BMS Usability

Many customers have BMS maps in mainframe applications that need to be duplicated if the application will be executing in CICS/OS2. These maps can be redefined in CICS/OS2 via standard macro source, as would be used on the host. This BMS macro source is then translated by CICS/OS2 into a form that the product can utilize. The command for the translation is supplied with the product.

In addition, some customers have used SDF (Screen Definition Facility) on the host to avoid native BMS macros. This development facility is not provided in the CICS/OS2 environment and, therefore, cannot be used to develop maps. The mainframe product, however, has the ability to produce BMS macro definitions as output and can be used to create the MAP definitions. These definitions can then be downloaded to CICS/OS2 where they would be translated.

A few dangers exist with this process. First, the maps created via SDF may contain more than minimum function BMS, which would not be supported by CICS/OS2. Second, SDF allows some function within the development tool that cannot translate into native BMS macros. These maps, then, could not be ported into CICS/OS2. So, while many maps may be downloaded from the mainframe environment, some may not be applicable for CICS/OS2.

8.5 BMS Hardware Issues

The entire discussion of BMS constantly returns to device constraints and compatibility issues. While BMS "frees" the programmer from device awareness, it does not entirely relieve the application from limitations of some devices. The discussion of the QUERY feature identified limitations within only one terminal type — the SNA LU2. Not all LU-type 2 devices are alike. How, then, can BMS expect to accommodate all the unique devices that may be found in an installation's network?

This section will deal with specific hardware issues that an application may need to be aware of. While this is certainly not a complete list, it will hopefully identify may hardware exceptions that may need to be considered.

8.5.1 Light Pen Selectable Fields

As documented in the APRM, there are two kinds of light pen detectable fields: immediate and deferred. A deferred field (also known as a selection field) contains a "?" in the first byte, and is, therefore, the designator character. An immediate field (also known as an attention field) contains a blank (X"40") in the first byte. If selected, the device sends an AID plus the contents of the field, returning the first byte as X"FF" to indicate that the field is a light pen field.

While the immediate field will cause an attention to be set and, therefore, cause the data stream to be sent, a deferred field will set an MDT (modified data tag) on, but no attention. Another action, such as an ENTER, must be used to cause transmission.

Additional information can be located in GA23-0061. The 3274 Control Unit Description and Programmer's Guide, since this is truly a hardware-related issue.

8.5.2 IBM 8775 Display Terminal

This specific device is used in many CICS installations and contains support for the MSR (magnetic slot reader). An MSR reads data from magnetic cards, and the 8775 allows the application to control functions of the reader.

This control is accomplished via the MSR options of the BMS commands such as SEND MAP, SEND TEXT, and SEND CONTROL. In addition, Trigger Field Validation is available for these devices. Via BMS functions, input can be initiated to an application program prior to the completion of the map. The trigger field is transmitted to CICS as soon as it has been modified, and the cursor is moved to the next field.

While Trigger Field Validation is supported for the 8775 terminal, it is not available to other 3270-type devices. Full documentation on this facility is provided in the APRM in the chapter covering Standard Function BMS.

8.5.3 Programmed Symbols (PS)

Some devices have the ability to support Programmed Symbols (PS). These devices include the IBM 8775, some 3278 and 3279 models, 3290, and the IBM 5550. PS capability allows additional symbol support, with up to six 191-character symbol sets. Characters in various fields can be selected from these different symbol sets. Of course, the device must be defined to CICS as EDS, with PS feature, and the definition of the symbols must be available to the terminal.

The PS attribute is required for Japanese Kanji characters with double byte data output. The IBM 5550 device supports Japanese Kanji output and uses the double byte data PS support for full implementation via BMS. The document SH18-0083 is available for further information concerning CICS support of the IBM 5550.

8.5.4 IBM 3290 Full Screen Support

Some installations use the IBM 3290 in full screen mode, with a screen size of 62 × 160. CICS supports this device via the terminal definition ALT SCREEN (62 × 160) and the transaction definition ALT SCREEN. Of course, the applications would then have specific BMS maps with this alternate screen size implemented. Some problems may be experienced when diagnosing problems with these applications.

If the programmer uses CEDF (execution diagnostic facility), care must be taken since CEDF was not designed to support any nonstandard screen sizes. EDF can execute in single or dual terminal mode. In single terminal mode it does not support the extended data stream and, therefore, extended attribute functions required by the IBM 3290. These functions are only available in two terminal mode, which must be used to diagnose any application problems on the device.

8.5.5 LYTYPE3 vs. LYTYPE1

CICS applications can utilize two different types of printers: LUTYPE1 or LUTYPE3. LUTYPE1 printers are also called SCS printers (SNA character string). These SCS printers receive data with SCS control codes rather than 3270 data streams (also known as orders). This difference in the generation of data streams may be advantageous to some applications, since SCS printers function similarly to line printers with forms control. This provides more flexibility in the formatting of output, since SCS printers do not respond to 3270 commands (such as WCC, write control character). Data is printed, and forms control is executed, as it is received within the data stream.

The LUTYPE3 printer uses 3270 data streams with controls for buffer addresses and print formatting (such as new line and form feed). While SCS printers execute forms control as it is detected within the data stream, non-SCS printers store print format commands in the buffer along with the data and are executed during the print operation. The application controls the print operation via an output command to the printer followed by a WCC. This WCC contains two flags to control printing — the start bit and the format bit.

Programmers should remember that since LUTYPE3 devices format data via SBA orders, any null lines are suppressed during the actual print operation. Also, applications that are coded for one type of printer may need to be recoded if moved to another type of device, especially if they are written via non-BMS mapping.

8.5.6 Protocol Converters

Installations must be aware of limitations in many network-attached devices. Since some printers must be connected, although locally via protocol converters, these "black boxes" do not support all functions of devices that are natively attached (for example, via an IBM 3174 controller).

While display devices may be defined to CICS as LUTYPE2, using standard 3270 data streams, the protocol converter may not provide all 3270 function. One example is the IBM 3708, which does not provide support for BMS partitions and windows. The WSF (write structured field) is required for partition support, and the command is not supported by the protocol converter.

In addition, many "converters" may attempt to emulate function and dilute the effect. Most standard functions are supported, but many enhanced functions and extended data stream attributes may be affected. Be sure to investigate support for any control of conversion units that may be used to support CICS devices.

8.6 Multiple BMS Maps

Many programmers create displays that are more than one logical or physical map. In addition, BMS contains support for partitioning of the display, which can be utilized to divide the display into as many as eight areas. As the application writes to the partitioned display, each partition is treated as separate and individual from the others. This allows the application to send data from different programs to individual partitions, producing output from multiple input sources.

CICS manages a partitioned display via definitions called "partitioned sets." The partitioned set is created via BMS macros defining each partition, which are then loaded dynamically when the data is first sent to the display, or via the BMS command SEND PARTNSET. Complete documentation on partitioning can be found in the Application Programmers' Reference Manual in the section on Standard Function BMS.

CICS also (within partitioning) supports the mapping of data from multiple BMS maps. In other words, data can be received from more than a single map and placed into a final map. The recommended technique to accomplish this result is via the terminal control RECEIVE command. The RECEIVE would receive and store the data for later use. When retrieving the stored data, the RECEIVE MAP command would require the FROM and LENGTH options to transfer the data from the data area into the final location.

These advanced techniques provide additional function; however, they require additional CICS resources, complex programming, and can produce elongated response times.

Any new programs that require enhanced mapping should research the applicability of CUA. In the IBM application development arena, recommendations are being made for all installations to become familiar with the Common User Access (CUA). Designing applications for CUA means that all applications, independent of the location or environment of execution, will provide the same results to the user. In complex installations, CICS applications may execute on a mainframe or a PS/2. The application can be designed to produce a common access, or display, regardless. More complete coverage of CUA issues can be found in Section 8.7.

8.7 CUA Issues with BMS

In a "true" SAA environment, cooperative processing applications can be "ported" into another SAA system and be executable with minor changes. The application presents one "view" to the terminal operator, regardless of which SAA platform it is executing on. One attempt to provide this "portability" and consistency of presentation is CUA. If the User Access is indeed Common, the application is not responsible for "awareness of location." In simple terms, the user need not know if the application is running under MVS/ESA or OS/2.

What is CUA? One of four basic elements of SAA, CUA attempts to:

. . . define the basic elements of the end user interface and how to use them. The primary goal is to achieve (through consistency of user interface) transfer of learning, ease of learning, and ease of use across the range of IBM SAA applications and environments.

While this is an honorable objective, most customers have already realized that it is not an easily achievable one. There *are*, however, some techniques that can be utilized to begin heading in the proper direction.

CICS BMS (Basic Mapping Services) has been the facility for terminal screen mapping from the beginning. There have been slight enhancements (such as Extended Data Streams), but for the most part, BMS has remained "functionally stable." The 3270 terminal has produced few exciting changes in the life of the device (remember when color was first introduced?). Finally, a new technology arrived and was heralded as the Intelligent Work Station. The IWS led to some new terminology when referring to the old 3270s (they were always called "dumb" terminals anyway).

Non-IWS devices can now be labeled as MFI (Mainframe Interactive), NPT (Nonprogrammable Terminal), or a number of other less complimentary designations. The fact remains that MFI or NPT devices cannot perform IWS functions.

8.7.1 Designing for CUA

So how are customers going to use BMS to begin CUA conformance? While BMS has limitations, there are techniques that can be used to begin conforming to CUA design. The major difference between current BMS screens and CUA screens is the panel layout and presentation elements of the model. A CUA screen contains Object/Action or Action/Object design. The latter is possible, even with BMS, if the panel is designed properly.

The most important facet of CUA is to create a consistent presentation in all screens. CUA screens contain the following standard elements:

Panel Title
Entry Fields

Scrolling Areas (when used)
Message Area
Command Area
Function Key Area

In addition, the screens should (across all applications) provide common command and function key assignments with online HELP available at any time. Anyone who has been in data processing for any length of time has been frustrated with inconsistent PF key assignments from one application to the next.

Use of these simple techniques, creating consistent and easily accessed screens across all applications, will begin compliance with CUA requirements. If properly designed, the application will be in optimum position to exploit IWS features when possible, such as Presentation Manager services in CICS/OS2.

8.7.2 PM in CICS/OS2

This is the first true implementation of expanded facilities for CICS screen displays. An application in CICS/OS2 can call PM services and exploit all available technology such as mouse cursor support and graphics. Of course, BMS will never do those things, even under CICS/OS2. Why redesign BMS when PM is already there? Some customers are starting to design BMS screens to "simulate" the PM services. BMS provides no true windowing support, but can be designed with overlay maps to imitate the window style. Once users become accustomed to observing windows in the displays, they may be more accepting of CICS/OS2's use of PM. Porting the application to the IWS will allow the CUA screen to remain intact and, again, provide a consistent view of the application.

8.7.3 CUA Documentation

Any installations that wish to begin CUA design in their BMS maps may wish to acquire existing documentation. The only two manuals currently available are SC26-4583 SAA CUA Basic Interface Design Guide and GG66-3115 SAA CUA Application Design Guidelines for CICS BMS.

8.8 Miscellaneous BMS Issues

The topics covered in this section deal with individual BMS concerns, those not covered in preceding headings. Although these items cannot address all possible BMS issues, they highlight some of the most popular questions raised concerning mapping facilities.

8.8.1 CSPS

The CICS-supplied transaction CSPS is used to route pages to a target terminal via the BMS Routing Facility. This facility can be used for developing message or broadcast applications. While multiple partition messages cannot be transmitted, routing can be helpful within a CICS system for notification of users, when necessary. The messages can be delayed, as with an ICE (interval control element) task, if necessary. Realize, however, that BMS generates a data stream for each terminal in the route list and is usually stored in CICS temporary storage.

This could result in an increased use of temporary storage, especially if a large number of terminals are identifed as targets for the message. CICS limits the number of terminals to which messages can be sent, and while a maximum cannot be defined, it is dependent on other operands specified in the ROUTE command. An ABMC abend will result if the limit is exceeded.

8.8.2 Security Protection of BMS Maps

Since CICS can only protect (check authorization) for resources such as programs, file, queues, etc., BMS maps cannot be secured via standard authorization facilities. External security managers, such as RACF or other vendor products, do not recognize BMS maps as resources within their control.

The only way an installation could protect BMS maps would be to code some logic into the application to invoke internal security. Prior to map send, the application could (via the EIB fields) detect the userid or operator id and the transaction currently in control. The application could then, at that time, determine via an external table or installation-defined resource type whether authorization should be provided. No standard interface currently exists for BMS map security.

8.8.3 Floating BMS Maps

Most maps are positioned within a display with absolute values for line and column number as specified within the BMS map definition macro (DFHMDI). Minimum and standard function BMS maps allow only this type of map positioning.

In full-function BMS, maps can "float" or be positioned relative to the position of the previous map. These maps can be sent to the terminal until the page is full and a page overflow condition occurs.

The CICS APRM cautions programmers to avoid using this technique with RECEIVE MAP commands, since the map will be arranged within a clear page and previous relative locations may be invalid. Another technique could be used via multiple maps, as discussed earlier in this chapter. When a previous map is stored, the RECEIVE command can include the FROM and LENGTH options to retrieve the appropriate data and move into a new map.

8.8.4 RECEIVE ASIS with UCTRAN

For many versions and releases of CICS, programmers have struggled with the inflexibility of terminal upper-case translation (UCTRAN). This parameter must be coded at the terminal level and is, therefore, stored as bit settings within the terminal control block for the life of the terminal's existence within CICS. It is, therefore, a binary decision, to translate or not to translate, for each terminal. Many installations have subsequently coded their own assembler routines to search out this setting and "zap" the UCTRAN bits when necessary. This was (until Version 3 announcement) the only way to dynamically change the terminal to UPPER/LOWER case if UCTRAN=YES existed for the terminal.

For this reason, any input message that initiates a transaction is always translated to upper case if UCTRAN=YES is specified. The RECEIVE command with ASIS option applies only to input messages AFTER the transaction has originated.

Another issue complicating this process is the terminal auto-install process, which deletes the terminal definition at log off time and rebuilds the entry at next signon. Any routine to dynamically change the UCTRAN setting is lost when the terminal is deinstalled and must be reissued.

The CICS/ESA Version 3 announcement contains some relief in this category. Installations will now be able to specify UCTRAN requirements at the transaction level. The CEDA facility will contain a new PROFILE option with UCTRAN setting for any transactions requiring this specific PROFILE. See the CICS/ESA Version 3 Release Guide for more information.

PPT Definitions of MAPSETS with RES=YES

Customers have noted in the past that PPT definitions of USAGE=MAP caused the modules to be quickly deleted after use and constantly reloaded. This could be avoided with the RES=YES option, which caused heavily used maps to be loaded a single time and remain resident.

RDO specification of maps requires a MAPSET definition, but have no corresponding residency option. If the installation removes all table support of programs and maps, RES=YES is no longer available with RDO MAPSET. An alternative would be to use an application load table (ALT) for map residency if the volume dictated the need.

CICS Journaling

9.1 Journal Characteristics

CICS provides the ability to journal activities within the application and provide either an audit trail or a record of movement. Installations identify these journals to CICS via a journal control table (JCT), specifying several parameters to assist in performance and retention. Following are the most significant parameter issues dealing with the JCT.

9.1.1 BUFSIZE and BUFSUV

BUFSIZE (buffer size) is used by CICS during the creation of the journal record. Journal control uses this value to establish the size of the IOAREA and read length when it positions the pointer within the journal. Since the journals are RECFM=U, each write creates a block, rather than a single record. Each record cannot exceed the BUFSIZE. For this reason, the size of the buffer must be calculated to accommodate any user requests for journal write.

If the application is requesting an automatic journal write via the FCT (file control table) with the JREQ (journal request) parameter, the journal BUFSIZE must be calculated via:

> Maximum record length for the file
> + 72 bytes for the label record and system prefix
> + 8 bytes for the CICS filename
> + <u>n-255 bytes for the key of the record</u>
> = BUFSIZE for that journal

IBM recommends that the BUFSIZE be specified as the maximum value based on the device capability and the maximum that CICS will allow. The CICS Resource Definition Macro manual recommends 32767 (32K) or the track capacity, whichever is less. Since 3380 DASD has a track capacity of 47K (the new 3390s have an even larger track capacity), any journals written to 3380 devices cannot exceed 32K. For this reason, most IBM publications recommend 32K as the BUFSIZE value.

Although this will utilize additional virtual storage (32K for each journal specified), it will reduce the physical I/O requests necessary to write the journal records.

Double Buffering   CICS performs double buffering within the singly specified buffer. The journal control program writes only the "current" data from the buffer and accumulates additional data during the I/O within the unused portion. In other words, while journal control is moving data from the buffer during the write, any new data is written "behind" and within the same buffer. When the write is complete, the pointer is moved to the start of the buffer and the area is reused.

The effect of double buffering takes advantage of large buffers, especially with active journals. No action is required of the application program or any CICS parameters. This "double buffering" takes place automatically, and as the volume of journal requests increases, CICS will begin writing larger blocks. If the buffer size is set to 32760, the maximum average block size can approach half that, or 16K. For this reason, IBM recommends using BLKSIZE=32760.

BUFSUV   BUFSUV (buffer shift up value) is also specified in the JCT and provides a mechanism to avoid a full buffer for the journal. If CICS detects a full journal buffer, the system waits until the write is complete. This can produce poor performance, especially for the transactions waiting for this buffer.

The CICS Resource Definition Macro Manual recommends a value of 50%, while the CICS Performance Guide indicates 33–50% may be preferable. The buffer should be written as soon as possible, to avoid any wait conditions. If the CICS shutdown statistics indicate any WAITs, perhaps the 33% value should be considered. The reduction of BUFSUV will begin the buffer writes more frequently and produce smaller physical records within the block. If no WAITs are detected, a higher value may be recommended.

The normal rule is to specify BUFSIZE of 32K and the BUFSUV of half BUFSIZE or 16K. The price is virtual storage, since the buffers may be larger than otherwise chosen. The advantages include avoidance of full buffer conditions and the subsequent performance implications.

9.1.2 BLKSIZE

Block size, or BLKSIZE, was previously coded (before CICS/VS 1.7) in the JCL to allocate journals at a specific BLKSIZE. As discussed in the previous section, the journal control program writes a logical record to the journal as specified in the BUFSIZE parameter. Normally the buffer corresponds to the size of a block (or a multiple). In journal control, however, CICS now uses the BUFSIZE value for all I/O and requires that the journal be formatted to accommodate the maximum buffer.

Placing a DCB=BLKSIZE= keyword parameter within the JCL when creating or reformatting a journal will be disregarded by CICS. The journal formatting program, DFHJCJFP, has specific code to mandate the 32K BLKSIZE and will ignore any value within the JCL. By creating a journal of BLKSIZE=32767, RECFM=U, journal control will write records as variable length blocks, with a maximum size as specified with BUFSIZE within the JCT entry. Section 9.1.4 contains the sample JCL required to format these journals.

9.1.3 Journal Space Utilization

CICS uses space within the preallocated DASD journals as it writes blocks (in the 32K size as previously stated). After the journal is initially formatted, it will appear 100% full, since the formatting program writes (formats) records within the allocation to the end of the file.

After the journal is used (written into) and then closed, the end of file is positioned at the last block written. This will show in the VTOC (volume table of contents), indicating the percentage of used space. Consequently, if the journal was closed after normal CICS shutdown, or switched via the CEMT command, the journal would appear less than 100% full.

This "less than full" condition comes into play when CICS is restarted, and the journal extent is chosen by CICS. Further discussion about journal positioning at restart is covered in one of the future sections of this chapter.

9.1.4 Formatting DASD Journals

Before CICS can write any records into a journal, the allocated space must be formatted by the program DFHJCJFP. As previously stated, CICS mandates the size of the blocks (32K), and the RECFM of the dataset must be U (undefined). As CICS formats the journal (sometimes called an extent, if DASD), it writes dummy records into the journal until it reaches the end. The journal is then flagged available and can be opened by CICS at next startup. A typical example of a job to format a journal would be:

```
//JRNFMT JOB (ACCT),SYS.PROG,CLASS=A,MSGCLASS=X
//FORMAT EXEC PGM=DFHJCJFP
//STEPLIB DD DSN=CICS.LOADLIB,DISP=SHR
//JOURNAL1 DD DSN=CICS.JOURNAL1,DISP=(NEW,CATLG),
//       DCB=RECFM=U,UNIT=3380,
//       VOL=SER=CICSXA,SPACE=(TRK,(20,5))
```

Note BLKSIZE is omitted in the JCL since BLKSIZE is mandated by BUFSIZE in the JCT for the journal.

After the job is complete, CICS will return a message to the JES joblog indicating the format completion and the number of tracks available in the journal. If two disks are formatted, DISK2 can be used in the JCT to "switch" the journal to the alternate extent, allowing the first to be dumped (probably to tape) before the second one fills.

9.2 DASD vs. TAPE Journals

Installations have the ability to choose between directing the output of journals to either disk volumes or tape devices. While IBM does not recommend tape journaling, it can be done. Most installations allocate DASD journals, but this, of course, requires online storage which is usually in short supply. The next section will discuss some limitations of tape journals and also the process of dual DASD journaling.

9.2.1 Tape Limitations

While writing to tape journals is probably less expensive (DASD space costs vs. cost of tape reels or cartridges), tape journaling can be very inefficient. If journal output is directed to tape, the device(s) must be dedicated to the CICS system for the entire length of time that CICS is active. If the installation already has a shortage of tape drives for production batch jobs, this will only worsen the situation. In addition, I/O to tape is considerably slower than I/O to disk drives and could impact performance on a highly used CICS system.

3480 Tape Drives The new tape devices, 3480 cartridges, are significantly faster than the old tape reel devices, model 3420. The increased speed is due to a buffering technique used by the devices to increase transfer rates to the tape volumes. In addition, IBM has recently announced the IDRC (Increased Data Recording) feature, which further enhances speed and recording capability of the devices.

CICS cannot utilize the new features of the 3480s, however. In order to ensure all records directed to tape journals have been physically written before further processing continues, the 3480s must be utilized in unbuffered mode. This negates most of the performance enhancements of the 3480s. The cartridges would certainly accommodate more records than the tape reels, but would not perform nearly as well as DASD journals.

9.2.2 Dual Disk Journals

Most installations utilize disk journals, with the option:

JTYPE=DISK2

to allow CICS to alternately use two datasets. When one journal becomes full, a message is produced, and CICS begins writing into the alternate journal. Hopefully, before the second journal is filled, a batch job is run to dump the journal records from the primary journal (probably to tape) and allow this journal to be reused. With many automated operations products, this message can be intercepted and the batch job be automatically initiated. Depending on the activity of the journal, the size of each dataset should be adequate to continue this switching and clearing of the journal records at appropriate intervals. More information is available pertaining to the advantages of dual disk journaling in the CICS/MVS Recovery and Restart Guide.

9.3 Journal Processing Options

Many options can be chosen for both system and user journals that enhance application use of journaling. This chapter has already discussed the options concerning tape and disk journals, but the installation has additional options that can be utilized to facilitate journaling.

9.3.1 DTB vs. Journaling

If an installation wishes to make a resource (such as a file) recoverable, there are multiple parameters that can be utilized to provide recovery. Realize, however, that truly recoverable resources, those requiring full integrity, should be directed to a dedicated data base manager, such as DB/2 or DL/I.

In the PCT (program control table), the transaction can be specified as

DTB=YES

indicating that CICS should back out uncommitted changes made to a resource if the transaction terminates abnormally. Using RDO (resource definition online), transactions are automatically assigned this mode since the parameter no longer exists. The philosophy behind the new default is that the transaction should not specify recovery; the resource itself should be specified recoverable.

This is obvious, even with the PCT parameter, since the DTB buffer is not acquired until a recoverable resource is changed. Specifying DTB will not produce recovery (or overhead) on a nonrecoverable resource. To specify recovery for a data set, the FCT (file control table) should be used.

In the FCT, the parameters used for recovery are:

```
LOG=YES
JID=nn          the journal identifier
JREQ=ALL        to journal all READ and WRITE
                ASY for asynchronous journaling of WRITEs
                RO for READ ONLY operations
                RU for READ UPDATE operations
                SYN for synchronous journaling of READ
                WN for WRITE NEW operations
                WU for WRITE UPDATE operations
```

Use of LOG=YES will allow backout and, therefore, recovery of incomplete changes to the file in case of transaction or system failure. The "before" image of the data is written in the system log (Journal 01) to enable this image to be recovered.

If a user journal is indicated (JID=nn), CICS records file activity for subsequent processing by the installation, such as data set recovery (also known as forward recovery) in case of file damage or loss. These journal records are not log records which can be used for backout, but journal records which show the I/O activity of the file during CICS processing.

For example, if a VSAM file was updated with new records, and an ABEND occurs, the system log would contain the keys for the added records and delete the records during backout processing. If the FCT entry for the file contained JREQ=WN, the image of the added records would be written to the user journal. During backout processing, the records would be deleted, but the journal would only reflect the deletions if JREQ=WN,WU were specified, thereby requesting WRITE UPDATE activity to the journal.

System Log Synchronization   As stated, if the resource has LOG=YES indicated, a "before image" is written to the system log for possible backout. For timing purposes, when a (recoverable) VSAM file is updated, the record (from the buffer pool) is physically written to the system log BEFORE the updated record is returned to the buffer. In most cases, the updated record is then "externalized" via a forced rewrite of the updated CI (control interval) to the DASD device by CICS. In this way, the system log always contains the most current updates to any record in case of failure. Only when the task ends, or a syncpoint is detected, does CICS then update the system log to synchronize the logical unit of work (LUW) with the successful completion of the update.

9.3.2 CICS Journals vs. SMF Records

Another option available in CICS journaling is the direction of the journals and the format of the records. All previous discussion of DASD journals utilized data sets that were allocated and preformatted with the journal formatting utility DFHJCJFP. One other option can be selected for the disk journal used by CICS to record monitoring information of all executed applications. If the journal entry in the JCT for journal 02 specifies

FORMAT=SMF
JTYPE=SMF

the output will be sent to the SMF (system management facilities) data sets. CICS does not perform any additional processing to direct the output of this journal to SMF, so the cycles required will be the same. As with performance of any journals, any degradation will be a factor of the actual activity (physical I/Os) and the size of the block being written. If the CICS shutdown statistics show buffer waits, the buffer size needs to be increased. If the statistics show "Buffer Fulls" on this journal, the blocks need to be increased to decrease the I/Os. One recommendation published by IBM states:

BUFSIZE = 2–4 times the largest MAXBUF + 80
BUFSUV = (BUFSIZE – (1.5 × MAXBUF + 80))

Any activity for tuning should attempt to decrease the activity by writing as much data within a single block. MAXBUF should be at least 2K and probably 4K, since a 4K page is normally a reasonable transfer of data for both CICS and the operating system. Installations sometimes choose to use SMF data sets, since they consolidate CICS performance data with all other performance records written by the operating system (RMF data).

9.3.3 Closing Journals

As with any resource, CICS allows an installation to utilize the master terminal transaction, CEMT, to close journals. Realize, however, that journals are *not* typical files, and use of this facility can disrupt the normal processing of applications writing to journals, especially disk journals. For most installations, the need to increase the size of any journal during CICS execution is impossible, since CICS will not reopen the journal with CEMT.

The only way CICS can reuse a journal after it has been closed is to process the entire scenario as one task. The task that closes the journal *must* be the same task that reopens the journal after it has been reinitialized. If the closing task is allowed to terminate, CICS will not allow another task to reopen that journal.

9.4 Journal Issues Relating to Restart

Use of journals, either system or user type, requires that the contents of these journals be protected in case of failure. In addition, the recovery of journal records must consider the type of startup that

CICS is experiencing. As previously stated, the recommended journal media is disk, with dual extents available for "swapping" back and forth. Realize that dual extents *do not* perform dual logging (as do data base managers) but rather allow the second extent (or journal) to be written into while the first can be copied to another media (usually tape).

If these user journals are not copied before being reopened, recovery of resources may become impossible and the integrity of the application lost.

9.4.1 CICS Catalog and Journaling

The CICS catalog (also known as the restart data set) contains information pertaining to the positioning of all journals. The catalog records which journal extent was the last one used during the previous execution of CICS. It also contains a flag called the "not ready for use" flag. This flag is set when the extent has been used (perhaps may have been filled) and is, therefore, not available to be used again until the flag has been reset. The flag is an attempt to protect the "used" extent from being written over before the data has been copied (archived). The flag is set in the catalog when the message

DFH4583 CICS JOURNAL nn PRIMARY/SECONDARY DATASET MAY BE COPIED REPLY 'Ynn' WHEN COPIED

is displayed. The catalog sets the flag and allows the extent to be archived while data is directed to the alternate extent. When the archival is complete and the operator responds to the above message, CICS writes a "ready for use" flag in the catalog and the extent is available when needed.

The customer may bypass the use of these catalog flags with the SIT (system initialization table) override:

JSTATUS=RESET

Use of this parameter will cause the status of the journal on the catalog to be ignored. CICS will use the journal that was active during the previous execution of CICS and begin writing after the last record written.

Of course, the catalog can only detect activity during the time CICS is active. If the system is shut down, and the journals are formatted (unknown to CICS), then the status of the journals and the flags within the catalog may not agree. If this is the case, CICS will not use any journal with the "not ready for use" flag in the catalog and will use the next extent, as indicated by the activity in the catalog.

9.4.2 Positioning of Journals During Restart

System Log   The system log (DFHJ01x) contains information for recovery and backout of changes made to resources in case of CICS failure. These records are used as input to the emergency restart process and are, therefore, most important during this type of restart. In "normal" startups, WARM or COLD, CICS positions this journal after the last record written in the active extent (according to the catalog) and then begins writing new data.

During EMERGENCY restart, CICS repositions this journal after the last record written at abnormal termination and opens it for recovery processing. The journal is then read backward and data is moved to the recovery file for backout processing. The process continues until all information pertaining to recoverable resources has been retrieved since the last activity keypoint in the log. These records will be input to recovery processing during restart. After all emergency restart processing has completed, CICS begins writing from the point of last keypoint.

User Journals   In the case of AUTO, COLD, or EMERGENCY restart, CICS will position all journals to begin recording after the last record written to the currently active journal. Of course, if the journals have been formatted, it will begin at the start of the first extent (the "A" journal, if dual). As CICS always uses the catalog to position journals, if the data set chosen conflicts with the information in the catalog, CICS will start at the beginning of the next extent.

In addition, a condition can arise where the last extent used is near the end of the volume. In this case, CICS attempts to write to a journal and determines that the record will not fit or the end of the journal is near. The record is not written into the existing extent, the DFH4583 message is displayed, and the next extent is opened to receive the data.

9.5 Enhancements to Journaling in CICS/ESA 3.1

There are substantial enhancements to the structure and content of journals in CICS/ESA 3.1. Application programs have many more reasons to use journals and include them in the design of potential and existing transactions.

9.5.1 Monitoring Enhancements

The facilities to monitor CICS activity have been substantially changed in CICS/ESA 3.1. New function has been added, and formats of the data have changed. The enhancements include:

• Transaction monitoring data cannot be directed to the CMF journals; they must be written into the MVS SMF datasets.
• A new utility program has been provided, DFHMNDUP, which creates a dictionary record into the dataset when data is extracted from SMF. This provides control information for processing of performance records.
• The data reduction program, DFH$MOLS, has been modified to include reports from data collected from the new monitoring domain.
• CSTT transaction has been replaced by enhancements to the CEMT transaction for control of monitoring and statistics options.

Additional enhancements to the programmable interface and monitoring exits provide more flexible and functional options.

9.5.2 VSAM Recovery

Customers have been struggling for years to attempt VSAM recovery and integrity. Most have migrated to DL/I or DB/2 for these functions, knowing that VSAM cannot ensure full integrity.

In CICS/ESA 3.1, enhancments to VSAM support include:

• A new method for automating the archive of CICS journals
• Additional EXEC CICS commands to control the backout and recovery status of VSAM files

As previously stated in this chapter, journals that contain recovery records for recoverable resources must be archived to ensure recovery. This is a purely manual process and often fails to accomplish the objective.

The new facility detects a full journal (closed for output) and automatically submits the archive job. CICS will not reuse the journal until archive has been completed. Rather than relying on operator intervention and decision, CICS now contains a JACD (Journal Archive Control Dataset) to control this submission and subsequent success. A new option in the JCL "activates" this journal archive process for any or all journals that require protection.

These two additions to monitor and journal functions are indeed welcome and will provide additional application enhancements for nondatabase resources.

Index

ABEND
    ABEND AKCS, 82
    avoiding AEY9, 159-161
    data exceptions, DB/2
        database, 174-175
    VSAM files, 82
Access control block, DL/I database,
    125-127
ADDRESS, Storage, 192-193
Addressability to internal areas, 38-
    39
Advanced Program-to-Program
    Communications, 36
AEY9 ABENDS, avoiding, 159-161
AKCW ABEND code, VSAM files,
    82
AS/400, VSAM in, 94
ASKTIME, 39
Assembler programs, CALLS to
    COBOL II from, 49
ASSIGN, Storage, 193
Attach interface module, DB/2
    database, DSNCLI, 171-171
Attention identifier (AIDs), 15-16
    available values for, 15
    uses of, 16
Automatic task initiation, 108
AUX, temporary storage and, 103-
    104

Base locator for linkage cell re-
    moval, 58
Basic mapping services, 213-232
    character translation, 231-232
    CICS/OS2, 222-223
    common user access, 227-229

basic elements, 228
    designing for, 228-229
    documentation, 229
    PM in CICS/OS2, 229
CSPS and, 230
extended data streams and,
    218-222
floating maps, 231
hardware
    IBM 3290 full screen sup-
        port, 225
    IBM 8775 display termi-
        nal, 224
    light pen selectable fields,
        224
    LUTYPE1 and LUTYPE3
        printers, 225-226
    programmed symbols, 225
    protocol converters, 226
map creation, screen definition
    facility, 216-223
multiple maps, 226-227
physical maps, 215
PPT definitions of MAPSETS,
    232
security protection, 230
SIT options, 213-215
symbolic maps, 215
Batch jobs, CICS and VSAM, 87-88
Block size, journal, 235-236
Buffer invalidate, data sharing,
    DL/I database, 132
Buffer shift up value, journal, 234-
    235
Buffer size, journal, 233-234

245